Evolutionary Economics and Social Complexity Science

Volume 18

The Japanese Association for Evolutionary Economics (JAFEE) always has adhered to its original aim of taking an explicit "integrated" approach. This path has been followed steadfastly since the Association's establishment in 1997 and, as well, since the inauguration of our international journal in 2004. We have deployed an agenda encompassing a contemporary array of subjects including but not limited to: foundations of institutional and evolutionary economics, criticism of mainstream views in the social sciences, knowledge and learning in socio-economic life, development and innovation of technologies, transformation of industrial organizations and economic systems, experimental studies in economics, agent-based modeling of socio-economic systems, evolution of the governance structure of firms and other organizations, comparison of dynamically changing institutions of the world, and policy proposals in the transformational process of economic life. In short, our starting point is an "integrative science" of evolutionary and institutional views. Furthermore, we always endeavor to stay abreast of newly established methods such as agent-based modeling, socio/econo-physics, and network analysis as part of our integrative links.

More fundamentally, "evolution" in social science is interpreted as an essential key word, i.e., an integrative and /or communicative link to understand and re-domain various preceding dichotomies in the sciences: ontological or epistemological, subjective or objective, homogeneous or heterogeneous, natural or artificial, selfish or altruistic, individualistic or collective, rational or irrational, axiomatic or psychological-based, causal nexus or cyclic networked, optimal or adaptive, micro- or macroscopic, deterministic or stochastic, historical or theoretical, mathematical or computational, experimental or empirical, agent-based or socio/econo-physical, institutional or evolutionary, regional or global, and so on. The conventional meanings adhering to various traditional dichotomies may be more or less obsolete, to be replaced with more current ones vis-à-vis contemporary academic trends. Thus we are strongly encouraged to integrate some of the conventional dichotomies.

These attempts are not limited to the field of economic sciences, including management sciences, but also include social science in general. In that way, understanding the social profiles of complex science may then be within our reach. In the meantime, contemporary society appears to be evolving into a newly emerging phase, chiefly characterized by an information and communication technology (ICT) mode of production and a service network system replacing the earlier established factory system with a new one that is suited to actual observations. In the face of these changes we are urgently compelled to explore a set of new properties for a new socio/economic system by implementing new ideas. We thus are keen to look for "integrated principles" common to the above-mentioned dichotomies throughout our serial compilation of publications. We are also encouraged to create a new, broader spectrum for establishing a specific method positively integrated in our own original way.

More information about this series at http://www.springer.com/series/11930

Yasuhiro Sakai

J.M. Keynes Versus F.H. Knight

Risk, Probability, and Uncertainty

Springer

Yasuhiro Sakai
Department of Economics
Center for Risk Research, Shiga University
Hikone, Shiga, Japan

ISSN 2198-4204 ISSN 2198-4212 (electronic)
Evolutionary Economics and Social Complexity Science
ISBN 978-981-13-7999-4 ISBN 978-981-13-8000-6 (eBook)
https://doi.org/10.1007/978-981-13-8000-6

This Springer imprint is published by the registered company Springer Nature Singapore Pte Ltd.
The registered company address is: 152 Beach Road, #21-01/04 Gateway East, Singapore 189721, Singapore

This book is dedicated to the memory of
Prof. Lionel W. McKenzie
Prof. Hirofumi Uzawa
Prof. Takashi Negishi
Toko, Tora, and Nao

Preface

"Natural disasters are most likely to visit us when they are least expected." This was a famous maxim told by Torahiko Terada (1878–1935), a distinguished Japanese scientist and essayist. Even after he passed away, his witty remarks have been reproduced so many times and are very influential even today.

According to Terada, a man in the street has an inclination to forget inconvenient truths such as earthquakes, wildfires, tsunamis, and volcanic eruptions. Wise words are not welcome to the ear. However, the nature itself will never forget those truths as if it would laugh at human nature of negligence and inaction. When natural disasters are least expected and almost out of our memory, they tend to visit us, thus constantly alarming the ferocity of nature. In short, a fearful natural disaster has a tendency to come to the forgetful human mind.

We must recall that many disasters are also man-made in modern times. Among man-made great damages are wars, epidemics, oppression, depression, mass unemployment, inequality, and hyperinflation. Speaking of myself, a large-scale air raid during the Second World War and an austere life during and just after the war are still retained in my memory. With the lapse of time, however, the number of older generations will decrease, and the one of younger generations will increase. As a result, the miserable memory of war times tends to gradually fade away among the people.

The theme of this book is simple and straightforward. In the history of economic thought, it is quite unfortunate that the serious problems associated with risk, probability, and uncertainty have been rather neglected so far. We have to point out, however, the presence of the two superstars who have energetically discussed the impact of risk and uncertainty on economic and human activities. They are J.M. Keynes (1883–1946), who was born with a silver spoon in the Old World, and F.H. Knight (1885–1972), who was born with a wooden spoon in the New World. They have very different backgrounds in many ways. It is in 1921, however, that both of them published apparently similar books of risk and uncertainty.

Keynes left the following impressive sentence to us in 1921: "In most branches of academic logic, such as the syllogism or the geometry of ideal space, all the arguments aim at demonstrative certainty. They claim to be conclusive. But many other arguments are rational and claim some weight without pretending to be certain. In Metaphysics, in Science, and in Conduct, most of the arguments, upon which we habitually base our rational beliefs, are admitted to be inconclusive in a greater or less degree. Thus for a philosophical treatment of these branches of knowledge, the study of probability is required" (Keynes, *A Treatise on Probability*, 1921, p. 3).

So wrote Keynes almost 100 years ago. Unfortunately, Keynes's contribution on probability and uncertainty has been more or less underestimated in the dark shadow of his more shining book, *The General Theory of Employment, Interest and Money* (1936). It should be noted, however, that in his 1937 article published 1 year later than the abovementioned book, he repeatedly emphasized an important role of uncertainty played in economic decisions: "By 'uncertain' knowledge, let me explain, I do not mean merely to distinguish what is known for certain from what is only probable. The game of roulette is not subject, in this sense, to uncertainty. ... Or the expectation of life is only slightly uncertain. The sense in which I am using the term is that in which the prospect of a European was is uncertain, or the price of copper... About these matters there is no scientific basis on which to form any calculable probability whatever. We simply do not know" (Keynes, "The General Theory of Employment, Interest and Money," *Quarterly Journal of Economics*, February 1937).

As Keynes has noted, we live in the world of uncertainty. We simply do not know. Undoubtedly, such philosophical view of Keynes on human conduct and the world affairs was also shared by his contemporary man, Knight. Indeed, Knight, an American hardheaded philosopher who had never met the British gentleman Keynes, wrote the following sentences in 1921: "Uncertainty must be taken in a sense radically distinct from the familiar notion of Risk, from which it has never been properly separated. The term 'risk' as loosely used in everyday speech in economic discussion...are categorically different ...It will appear that a measurable uncertainty, or 'risk' proper, as we shall use the term, is so far different from an unmeasurable one that it is not in effect an uncertainty at all. We shall accordingly restrict the term 'uncertainty' to cases of the non-quantity type. It is in this 'true' uncertainty, and not risk, as has been argued, which forms the valid theory of profit and account for the divergence between actual and theoretical competition" (Knight, *Risk, Uncertainty and Profit*, 1921, pp.19–20).

So wrote Knight almost 100 years ago. It is in the miracle year of 1921 that Keynes and Knight published apparently similar, but subtly different, books on the economics of risk, probability, and uncertainty. It is really interesting to see how Keynes' concept of probability and uncertainty can be compared to Knight's distinction between a measurable risk and a non-measurable uncertainty. As will be shown in the main text of this book, while they look somewhat similar in one aspect, they are definitely different in another aspect and sometimes even antagonistic.

In a more historical perspective, the relationship between Keynes and Knight is really complex and rather strange. It has an interesting history of separating, approaching, separating again, and approaching again. So, it is high time for us to investigate how and to what extent Keynes and Knight are similar (or different) in terms of vision, ideology, tool, and policy implications.

In the 1970s, the influential economist Galbraith once advocated the *First Age of Uncertainty*. Almost 50 years have passed since then. For those years, so many "black swans" or highly improbable events, a la Nassim Nicholas Taleb, took place successively. The fall of Berlin Wall in 1989 followed by the collapse of the Soviet Union, the bankruptcy of Lehman Brothers in 2008 followed by the Great Recession, and the outbreak of the Great East Japan Earthquake and Tsunami followed by the explosion of Fukushima nuclear generation in 2008 were surely among those black swans.

At present, we are supposed to live in the *Second Age* of Uncertainty. All the existing knowledge and doctrines are no longer reliable. As Keynes rightly said, we simply do not know. And as Knight noticed, we have to deal with the unfamiliar notion of true uncertainty distinct from the familiar one of risk. In order to solve so many difficulties and problems facing us today, the emergence of new superstars such as the new Keynes and the new Knight would urgently be needed. While this book deals with risk and uncertainty, one thing should be quite certain. We have to learn new lessons from old teachings. As the saying goes, where there is a will, there is a way!

The preparation of this book has been made possible by the Japanese Ministry of Education, Culture, Sports, Science and Technology through Grant-in-Aid for Scientific Research. Thanks are due to the late Professor Lionel W. McKenzie (Rochester) and Professor Hirofumi Uzawa (Tokyo, Chuo) and Professor Takashi Negishi (Tokyo, Aoyama) for their everlasting encouragement and the staff members of Center for Risk Research, Shiga University, for their generous assistance. I am also deeply grateful to Professor Kiichiro Yagi (Kyoto, Setsunan), Professor Yuji Aruka (Chuo), and other council members of the Japan Association for Evolutionary Economics (JAFFE) for their helpful advices and useful comments for doing my research for a long time. And last but not least, I would like to say special thanks to Mr. Yutaka Hirachi and other staff members of Springer Japan for their kind suggestions and constant encouragement.

Hikone, Shiga, Japan
3 May 2019

Yasuhiro Sakai

Contents

Part I History and Decision

1 How My Life and Work Have Been Influenced by J.M. Keynes and F.H. Knight: Introduction and Summary 3
1.1 The First Age of Uncertainty: Many Turbulent Events in the Twentieth Century 4
1.1.1 The Popular Book of J.K. Galbraith: Its Widespread Impact 4
1.1.2 The Fall of the Berlin Wall: Incredible Events beyond all Expectations 7
1.2 The Second Age of Uncertainty: The Return of the Old Masters and beyond 8
1.3 The Brief Outline of this Book 9
1.3.1 Part I: History and Decision 10
1.3.2 Part II: Market and Application 12
1.4 "Strong in the Rain": Final Remarks 14
References 14

2 On the Economics of Risk and Uncertainty: A Historical Perspective 17
2.1 A Long and Rich History: An Introduction 17
2.2 The Economics of Risk and Uncertainty: The Six Stages of Development 19
2.2.1 The Initial Age as the First Stage: Greatness and Suffering of Blaise Pascal 19
2.2.2 The "B-A" Age as the Second Stage: Daniel Bernoulli and Adam Smith on Risk 23
2.2.3 The "K-K" Age as the Third Stage: Keynes and Knight on Uncertainty 27
2.2.4 The "N-M" Age as the Fourth Stage: Von Neumann and Morgenstern on Strategy and Game 28

2.2.5 The "A-S" Age as the Fifth Stage: The Arrow-Akerlof-Spence-Stiglitz Quartet on Imperfect Information 29
2.2.6 The Uncertain Age as the Sixth Stage: The Return of Keynes and Knight and Beyond 30
2.3 J.M. Keynes and F.H. Knight on the Role of Uncertainty in Human Behavior 30
2.4 The Spirit of Geometry Versus the Spirit of Fineness: Final Remarks 34
References 36

3 J.M. Keynes on Probability Versus F.H. Knight on Uncertainty: Reflections on the Miracle Year of 1921 39
3.1 1921 as a Miracle Year: An Introduction 39
3.2 Keynes on Probability and Uncertainty 41
3.2.1 The Meaning of Probability 41
3.2.2 Keynes' Strange Chart of Probability: An Attractive Partial-Order Network 42
3.2.3 Keynes' Theory of Induction: Reappraisal of Several Case Studies 45
3.2.4 Keynes on Uncertainty: *The General Theory of Employment, Interest and Money* 47
3.3 Keynes Versus Knight: With Special Reference to Risk, Probability, and Uncertainty 49
3.3.1 Keynes on Probability and Uncertainty 49
3.3.2 Knight on Risk and Uncertainty 51
3.4 Hicks on Decision and Probability: How Hicks Was Influenced by Keynes and Knight 54
3.4.1 Economics on the Edges of Both Sciences and History . . . 54
3.4.2 Decision and Probability 55
3.5 Beyond Keynes and Knight: Concluding Remarks 58
References 59

4 Daniel Ellsberg on J.M. Keynes and F.H. Knight: Risk, Ambiguity, and Uncertainty 61
4.1 Daniel Ellsberg as a "Man in Paradox": An Introduction 62
4.2 Uncertainties that Are Not Risks 63
4.2.1 Keynes and Knight: Their Similar yet Different Views . . . 63
4.2.2 Arrow's Skepticism About Knight on Uncertainty 66
4.3 Ambiguity and Risk 68
4.3.1 Keynes on the "Two-Color Urn" Problem 68
4.3.2 Ellsberg on the "Three-Color Urn" Problem 70
4.3.3 Alternative Ways to Resolve Ellsberg's Paradox 72
4.4 Econs Versus Humans: Concluding Remarks 76
References 77

Part II Market and Application

5 Involuntary Unemployment Versus "Involuntary Employment": J.M. Keynes and Beyond . . . 81
5.1 J.M. Keynes, F.H. Knight, and Y. Takata: An Introduction . . . 81
5.2 Involuntary Unemployment a la Keynes . . . 84
5.2.1 A Very Terribly Written Book of Macroeconomics . . . 84
5.2.2 The Original Framework: The Aggregate Supply and the Aggregate Demand . . . 85
5.2.3 Involuntary Unemployment: A New Concept in the Labor Market . . . 88
5.2.4 Takata on Keynes: Another Look at Involuntary Unemployment . . . 91
5.3 "Involuntary Employment": Another New Concept Beyond Keynes . . . 93
5.3.1 Depression Economics: Old and New . . . 93
5.3.2 Unhappy Workers Dispatched by Outside Agencies . . . 94
5.3.3 N. Takahashi's New Approach to "Involuntary Employment": Looking Beyond Keynes . . . 96
5.4 The Impact of Piketty's New Book: Concluding Remarks . . . 98
References . . . 99

6 Frank H. Knight on Uncertainty and Profit: Manager Versus Entrepreneur . . . 101
6.1 M. Bronfenbrenner as "Prof. Sharp Tongue": Some Traces of F.H. Knight . . . 101
6.2 Risk, Uncertainty, and Profit: Knight's Theory of Trinity . . . 104
6.2.1 How Uncertainty Is Radically Distinct from Risk . . . 104
6.2.2 Three Types of Probability Situations . . . 106
6.3 Enterprise and Profit . . . 110
6.3.1 The Effects of Uncertainty on the Organization . . . 110
6.3.2 Manager Versus Entrepreneur . . . 111
6.4 Bronfenbrenner on "the Chicago School": Final Remarks . . . 112
References . . . 113

7 Frank H. Knight on Market Thinking: Reflections on the Logic and Ethics of the Capitalist Economy . . . 115
7.1 What Money Can and Cannot Buy: An Introduction . . . 116
7.1.1 Michael Sandel on the Moral Limits of Markets . . . 116
7.1.2 Gary Becker on the Economics of Marriage . . . 117
7.1.3 F. H. Knight Versus M. Friedman: H. Uzawa's Remark . . . 118
7.2 The Ethics and Ideology of General Equilibrium Theory . . . 119
7.2.1 The Life and Work of "Professor Fixed Point" . . . 119
7.2.2 The Brouwer Fixed Point Theorem . . . 121
7.2.3 The Equivalence Between the Walras Existence Theorem and the Brouwer Fixed Point Theorem . . . 122

7.3 Welfare Implications of General Equilibrium 125
7.3.1 The Impact of the Cold War on the Economics Profession 125
7.3.2 Market Equilibrium and Pareto Optimality 127
7.4 F. H. Knight's Strong Objections Against the Capitalist Economy 128
7.4.1 Knight's Unique Position: A Pluralist Insight 128
7.4.2 Knight's Strong Objections Against the Market Economy 129
7.4.3 Inheritance, Luck, and Effort: A Graphical Interpretation 131
7.4.4 Risk, Uncertainty, and Moral Hazard: A Graphical Analysis 133
7.5 The Disappointing Performance of the Economics Profession: . . . 134
References 135

8 An Application to Nuclear Power Generation: From Daniel Bernoulli to J.M. Keynes and F.H. Knight 139
8.1 "Strong in the Rain": Fukushima and Chernobyl 139
8.2 The Place of Risk and Uncertainty in Economics 141
8.2.1 People's Concept of Risk in Daily Life 141
8.2.2 Individual Decision-Making Under Risk: The General Framework 142
8.2.3 The Allocation Problem of a Power Plant 143
8.3 Nuclear Power Generation: The Interactions of Economic and Psychological Factors 145
8.3.1 The Two Opposite Views: Pro and Con 145
8.3.2 Psychological Factors: Their Effects on Payoff Matrices and Probabilities 147
8.4 A Generalization of the Expected Utility Theory: J.M. Keynes and F.H. Knight 149
8.5 Selection of Appropriate Projects in the World of True Uncertainty 152
8.5.1 Paul Slovic and F.H. Knight: Beyond Measurable Risks 152
8.5.2 Application of the Maximin Rule to the Selection of Power Plants 153
8.6 Louis Pasteur Versus Torahiko Terada: Concluding Remarks 155
References 156

Part I
History and Decision

Chapter 1
How My Life and Work Have Been Influenced by J.M. Keynes and F.H. Knight: Introduction and Summary

Abstract This chapter aims to serve as a plain introduction and brief summary of my new book entitled *J.M. Keynes* versus *Frank H. Knight: Risk, Uncertainty and Decision*. Speaking of myself, I have been a professional economist more than 50 years. For those long years, so many things and events, mostly beyond my expectations, have happened in both Japan and foreign countries. Although I was fortunately awarded a Ph.D. from Rochester, I was quite annoyed by the practical irrelevance of general equilibrium theory, a very elegant field of economic science, which I myself taught to my students at Pittsburgh in the 1970s. When Oscar Morgenstern visited Pittsburgh, he kindly advised me to turn my interest to the economics of risk and uncertainty, a newly rising subject promoted by my contemporaries. It was a rather surprising fact that while J.M. Keynes and F.H. Knight did classical contributions to risk and uncertainty theories in the same year of 1921, their relations to more modern theories including George Akerlof, Joseph Stiglitz, and Richard Thaler had not been fully elucidated. Clarifying the total picture of such connections is an important motivation of writing this paper.

According to J.K. Galbraith, we lived through the First Age of Uncertainty in the twentieth century. Around 1990, we witnessed the Fall of the Berlin Fall together with the Collapse of the Soviet Union. Since we experienced the Great Recession caused by the 2008 Lehman Shock, we entered the Second Age of Uncertainty in which the old masters such as Keynes and Knight had superbly returned with new costumes on the academic stage. Surely, we can learn new lessons from old teachings.

This chapter also gives the compact outline of this book. The book as a whole consists of two parts. The first part contains the first four chapters, being concerned with history and micro. The second part contains the following four chapters, dealing with market and application.

Keywords J.M. Keynes · F.H. Knight · Oscar Morgenstern · J.K. Galbraith · The First Age of Uncertainty · The Second Age of Uncertainty

Y. Sakai, *J.M. Keynes Versus F.H. Knight*, Evolutionary Economics and Social Complexity Science 18, https://doi.org/10.1007/978-981-13-8000-6_1

1.1 The First Age of Uncertainty: Many Turbulent Events in the Twentieth Century

1.1.1 The Popular Book of J.K. Galbraith: Its Widespread Impact

When the very popular book *The Age of Uncertainty* by John Kenneth Galbraith, then a distinguished Harvard professor, was published in 1977, I myself was quite excited in many ways. First of all, it was really a delightful surprise to me. I was then a young and ambitious researcher who had just returned to the Land of the Rising Sun after receiving a Ph.D. in economics from the University of Rochester and later teaching a sequence of theory courses at the University of Pittsburgh. Although my research major was general equilibrium theory at Rochester, my teaching experience at Pittsburgh gave me a strong impetus to shift my academic interest to more applied fields.[1]

I vividly remember my exciting meeting with Oscar Morgenstern, a famous pioneer of the theory of games, who happened to come to Pittsburgh in 1973 in order to give us a general lecture on the history of economic theories. Being among the enthusiastic audience to listen to his lecture, I took a courage to ask a rather pointed question to him:

> Professor Morgenstern, I have been so impressed by your instructive lecture today. To tell the truth, however, I am not so happy about the present state of economic science. It seems that there exists a big gap between the abstract assumptions of theory and the harsh facts in reality. In order to fill in the gap, I would strongly feel the necessity to establish a new approach to socio-economic problems today. If you have some suggestions in this direction, please let me know.

Morgenstern at first appeared to be perplexed a bit, but soon composed himself. Then he kindly began to answer my question:

> Oh, Mr. Sakai, you look still young and have a lot of potential. I can tell you that fortunately, there now appears a new wave of economic thinking, that is the economics of uncertainty promoted by a group of young economists like you. Why don't you join the group right away?

The keyword "uncertainty" sounded to me like a sort of revelation or "Sermon on the Mount." What is uncertainty all about? Since then, I shifted all my energy into an investigation into the economics of risk and uncertainty although I had already read several articles by George Akerlof, Michael Spencer, and Joseph Stiglitz. Surely, they were all my contemporaries, so that I hopefully could join the "promising club of uncertainty."

---

[1]Galbraith (1977) was one of the most popular books in economics written in the 1970s, being also the subject of a television series which broadcasted not only in the USA and the UK but also in many other countries. The title "The Age of Uncertainty" per se was a very catchy word; thus helping to someway clear up people's uneasiness about the political economy caused by the great Watergate Scandal at Washington, D.C. People wanted to find a ray of hope in the dark and uncertain world.

I was then teaching a general equilibrium course at Pittsburgh. One day, a female student from Turkey asked me a very pointed question like this:

> Dr. Sakai, I am so impressed by the way you taught us general equilibrium theory. We have enjoyed by seeing the power and beauty of Kakutani's fixed point theorem, a mathematical tool to show the existence of competitive equilibrium. As you may know well, sir, I am not from well-advanced countries like the U.S. and Japan, but alas, from a less advanced country. I wonder whether and to what extent your general equilibrium lecture is applicable to the betterment of my home country. Please let me know.[2]

To tell the truth, this question gave me a shock, sounding like a thunder out of blue. The questioner was a bright and beautiful female student from an agricultural country, who had been very attentive to my graduate course. It seemed that she wisely hit the mark. I myself was then a professor lecturing her. So I tried to hide my true feeling before her, barely making the following answer:

> Oh, this sounds a very clever question. My country, Japan, is not so advanced as the United States either. As a matter of fact, there exist dual structures in Japan, namely, advanced and backward sectors. So speaking of myself, I am not in a position to strongly believe that the general equilibrium stuff can straightforwardly be applied to my home country. Well, all the students, I would like to say this! Now let us study together to carefully examine the applicability of pure economic theory to more complicated economies as they really are.

Although I managed to somehow escape from the pointed question from one of my graduate students, I nevertheless could not completely escape from a sort of feeling of shame. Why on the earth did I feel shameful then? To tell the truth, I pondered over such a serious problem, seeking the right answer for some time. Several years later, when I was walking around the Peace Memorial Park in Hiroshima, Japan, the popular book of Galbraith (1977) unexpectedly caught my eyes. Surely, we are now living in the Age of Uncertainty!

Galbraith wisely remarked:

> We would contrast the great certainties in economic thought in the last century [meaning the nineteenth century] with the great uncertainty with which problems are faced in our time. In the last century capitalists were certain of the success of capitalism, socialists of socialism, imperialists of colonialism, and the ruling classes knew they were meant to rule. Little of this certainty now survives. Given the dismaying complexity of the problems mankind now faces, it would surely be odd if it did. (Galbraith 1977, p. 7)

In the light of economic thought, Galbraith said that there existed a clear dividing line between the nineteenth and the twentieth centuries. In the nineteenth century, the problems we faced could be posed and solved with full certainty. Although the

---

[2]Shizuo Kakutani was a very famous mathematician who was born in Japan and later immigrated to the USA. He once served as a research assistant to von Neumann and Oscar Morgenstern when they were jointly writing the great book *The Theory of Games and Economic Behavior*. Kakutani's fixed point theorem is so powerful that it can be applied to many economics fields including game theory, general equilibrium theory, and oligopoly theory. In 1969, I myself met Professor Kakutani at the University of Rochester, who made a very exciting seminar, inspiring so many participants. This was surely one of my fond memories in my graduate student days in the USA. Hirota (2004) vividly describes the life and work of Kakutani.

relations between capitalists and socialists were antagonistic, each party believed in its victory over the other; namely, capitalists were certain of the success of capitalism and socialists the victory of socialism. Water is water, and oil is oil: they never mix well. In contrast to this, the situations faced in the twentieth century were so complicated and inscrutable that they could never be solved with firm confidence. Capitalism and socialism were engaged in real battles globally.

In my student days in Japan, there existed two popular yet opposing textbooks in economics—the "red text" and the "blue text." What we called the red text was represented by *Economics Textbook* (1958) published by the Russian Academy, the most authoritative agency of the socialist bloc. The problem of "socialism versus capitalism" constituted the central theme of the red text. In fact, the bulky text took pride in a through and comprehensive investigation of such comparative economic studies, thus reaching the following definite conclusion:

> We have thus far discussed the whole processes of economic development of a society. As a result, we have reached the most important conclusion that from a historical viewpoint, capitalism is destined to collapse whereas socialism is marching for its final victory over capitalism. There should be no other way! We are so confident of such historical inevitability (U.S.S.R. Academy Economics Institute 1958, p. 1050).

In contrast to the powerful and boastful red text, the blue text, presumably being regarded as a strong rival, seemed to be rather modest and even hesitant. To take an instance, Paul A. Samuelson (1967) wrote the world-popular textbook *Economics*, a typical "blue text" defending the American capitalist bloc, which fully argued alternative economic systems in its final chapter. Comparing relative economic growth of the USA and the U.S.S.R., he rather boldly depicted a very interesting diagram like Fig. 1.1.

In this figure, all indexes are based on the USA real GDP for 1960 = 100 and the U.S.S.R. real GDP for 1960 = 50. This means that in terms of DPP, the USA is approximately twice as big as the U.S.S.A. Note that each country has its own range of economic growth after 1960 onward, which appears to be widening every year until 2000. In other words, each range is enclosed by the two bounds—the upper bound based on the optimistic scenario and the lower bound based on the pessimistic scenario. While the USA apparently leads the U.S.S.R. in the first half of the 1970s, the economic gap between the two countries begins to be serious challenged in its second half since the "American range" and the "Russian range" are overlapped. Such an overlapping area is gradually widening until 2000. Samuelson thinks that as of 2000, the upper bound of the U.S.S.R. will possibly exceed that of the USA, thus boldly predicting a possibility, though it is rather faint, that Russia will overtake America.[3]

[3]Samuelson honestly acknowledges that Fig. 1.1 per se is not exactly depicted: the range of estimates shown there can no claim to accuracy, but they may roughly portray the nature of the strong challenge of the U.S.S.R. against the USA. Although Samuelson compared the two economies in terms of GNP (Gross National Product), I employed a more modern term GDP (Gross Domestic Product). The deference between GNP and GDP is statistically so small that it can safely be interchangeable in rough comparison of the two economies.

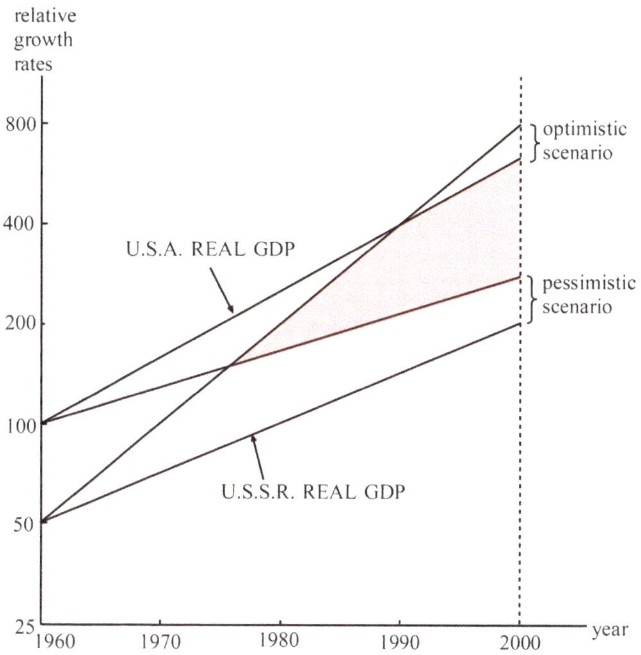

Fig. 1.1 Samuelson's prediction on the USA versus the U.S.S.R.

Although I was myself more impressed by the powerful red text than the moderate blue text, I nevertheless decided to go to the USA so that I could continue my graduate study without unduly political and psychological interruptions. I just wanted to get out of the Japanese university disturbance in the 1960s, thus daring to jump into the core of the capitalist economy. This is the brief story of why I went abroad midst the Cold War and how I became a serious researcher of the economics of risk and uncertainty.[4]

1.1.2 The Fall of the Berlin Wall: Incredible Events beyond all Expectations

History sometimes does something cruel. Indeed, as the real history told us, a sequence of so many incredible things and events happened beyond all expectations. As I mentioned above, alas, Samuelson's prediction abruptly ended around 2000. He seemed to think that he could safely extend the prediction well beyond the twenty-

[4]In an important book, Tsuru (1961) posed the question whether or not capitalism had changed since the 1960s. He thought that the distinction between capitalism and socialism as a social system was still effective and reserved a further investigation.

first century, at least as far as 2050. As we know so well, however, no person on the earth should be perfect and almighty: even Samuelson seemed to fail to come up to his prediction.

Against the wildest expectations of everyone including Samuelson, the invincible Berlin Wall collapsed all of a sudden in 1989, being followed by the total collapse of the mighty Soviet Union into so many independent countries in 1991.

> The Wall has collapsed completely! It is just gone! You'll see that we can now come and go so freely in Berlin!

This is the lively conversation I heard among the people when I attended the Berlin international economic conference in 1993. Once so many people in the Eastern Europe strongly believed in the total victory of capitalism over socialism. What they really experienced in Berlin, however, went just in the opposite direction, contradicting the way of thinking based on the authoritative red textbook. The real state of affairs may not proceed so dogmatically!

1.2 The Second Age of Uncertainty: The Return of the Old Masters and beyond

It was in the dreadful year of 2008 that the world economy faced the most serious crisis since the Great Depression of the 1930s. In fact, share prices plunged throughout the world; in particular, the USA lost 33.8% of its value in that single year. The seemingly mighty Lehman brothers collapsed, being followed by the total collapse of Yamaichi security company in Japan. Some economists tended to call the financial crisis of 2008 the Great Recession named after the famous Great Depression.

The Queen Elizabeth used to keep a large portion of her huge wealth in the form of stocks and securities. All of a sudden, the Great Recession took place, hitting the wealth of the British monarchy very harshly: the personal of the Queen's fortune was then estimated to have fallen £25 in the 2008 credit crunch. This was really an intolerable shock to the Queen!

In 2008, at the opening of a new building at the London School of Economics, the Queen uncharacteristically asked the following brief yet sharp question to the audience, including Professor Luis Garicano, then the director of research at the LSE:

> If these things were so large, how come everyone missed it?

Professor Caricano apparently got off-guard, thus just answering the Queen:

> In every stage, someone was relying on somebody else and everyone thought they were doing the right thing.

This episode was summed up as the simple sentence "Sorry Ma'am—we just didn't see it coming." More academically, I would rather like to say that we are now living in the Second Age on Uncertainty. In this connection, Posner (2009) eloquently remarked in a rather long sentence:

> I also emphasize some points that have received relatively little coverage in other accounts: the depression's political dimensions, the disappointing performance of the economics profession in regard to anticipating and providing guidance to responding to the depression, how ideology can distort economic policy, the inherent limitations of depression economics, how the self- interested decisions of rational businessmen and consumers can give rise to a depression (so there is no need to look for psychological explanations), and how the failure of officials and economists to anticipate the financial crisis and prevent its ripening into a depression echoes the failure of other officials and other professionals in anticipate and prevent other catastrophic events, like the Pearl Harbor or 9/11 attacks or the devastation of New Orleans by Hurricane Katrina. (Posner 2009, Preface, pp. xiv - xxv)

Perhaps, I do not need to add to Posner's remark. I just want to confirm here the disappointing performance of economic profession as an anticipating guidance to the Great Recession of 2008. It is quite interesting to see that the scale of the Economic Crash is likened to the Pearl Harbor air raid in 1941, the December 11 airplane attacks to the Twin Towers in New York, the Hurricane Katrina disaster, and the like.

Many people may believe that the collapse of the Soviet Union in 1991 shows the fundamental failure of socialism as well as an overwhelming victory of capitalism over socialism. The crisis of 2008, however, teaches us that the capitalist victory is not quite clear. A failure, if not the failure, of capitalism should be a very fashionable topic again in the academia. In short, we are now living in the Second Age of Uncertainty in which the rivalry between capitalism and socialism, or more exactly the one between market and organization, is still alive in many forms. We look forward to the return of the old masters including J.M. Keynes and F.H. Knight. Of course, we should not simply imitate the old teachings, nor apply them to new realities. Simple imitations and rude applications do not work here! We must do something else; we rather must go beyond those masters in a variety of ways toward the new horizon of integrated social science.

1.3 The Brief Outline of this Book

The great dramatist William Shakespeare (1564–1616) once remarked: "All's well that ends well." Well, this may be true, but not always so. This book focuses on risk and uncertainty, with special reference to J.M. Keynes and F.H. Knight. Although the two great men, Keynes and Knight, are in a sense the past economists, they are nevertheless still alive academically and will be very much so. Insofar as they are immortal, any book on their works should have no end at all; it will be wide open forever in the future. So I would rather like to change Shakespeare's golden saying in the following way: "All's well that ends nowhere."

As both Keynes and Knight constantly emphasized in their eternal works, everything is uncertain and unpredictable. This book is written in line with the uncertainty sprit a la Keynes and Knight. So let me write down the outline of this book right here.

This book consists of two parts. The first part contains the first four chapters from Chaps. 1, 2, 3, and 4, dealing with history and decision. The second part contains the following four chapters from Chaps. 5, 6, 7, and 8, turning to market and application. More detailed discussions of each chapter will be given in the subsections to be specified below.

1.3.1 Part I: History and Decision

Part I is expected to have a threefold purpose. First of all, it aims to serve as a comprehensive introduction to the whole content of this book. Second, it will discuss the economics of risk and uncertainty in a historical perspective. The six stages of its development will be carefully described and mutually compared. Third, it will deal with the micro foundations of such economics, with focus on the similarity and differences between J.M. Keynes and F.H. Knight, the two superstars of uncertainty economics. Besides, Daniel Ellsberg will be single out as a scholar in paradox, and his work on ambiguity will intensively be examined in relation to Keynes and Knight.

So far, we have lived in the two ages of uncertainty. The First Age of Uncertainty was energetically pointed out by John Galbraith, and the Second Age has started with the 2008 Lehman shock. Living through in those two ages gives us a strong incentive to write an academic work like this book.

On reflection, the economics of risk and uncertainty has a long history over 300 years. The purpose of Chap. 2 is to systematically summarize and critically reevaluate it, with special reference to John M. Keynes and Frank H. Knight, the two giants in modern times.

In our opinion, there are the six stages of development, with each stage vividly reflecting its historical background. The first stage, named the "Initial Age," corresponded to a long period before 1700, the one in which statistics was firmly established by Blaise Pascal, a famous mathematician and deep thinker, as a branch of mathematics. Unfortunately, economic theory per se was not well developed, however.

The second stage, called the "B-A" Age, covering the period from 1700 to 1880, was characterized by the two superstars, Daniel Bernoulli and Adam Smith. While Bernoulli was a member of the noted family of mathematical geniuses, Smith was an independent thinker and often called the Founding Father of Economic Science.

The third stage from 1880 to 1940 could be named the "K-K" Age because it was dominated by J.M. Keynes and F.H. Knight. It is those superstars that paid much attention to the critical difference between uncertainty and risk, thus seriously investigating the special role of the former, not the latter, in the working and performance of the market economy.

The fourth stage, called the "N-M" age, eyewitnesses the birth of game theory, with von Neumann and Morgenstern being its foundering fathers. It is quite remarkable to see that game theory was the product of collaboration of a distinguished mathematician and an outstanding economist.

The fifth stage from 1970 to 2000, named the "A-S" Age, was characterized by several distinguished scholars with the initials of their surnames "A" or "S." They included Kenneth Arrow, George Akerlof, Michael Spence, and Joseph Stiglitz. Fortunately, the initial of my name happens to have the initial "S."

Finally, in 2000 and onward, while many doubts have been raised about the existing doctrines, new approaches have not emerged yet, thus being named the "Uncertain Age." Both real economies and economic science are involved in so many uncertain factors. The important question of whether and in which way we can duly deal with them remains to be unanswered.

The relationship between Keynes and Knight seems to be complex and even strange. It has an interesting history of separating, approaching, separating again, and approaching again. As the saying goes, two cocks in one yard do not agree. This seems to be a historical destiny.

The purpose of Chap. 3 is to intensively discuss and carefully compare J.M. Keynes and F.H. Knight with respect to risk, probability, and uncertainty. It is in 1921 that both of them published apparently similar books on the economics of risk and uncertainty. While Knight's contribution on risk and uncertainty is now well recognized, Keynes's accomplishments on probability and uncertainty have been rather ignored in the shadow of his most famous book *The General Theory of Employment, Interest and Money* (1936). This paper aims to focus on his earlier yet equally important book *A Treatise on Probability* (1921), thus shedding a new light on his outstanding ideas and everlasting influences on his later work including *The General Theory of Employment, Interest and Money*. It is really interesting to see how Keynes's concept of probability and uncertainty can be compared to Knight's distinction between a measurable risk and a non-measurable uncertainty. This chapter also contains some new materials such as J.R. Hicks on decision and probability, thus intensively discussing how Hicks has been influenced by the two predecessors, Keynes and Knight.

Chapter 4 will focus on the life and work of Daniel Ellsberg, with an intensive discussion on his relation to J.M. Keynes and F.H. Knight, the two pioneers of the economics of uncertainty. Ellsberg seems to be a man in paradox. When he was young, he was an outstanding researcher at Harvard University and later at the RAND Corporation; at the December 1960 Meeting of the Econometric Society in 1960, he presented his remarkable paper in which he successfully demonstrated what we could call the Ellsberg paradox against the traditional expected theory a la Daniel Bernoulli and von Neumann. Although it was published with the title "Risk, Ambiguity, and Decision" in the November 1960 issue of the *Quarterly Journal of Economics*, it was not paid due attention for a long time. It was partly because he was so preoccupied in the 1960s and onward by letting the general public know the Pentagon papers that he could virtually have no time left to engage in purely academic activities. In the twenty-first century, however, the times have changed in favor of Ellsberg: we can see the dramatic return of interest in decision-making under ambiguity.

More specifically, we will first deal with uncertainties that are not risks. Kenneth Arrow's skepticism about Knight on uncertainty will be paid due attention. We will then turn to the concept of ambiguity that was first introduced by Ellsberg. Both the two-color problem and the three-color problem will systematically be examined by help of numerical representations. We will finally discuss many alternative ways to solve the so-called Ellsberg paradox. Presumably, the Keynesian approach by means of interval-valued probabilities will be shown to be very simple and highly effective. In our opinion, the most amazing Ellsberg paradox lies in the fact that an accomplished economist specialized in the aversion of risk and uncertainty dared to make a personal choice to risk everything such as degrading his social fame and putting him in prison for a long period. Surely, the intellectual legacy of Ellsberg himself seems to be an intriguing research in paradox.

1.3.2 Part II: Market and Application

Part II consists of four chapters, from Chaps. 5, 6, 7, and 8: it is a multipurpose chapter. It will analyze the working and performances of labor market equilibrium (or disequilibrium), the firm's equilibrium with profit, and the general equilibrium with many market interactions, with an important application to nuclear power generation with due considerations of psychological factors.

Chapter 5 is concerned with the important question of how and to what extent the great economists such as J.M. Keynes, F. H. Knight, J.R. Hicks, P. A. Samuelson, Y. Takata, and M. Morishima have been intermingled with each other. Our discussion focuses on the two key concepts in the labor market—involuntary unemployment and "involuntary employment." On the one hand, there are so many persons in the street who are willing to work at the existing wages but cannot find jobs because of a shortage of the effective demand as a whole. This is clearly the issue of involuntary unemployment, which has been energetically tackled by J. M. Keynes and his followers since the 1930s.

On the other hand, since the 1990s, there also have emerged so many people who must work unwillingly for their survivals at the minimal level of wages. This is a new issue of "involuntary employment" or "non-regular workers," which has recently been investigated by Nobuaki Takahashi, a rising Japanese economist. Although the Takahashi approach is an attractive one, it nevertheless seems to remain at the embryo stage, thus requiring further developments in many ways. I believe that the second Keynes would urgently be needed.

Chapter 6 aims to carefully discuss how Frank H. Knight, the "Grand Old Man" of Chicago, dealt with uncertainty and profit, with special reference to manager versus entrepreneur. Frankly speaking, Knight himself was a sort of man in paradox, having a dualistic view and adopting an eclectic approach. In order to shed a new light on his life and work, we first argue that there possibly exist some traces of the great Knight in the words and deeds of Martin Bronfenbrenner, once one of Knight's students at Chicago. Then we focus on the clear-cut distinction between risk and uncertainty. According to Knight, non-measurable uncertainty must radically be different from measurable risk: only uncertainty, but not risk, enables the entrepreneur to acquire true profit as its reward. In contrast to the manager who are doing just routine jobs every day, the entrepreneur dares to engage in new venturous activities, thus playing the central figure of the capitalist system. At present, we live in the new age of uncertainty. As mentioned before, the second Knight is urgently needed.

The purpose of Chap. 7 is to shed a new light on the working and performance of the market economy from a pluralistic viewpoint. To this end, I first pay attention to the general equilibrium theory a la L.W. McKenzie, K. J. Arrow, and G. Debreu. Whereas this theory seems to be established on the foundation of solid logic and advanced mathematics, the existence of special ethics and ideology behind the scenes should not be forgotten. I next reexamine the thought of Frank H. Knight, who has raised a strong objection against glorification of the market economy by the neoclassical economists.

In the late 1960s, I myself was a graduate student at the University of Rochester. I still recall the touching moment when Professor McKenzie, finally succeeding after a long struggle to prove the existence of a competitive economy by help of a mathematical theorem of fixed point, posed a bit in a class and said quietly, "it's so beautiful!" The world was then in the midst of the Cold War and divided into the two powerful blocs: namely, the socialist bloc dominated by the Soviet Union and the capitalist block led by the USA. McKenzie's complacent whispering sounded like the victory declaration of capitalism over socialism.

Around 40 years have passed since then. It seems that the "Academic Cold War" between Marxian economics and modern economics is now over. At the same time, the ethics and ideology of general equilibrium looks surely fading away although it is not completely vanished. It is our sincere regret, however, that the new, synthetic social science to replace the existing dogmatic doctrines are not in sight yet. A completely new approach with the Knightian spirit and/or the Keynesian sprit would eagerly be awaited.[5]

Chapter 8, the final chapter of this book, aims to discuss the problem of nuclear power generation from the viewpoint of the economics of risk and uncertainty. Although we have experienced the two major nuclear disasters, Chernobyl and Fukushima, in recent times, it is quite unfortunate that risk-economic studies in nuclear power generation have been disappointingly rare so far. This could show intentional neglect in the academic circle.

[5]After witnessing the crisis of 2008, Paul Krugman (2008) has remarked that "John Maynard Keynes, the economist who made sense of the Great Depression, is now more relevant than ever" (Krugman 2008, p.190). Michio Morishima, perhaps the greatest economist who Japan has ever produced, has published an important book with the sensational title "Why will Japan Collapse?" Morishima (1999) has advocated the necessity of establishing a sort of interdisciplinary and comprehensive research in social science—what he once called a "symphonic social science"—a true synthesis of economic science, sociology, education science, history, and the like. I myself believe that the synthesis must include natural science such as biology, physics, and life science as well.

The purpose of Chap. 8 is to duly mend such a regrettable tendency. Before 11 March 2011, there were many people who more or less believed in the myth of absolute safety. The Great East Japan Earthquake, however, has completely changed their concept of risk for nuclear power generation, thus requiring a completely new risk-economic approach to nuclear energy. As the saying goes, we can learn new lessons from old teachings: we have to reexamine the economics of J.M. Keynes and F. H. Knight. Surely, there remain many new possibilities for future research.

1.4 "Strong in the Rain": Final Remarks

Kenji Miyazawa (1896–1933) was a very popular Japanese writer who spent his whole life in Iwate Prefecture, one of the stricken areas of the 2011 Great East Japan Disaster. By writing the famous poem "Strong in the Rain," the wise man Miyazawa (1931) has left an everlasting memory to all the people until today:

> Strong in the rain.
> Strong in the wind.
> Strong against the summer heat and winter snow.
> He is healthy and robust.
> Unselfish.
> He never loses his temper.
> Nor the quiet smile on his lips. (Miyazawa 1931)

In the twentieth century, we lived through the First Age of Uncertainty. So many unexpected things and events happened. In the twenty-first century, we are now living in the Second Age of Uncertainty. We have to do our best to live through so many kinds of fluctuations and turbulences which will come in the new century.

As Miyazawa rightly said above, we must be strong enough to deal with any kind of risk, ambiguity, and uncertainty. We must be strong in the rain and in the wind. Likewise, we must be strong against earthquakes and depressions.

One final word. I strongly hope that this book will serve as a helpful guide to a newly integrated theory of risk and uncertainty that should be built on the basis of J.M. Keynes and F.H. Knight. I am sure that we can learn a variety of new lessons from a set of old teachings. Life is a challenge! As the saying goes, where there is a will, there is a way!

References

Galbraith JK (1977) The age of uncertainty. Houghton Mufflin Co, Boston

Hirota M (2004) The life and work of Professor Shizuo Kakutani, with special reference to his contributions to mathematics and economic theory. Econ Semin J, 597, Nihon Hyoron Publishers, pp 10–11. (in Japanese)

Krugman P (2008) The return of depression economics and the crisis of 2008. Penguin Books, London

Miyazawa K (1931) Strong in the rain (in Japanese). Translated by Japan Medical Association and contained in Nabeshima N (ed) (2007) The world of Kenji Miyazawa. Ryukoku University Press, Kyoto

Morishima M (1999) Why will Japan collapse? Iwanami Shoten Publishers, Tokyo. (in Japanese)

Posner RA (2009) A failure of capitalism: the crisis of 2008 and the descent into depression. Harvard University Press, Cambridge, MA

Samuelson PA (1967) Economics: an introductory analysis, seventh edition. McGraw-Hill, New York

Tsuru S (ed) (1961) Has capitalism changed?: an international symposium on the nature of contemporary capitalism. Iwanami Shoten Publishers, Tokyo

U.S.S.R. Academy Economics Institute (ed) (1958) Economics textbook, 3rd rev edn. Moscow. (in Russian) Japanese Translation (1960)

Chapter 2
On the Economics of Risk and Uncertainty: A Historical Perspective

Abstract The economics of risk and uncertainty has a long history over 300 years. This chapter aims to systematically summarize and critically reevaluate it, with special reference to John M. Keynes and Frank H. Knight, the two giants in modern times.

In our opinion, there are the six stages of development, with each stage vividly reflecting its historical background. The first stage, named the Initial Age, corresponds to a long period before 1700, the one in which statistics was firmly established by B. Pascal as a branch of mathematics but economic theory per se was not well-developed. The second stage, called the "B-A" Age, covers the period from 1700 to 1880, is characterized by the two superstars, Daniel Bernoulli and Adam Smith. The third stage from 1880 to 1940 may be named the "K-K" Age because it was dominated by J.M. Keynes and F.H. Knight. The fourth stage, called the "N-M" Age, eyewitnesses the birth of game theory, with von Neumann and Morgenstern being its foundering fathers. The fifth stage from 1970 to 2000, named the "A-S" Age, is characterized by several distinguished scholars with their initials "A" or "S." Finally, in 2000 and onward, while many doubts have been raised about existing doctrines, new approaches have not emerged yet, thus being named the Uncertain Age.

The relationship between Keynes and Knight is complex and even strange. It has a history of separating, approaching, separating again, and approaching again. As the saying goes, a new wine should be poured into a new bottle. We would urgently need a Keynes and/or a Knight toward a new horizon of the economics of risk and uncertainty.

Keywords Economics of risk and uncertainty · Bernoulli · Keynes · Knight

---

This chapter is largely based on Sakai (2019).

Y. Sakai, *J.M. Keynes Versus F.H. Knight*, Evolutionary Economics and Social Complexity Science 18, https://doi.org/10.1007/978-981-13-8000-6_2

2.1 A Long and Rich History: An Introduction

On 5 November 2008, Queen Elizabeth attended the opening ceremony for a new academic building at the London School of Economics. After being briefed by academics at the LSE about the turmoil and crisis on the international stock market, the Queen suddenly asked to the professors the question: "Why did nobody notice it?" In spite of the fact that these depressive things were so large, the Queen wondered why everyone in the academic circle failed to foresee the crisis. Then Professor Luis Garicano, director of research at the management department, had very hard time to explain the origins and effects of the credit crunch. He barely managed to tell the Queen, "At every stage, someone was relying on somebody else and everyone thought that they were doing the right thing."[1]

In hindsight, history tells us that in 2008 the people around the world were in the midst of the biggest crisis since the infamous Great Depression of the 1930s. As was clearly pointed out by Posner, a noted Harvard professor, we have shockingly seen disappointed performance of the economics profession in regard to anticipating and providing guidance to responding to the depression.[2]

We now live in the age of uncertainty. As Beck (1986) has rightfully noted, we could also say that we live in Risk Society. While most of swans are surely white birds, there are nevertheless a considerable number of *Black Swans* in modern society. According to N.N. Taleb (2007), "Black Swan logic makes *what you don't know* far more relevant than what you do know. Consider that many Black Swans can be caused and exacerbated *by their being unexpected.*" Presumably, the 2008 credit crunch which surprised the Queen as well as the economics profession was one of those Black Swans. Taleb proceeds to say that a Black Swan is an event with the following three attributes. First, it lies outside the realm of regular expectations, because nothing in the past can convincingly point to its possibility in the present. Second, it may sometimes carry an extreme impact as was illustrated by the Great Depression in the 1930s and the financial crisis in 2008. Third, human nature makes us concoct some explanations and even excuses only after the event happened.

We now believe that it is high time to systematically summarize and critically reevaluate the long history of the economics of risk and uncertainty. Carrying out such a mission is certainly the main goal of this paper. The contents of the paper are briefly described as follows. In Sect. 2.2, we carefully survey the economics of risk and uncertainty from a historical perspective. We will show that there are six stages of development, with each stage reflecting its historical events. In Sect. 2.3, we will focus on Keynes and Knight, the two great economists in modern times. While they both can be regarded as pioneers of non-measurable uncertainty, their relations are

[1]For details, see Pierce (2008).

[2]For details, see Posner (2009). Also see Borch (1968), Fellman (1995), Leibnitz (1703), Mizushima (1995), Morishima (1994, 1999), Negishi (1989), Ogura (1980), Sakai (1985, 1990, 1996), Schumacher (1973), Shackle (1949), Skidelsky (2009), Soros (1998), and Thaler and Sunstein (2009).

rather complex and even strange. Their positions are separating in one time yet approaching in other times. We will attempt to shed new light on their delicate relationship. And some final remarks will be made in Sect. 2.4.

2.2 The Economics of Risk and Uncertainty: The Six Stages of Development

The economics of risk and uncertainty has a long history over 300 years. In this section, we would like to systematically summarize and critically reevaluate it. In our opinion, as is seen Table 2.1, there are the six stages of development, with each stage corresponding very well to its historical background. The first stage, named the Dark Age, refers a long period before 1700. The second stage, called the "B-A" Age, covers the period from 1700 to 1880, and the third stage from 1889 to 1940 may be named the "K-K" Age. While the fourth stage can be called the "N-M" Age, the fifth stage from 1970 to 2000 may be named the "A-S" Age. Finally, in 2000 and onward, we step into the sixth stage where we are supposed to live in the Uncertain Age.[3]

2.2.1 The Initial Age as the First Stage: Greatness and Suffering of Blaise Pascal

Concerning the economics of risk and uncertainty, as is seen in Table 2.1, the first stage of its development corresponded to a long period before 1700. Although statistics as a branch of mathematics was firmly established by Pascal and Fermat, economic theory was not well-developed yet. So we would like to regard this first stage as the Initial Age. Regarding its outstanding historical events, we can point out the around-the-world trip by F. Magellan, a Portuguese adventurer, for the period 1519–1522, the opening of London stock exchange, the establishment of British East India Company in 1600, and the opening of Lloyd coffee shop as a forerunner of marine insurance company in 1688. Remarkably, a big fire took place in Tokyo in 1657, being followed by another big fire in London in 1665. Therefore, the Initial Age was well-characterized by risky ventures by adventurers with animal spirits and risk-sharing management by stock and insurance companies.

It is noted that the period of around 300 years before 1700 can be regarded as the era of the merchants, namely, the one which was called mercantilism or the mercantile economy. In fact, the merchants of seventeenth-century Osaka were even able to carry out very sophisticated mercantile dealings such as futures trading.

[3]There have been still very few books and papers that discuss the history of the economics of risk and uncertainty. A modern and systematic approach to the history was provided by Sakai (2010). Also see Borch (1968) and Greer (2000).

Table 2.1 The economics of risk and uncertainty: the six stages of development

Age	Economics of risk and uncertainty	Historical events
I. Initial Age	Statistics is established by **Pascal**, Fermat	Around-the-world trip by Magellan (1519–1522)
		London stock exchange (1566)
	Economic theory is not well-developed yet	British East India Company (1600)
		Tokyo big fire (1657), London big fire (1666)
		Lloyd coffee shop (1688)
1700		
II. "B-A" Age	**Daniel Bernoulli** (1738)	American Independence (1776), French Revolution (1789)
	Adam Smith (1759, 76)	Meiji Revolution (1868)
	Laplace (1812)	Tokyo marine insurance (1879)
1880		
III. "K-K" Age	Marshall (1890)	First World War (1914–1918), Russian Revolution (1917)
	Keynes (1921, 36), **Knight** (1921)	Great Kanto earthquake (1923), Great depression (1929)
	de Finetti (1937), Shackle (1938, 1949)	Second World War (1936–1945)
1940		
IV. "N-M" Age	von **Neumann/Morgenstern** (1944)	Hiroshima atomic bombing (1945)
	Nash (1951), Selten (1970)	People's Republic of China (1949), Cuba crisis (1962)
	Friedman/Savage (1948), Allais (1953)	Sputnik in the space (1964)
	Simon (1957), Tobin (1958)	Man on the Moon (1969)
	Stigler (1961), Pratt (1964)	Violent student movement (1968–1969)
1970		
V. "A-S" Age	**Arrow** (1970), **Akerlof** (1970)	Second economics crisis by Robinson (1971)
	Spence (1974), **Stiglitz** (1975)	Oil crisis (1973, 1978–1979)
	Hurwicz (1973), Sandmo (1970)	Chernobyl nuclear disaster (1986)
	Tversky/Kahneman (1974)	Soviet Union collapses (1989)
	Black/Sholes (1973), Author (1994)	Kobe great earthquake (1995)
2000		
VI. Uncertain Age	Piketty (2013)	Lehman shock (2008)
	Old doctrines are shaky	Fukushima nuclear disaster (2011)
	New approaches to be awaited	Unpredicted events to come

Unfortunately, in these three centuries of mercantilism, economic theory did not have a famous spokesman, none such as Adam Smith, Alfred Marshall, Karl Marx, and J.M. Keynes in later years.[4]

Mathematics has a longer history than economic theory. In this Initial Age, statistics as a branch of mathematics was firmly established by the two great men of mathematicians—P. Fermat (1601–1665) and B. Pascal (1623–1662). In connection with the risk theory and its implication to human behavior which constitute the main subject of this paper, Pascal would perhaps be one of the most remarkable persons in the whole history of mankind. He was not only a very famous mathematician, but also a first-rate philosopher and an excellent essayist. According to E.T. Bell, a noted historian of mathematics, Pascal was perhaps the greatest might-have-been in the history of mathematics. "If ever a wonderfully gifted man buried his talent, Pascal did; and if ever a medieval mind was cracked and burst asunder by its attempt to hold the new wine of seventeenth-century science, Pascal was. His great gifts were bestowed upon the wrong person" (Bell (1937), p. 74). We would like to add that Pascal was perhaps one of the greatest might-have-been in the history of the science of human behavior: he would perhaps have cracked a medieval mind by his attempt to establish a new wine of risk science.

P. S. Laplace (1749–1827), a noted mathematician, once remarked:

> We see … that the theory of probability is at bottom only common sense reduced to calculation; it makes us appreciate with exactitude what reasonable minds feel by a sort of instinct, often without being able to account for it. … It is remarkable that this science, which originated in the consideration of games of chance, should have become the most important object of human knowledge.[5]

Yes, it would appear that the theory of probability is at bottom only commonsense reduced to calculation. This is a viewpoint commonly shared by classical statisticians. The position of modern probability is different from the classical one since the former thinks that probability cannot simply be reducible to common sense; it should something more than mere calculation.

The founders of the classical theory of probability were Pascal and Fermat. The initial problem, called the "problem of points," was originally proposed to Pascal by his friend de Méré, a professional gambler, and successfully solved by the close correspondence between the two mathematicians, Pascal and Fermat. Let us suppose that each of the two players gambling with dice must gain a certain number of points to win the game. And suppose that because of some reasons, they have to discontinue the game before it is finished. Then the question that would naturally arise is how the stakes should be divided between the two players. It was Pascal and Fermat who jointly analyzed the chance of winning or losing by help of the consideration of probability.[6]

---

[4]For this point, see Galbraith (1987) and Hicks (1969).

[5]For details on Pascal and Laplace, see Bell (1937), Chapter 5. Laplace's dramatic life was described by Bell as "from peasant to snob."

[6]It should be noted that the original writings of Pascal (1656) were occasionally unclear and unnecessarily repetitive to the modern mind. While its English translation by Trotter (1910) is available, the Japanese translation by Matsunami (1965) is more instructive than the English one since Matsunami offers the reader a series of helpful translation remarks.

Table 2.2 Pascal's final problem: "God is" or "He is not"?

Alternative states	"God is"	"He is not"
Probability	p	$1-p$
Utility	∞	n
Expected utility	∞	$(1-p)\,n$

Pascal made the important application of probabilities which for his time was very practical as well. Interestingly enough, this is the very fundamental problem of whether "God is" or "He is not." According to his eloquent yet classical expressions, Pascal once wrote:

> Let us say, 'God is', or 'He is not.' To which side shall we incline? Reason can decide nothing here. There is an infinite chaos which separate us. A game is being played at the extremity of this infinite distance where heads or tails will turn up. What will you wager? According to reason, you can neither the one thing nor the other; according to reason, you can defend neither of the proposition. ...... Yes; but you must wager. It is not optional. You are embarked. Which will you choose then? ...... Let us weigh the gain and the loss in wagering that God is. ... There is here an infinity of an infinitely happy life to gain against a finite number of chances of loss, and what you stake is finite. It is all divided; wherever the infinite is here and there is not an infinity of chances of loss against that of gain, you must divide. (Pascal (1656); Trotter (1910), p. 47)

Unfortunately, Pascal's expressions seem to be speculative and unclear, so that the modern mind needs to have much patience for full understanding. In our opinion, an expected utility interpretation would be very helpful in grasping the Pascal's final problem. In Table 2.2, there are two alternative states: "God is" and "He is not." Let us suppose that the probability that the "God is" and the one that "He is not" are, respectively, denoted by p and $(1-p)$. Presumably, the value of p is a very small fraction, but it is not zero.

Theoretically speaking, there are two possibilities: "God is" and "He is not." On the one hand, Pascal claims that if "God is," then "an infinitely happy life to gain" will be promised; whence its utility can be expressed as an infinity: U (God is) $= +\infty$. Since the expected utility is equal to the product of probability and utility, we must have EU (God is) $= p \times \infty = \infty$. On the other hand, if "He is not," then the amount of utility achievable is as much as n, a certain finite number: U (He is not) $= n$. As a result, we obtain EU (He is not) $= (1-p)\,n < \infty$. Since an infinite number is greater than any finite number, the value of EU (God is) exceeds the one of EU (He is not). So Pascal concludes that there is no time to hesitate but decide to wager that God is.

Pascal as a "thinking reed" put all his energy into the final problem, namely, the one whether "God is" or "He is not." In the above, we have attempted to provide a modern interpretation by help of the expected utility theory. It was Daniel Bernoulli who systematically developed the powerful theory of risk almost 100 years later than Pascal.

2.2.2 The "B-A" Age as the Second Stage: Daniel Bernoulli and Adam Smith on Risk

If we make a bird's-eye view of the history of the economics of risk and uncertainty, we find that there existed the two great pioneers for the period from 1700 to 1880: Daniel Bernoulli (1700–1782) and Adam Smith (1723–1790). They were both outstanding contemporaries of the eighteenth century. And Laplace (1812) was an outstanding successor of Pascal and Fermat in the field of mathematical statistics.

In this period, we had big political upheavals such as American Independence (1776), French Revolution (1789), and Meiji Revolution (1868). It is also noted that the opening of Lloyd coffee shop in London stood out as the beginning of modern insurance company.

Daniel Bernoulli was then regarded as one of the most famous mathematicians after the death of Isaac Newton (1642–1727). Besides, quite fortunately, he could have a plenty of pastime for gambling, which presumably led him to establish the fundamental theory of human decision-making under risk: indeed, he might occupy the position of the "father of risk economics." While Smith was well known as the author of *The Wealth of Nations* (1776), the greatest economics book ever written in human history, it would be a pity that he has been a rather forgotten man in the field of risk and uncertainty. It is high time to shed new light on the "side jobs" of those two giants who greatly contributed to the formation of the second stage: the "Bernoulli-Adam" Age or simply the "B-A" Age.[7]

St. Petersburg, once the capital of the mighty Russian Empire, was artificially built by Peter the Great at the beginning of the eighteenth century, at the swampy mouth of the Neva River. There stood the famed statue *The Bronze Horseman* whose greatness was documented by a narrative poem written in 1833 by Aleksandr Pushkin, a respected Russian poet. At this time, scientific academies of high prestige existed in several cities such as Paris, London, Rome, and Bologna. When Peter the Great determined to construct the Petersburg Academy, a Russian equivalent of the Paris Academy, he enthusiastically invited a group of first-rate scientists from Western Europe, among whom were Daniel Bernoulli and Leonhard Euler, very close friends and highly productive mathematicians.[8]

Which is the most deciding factor in the emergence of genius, nature or nurture? This would certainly be one of the most intriguing questions to ask. While this constitutes a still unsettled controversy, the most striking case has been provided by the mathematical Bernoulli family. This family produced eight first-rate mathematicians over three generations. Take a look at Fig. 2.1. Out of the number of ten persons indicated there, those eight persons framed by squares were noted mathematicians. One exception was Nicholas Senior (1623–1708), who headed the family

[7]A notable exception was Alfred Marshall (1890), the man of "cool head but warm heart," carefully recorded Bernoulli's work in risk theory in a mathematical appendix of his great lifework.

[8]The establishment and development of the Petersburg academy was well described by Fellmann (1995) and its English translation (2007).

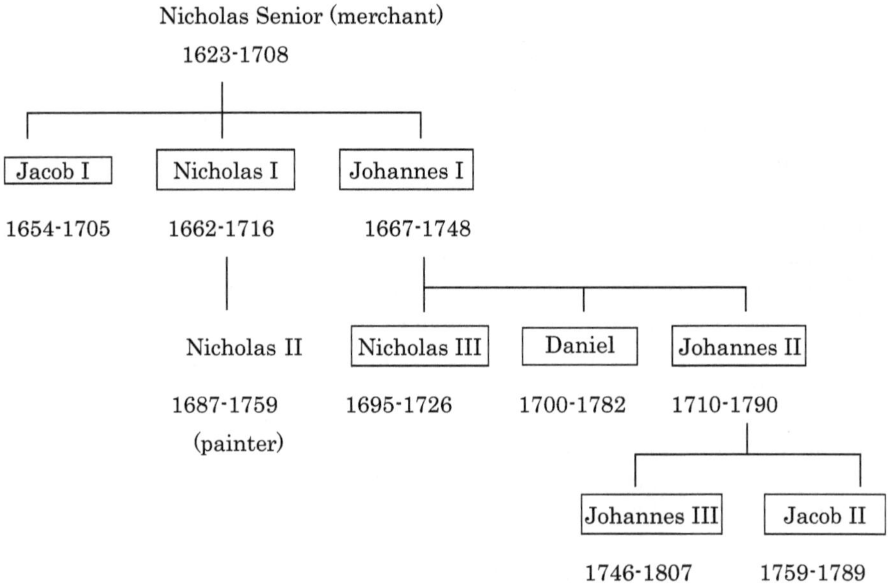

Fig. 2.1 The family tree of the mathematicians of Bernoulli

tree and was a great merchant as his father and grandfather had been. Another exception was Nicholas II, who was a son of great mathematician Nicholas I and was not a mathematician at all but a very good painter.[9]

Daniel Bernoulli, a grandson of Nicholas Senior and also a noted mathematician, dared to leave Basle, Switzerland, toward the capital of the Russian Empire, becoming a professor of mathematics at the Petersburg Academy. His academic work was vast and productive, including differential equations, probability, and many other problems in applied mathematics. Considering the harsh weather and his loneliness in Petersburg, it would perhaps be no wonder that he found much interest in gambling and its related topic of individual decision-making under risk.

It is in 1738 that he published an epoch-making article in Latin, which is now regarded as the beginning of the modern theory of risk aversion and expected utility. Bernoulli considered the following coin-tossing game shown in Table 2.3.[10]

[9]For the family tree of Bernoulli, see Bell (1937).

[10]Following the academic custom at that time, Bernoulli (1738) was originally written in Latin on the academy bulletin of the Petersburg academy and had been almost forgotten since then. It is after 200 years that its English translation was published in *Econometrica* (Vol. 22, No.1, 1954) and built up a solid reputation as a monumental work.

Table 2.3 Bernoulli's coin-tossing game: heads or tails?

Events (coin tossing)	$i = 1$	$i = 2$	$i = 3$	......	$i = N$	......
Prizes (100 dollars)	2	4	8	......	2^N	......
Probability	1/2	1/4	1/8	......	$1/2^N$	......
Expected prizes	1	1	1	......	1	......
Expected utility	$(1/2)U(2)$	$(1/4)U(4)$	$(1/8)U(8)$	......	$(1/2^N)U(2^N)$	......

Remark. We suppose that the head appears for the first time after the i- th toss

Now let us toss a brand-new coin. Then we will find the two possibilities, "head" and "tail." If we find the head, you get 200 dollars as a prize and stop the game. If you find the tail, we continue to toss it again until you find the head. Now suppose that the head appears at the first time after the i -th toss ($i = 1,2,3,\ldots, N,\ldots$). Then, as is seen in Table 2.2, the following sequences of probabilities and prizes will appear:

Probability:	1/2	1/4	1/8	......	$1/2^N$	......
Prizes (100 dollars):	2	4	8	......	2^N	......

Since the expected prize is equal to the product of probability and prize, and the expected utility, the one of probability and the *utility* of prize, the following sequences of expected prizes and *expected utility* will come out:

Expected prizes:	1	1	1	......	1	......
Expected utility:	$(1/2)U(2)$	$(1/4)U(4)$	$(1/8)U(8)$	......	$(1/2^N)U(2^N)$	......

Now let us assume that if we want to participate in the coin-tossing game aforementioned, we have to pay a certain amount of entry fee, say one million dollars. The question which would naturally arise to our mind is whether or not we are really willing to play the game. Since one million dollars are no doubt a huge amount of money, common sense would tell us that the answer should definitely be negative. If we rely on the expected prizes, however, the opposite answer would come out. In order to prove this, let us look at the fourth line of Table 2.3. Then we will immediately see that the total sum of prizes obtainable from the game is given by

$$E\Pi \equiv 1 + 1 + 1 + \cdots + 1 + \cdots = +\infty, \tag{2.1}$$

which is the amount of money larger than one million dollars. Therefore obeying the simple rule of expected prizes, we should by all means play the game. Do not play the game *emotionally*, but do play it *theoretically*! Such a counterintuitive result is often called the St. Petersburg paradox.

In order to get out of the paradox, we ought to introduce a new decision rule that is completely different from the rule of expected prizes. Bernoulli was brave enough to replace the old rule of expected prizes by the new rule of *expected utility of prizes*:

$$EU \equiv (1/2)U(2) + (1/4)U(4) + (1/8)U(8) + \cdots\cdots + \left(1/2^N\right)U\left(2^N\right) + \cdots\cdots \tag{2.2}$$

In a historical perspective, Bernoulli was a very practical man in the sense that he wisely employed a very convenient logarithm function: $U(x\ ) = \log x$. Then the expected utility of playing the game can easily be calculated as follows:

$$\begin{aligned} EU &\equiv (1/2)(\log 2) + (1/4)(\log 4) + (1/8)(\log 8) + \cdots\cdots + \left(1/2^N\right)\left(\log 2^N\right) + \cdots\cdots \\ &= \left\{(1/2) + (2/4) + (3/8) + \cdots\cdots + \left(N/2^N\right) + \cdots\cdots\right\} (\log 2) \end{aligned} \tag{2.3}$$

If we let $A = \{(1/2) + (2/4) + (3/8) + \ldots\ldots + (N/2^N)\}$, then it is not hard to find that $A - (1/2)A = 1$, implying that the value of A is just two. Therefore, the expected utility of playing the game is shown by *EU* (playing the game) = 2 (log 2) = log 4.

It is recalled that the (expected) utility of the entry fee of coin tossing is shown by *EU* (paying the entry fee) = log 100. What we have learned from the above calculations is the importance of a comparison of the two values, namely, log 4 and log 100. Since the value of log 4 is definitely smaller than the one of log 100, we should not play the coin-tossing game, which is apparently a reasonable conclusion. Thus Daniel Bernoulli, a man of mathematical genius, has at last succeeded in solving the St. Petersburg paradox!

We are ready to turn another towering giant in "B-A" Age, namely, Adam Smith. In contrast to Daniel Bernoulli who was born with a silver spoon in Central Europe, Adam Smith was born with a wooden spoon in a small village of Scotland, far away from the center of Europe. Under the influence of David Hume (1739), a noted philosopher of skepticism, Adam Smith published two great books, *The Theory of Moral Sentiments* (1759) and *The Wealth of Nations* (1776).

Smith (1759), his first great book, was an outstanding breakthrough on moral philosophy. The book asserted that both moral ideas and human actions were produced by our very nature as social creatures. Concerning the special relationship between self-interest and sympathy, Smith (1759) began with the following famous assertion:

> How selfish soever man may be supposed, there are evidently some principles in his nature, which interest him in the fortunes of others, and render their happiness necessary to him, though he derives nothing from it, except the pleasure of seeing it. Of this kind is pity or compassion, the emotion we feel for the misery of others, when we either see it, are made to conceive it in a very lively manner. (Smith, 1759, p. 9)

Smith (1776), his second great book, was no doubt a historical landmark on economic science. There he boldly assumed that a man pursued his self-interest first without due consideration of the interests of others and discussed the question how and to what extent the whole economy worked as the interactions of those selfish persons. So on appearance, the first book *Moral Sentiments* was somehow at odds with the second book *Wealth of Nations*. We believe, however, there should have been no contradictions whatever between those two books because they were really the products of the same brilliant brain. We must bear in mind that Smith was a professor of moral science at the University of Glasgow, whence paying attention on the moral behavior of the *Total Man*, or the man who could be influenced by many factors such as emotions, justice, power, and economic gains. This was really the research subject of the first book. If we narrowed our scope on the material side only, the Total Man may have shrunk to the *Economic Man*, or the man who was so self-centered and sought his own material wealth. This was apparently the main subject of the second book. We should point it out, however, that even in the second book, the behavior of the Total Man appeared here and there, thus exceeding the limited scope of the Economic Man. Putting it differently, Smith shrewdly succeeded in introducing the noneconomic aspects of the first book into the economical second book. Such a mixture of economic and noneconomic factors became quite clear when he turned his attention to his pet problem of how a man in the street behaved under the conditions of risk and uncertainty.

In the second great book, Smith once remarked:

> The chance of gain is by every man more or less over-valued, and the chance of loss by most men under-valued . . . (Smith 1776, p. 107)

According to Smith, on the one hand, the universal success of lotteries told us that a man tended to overvalue the chance of gain. Objectively speaking, there was a very small hope of gaining some of great prizes. The man nevertheless wished to participate in a lottery in order to make rich quick. This showed that a man may sometimes be motivated emotionally rather than economically. On the other hand, the chance of loss was frequently undervalued. In the time of Smith, although sea risk were alarmingly high, the proportion of uninsured ships to those insured was much greater. This evidently demonstrated people's neglect of insurance on shipping and also on houses.

The problem of making a bridge between the Total Man and the Economical Man has been one of main targets of investigation since Smith. To tell the truth, it still remains unsolved even today.

2.2.3 The "K-K" Age as the Third Stage: Keynes and Knight on Uncertainty

Regarding the history of the economics of risk and uncertainty, the period from 1880 to 1940 could be characterized as the "K-K" Age or the age in which J.M. Keynes (1883–1946) and F.H. Knight (1885–1972), somehow unusual pupils of Alfred Marshall (1842–1924), revolutionized the main stream of economic theory by first dealing with the new factor "uncertainty" as distinct from the old factor "risk."

The relation between Keynes and Knight was so delicate and complex that it could not be described by a single passage. It was really described as a sequence of separating, approaching, separating again, and approaching again. So it would be a good idea to spare one full section, namely, the next section, for a fuller discussion on this subject.

We would like to point out that both Keynes and Knight were contemporaries and lived through the two world wars, the First World War (1914–1918) and the Second World War (1939–1945). In this inter-war period, people's lives were greatly affected by many serious incidents including Russian Revolution (1917), Great Kanto earthquake (1923), and the outbreak of Great Depression (1929) and its aftereffects.

2.2.4 *The "N-M" Age as the Fourth Stage: Von Neumann and Morgenstern on Strategy and Game*

The fourth stage was set up by the overwhelming rise and striking development of the new field of game theory. In fact, Von Neumann and Morgenstern (1944) were the culmination of the joint work of the two outstanding scientists in different fields—applied mathematics and economic theory. So we could call this stage the "N-M" Age by noting the initials of the authors.[11]

As was systematically discussed by Sakai (1982, 2019), their ideas were still further developed by Nash (1951), Selten (1970), and others. Besides, individual behavior under risk was carefully studied by Friedman/Savage (1948), Allais (1953), Tobin (1958), Stigler (1961), and Pratt (1964).

Without getting into details, we would like to point out that in this "N-M" Age, we saw a series of extraordinary things such as atomic bombing in Hiroshima and Nagasaki (1945), the rise of People's Republic of China (1049), the Cuba crisis between the capitalist bloc and the socialist bloc (1962), the Russian spaceship Sputnik in the space (1964), the first man on the Moon by American space project (1969), and the frequent occurrence of violent student movements (1968–1969). Needless to say, those events were more or less the products of the so-called Cold War between the two blocs aforementioned.

We would to add that another sort of Cold War took place on the academic front as well. *Das Kapital* (1867) by Karl Marx had been regarded as a Bible for a long time. It told us how the socialist economy of the Soviet Union was economically and morally better than the capitalist economy of the USA. In our opinion, the mathematically powerful theory of games and its elegant application to general equilibrium theory served very well as the perfect justification for the superiority of capitalism over socialism. As philosopher Emmanuel Kant noted, people tended to seek the nice combination of the three virtues, truth, justice, and beauty![12]

---

[11]The collaboration between Morgenstern and Von Neumann was one of the most interesting stories ever told in the history of economic theories. See Morgenstern (1976).

[12]During the Cold War, a great number of papers on game theory and general equilibrium theory were financially supported by military-related funds such as the Office of Naval Research Logistics Project. We should always remember that the Cold War carried out not only militarily but also ideologically.

2.2.5 The "A-S" Age as the Fifth Stage: The Arrow-Akerlof-Spence-Stiglitz Quartet on Imperfect Information

While game theorists were mainly concerned with measurable risk rather than non-measurable uncertainty, a group of clever economists looked at human interactions from a different angle. Remarkably, in the 1970s, explosion on papers on uncertainty and imperfect information took place as exemplified by Arrow (1970), Akerlof (1970), Spence (1973), and Stiglitz (1975). Since the initials of those authors were "A" or "S," it could be appropriate to call this fifth stage the "A-S" Age.[13]

If we follow the popular expression of Taleb (2007), then the period from 1970 to 2000 contained so many "black swans" or highly improbable events such as the first oil crisis (1973), the second oil crisis (1978–1979), Chernobyl nuclear disaster (1986), the collapse of the Soviet Union (1989), and Kobe great earthquake (1995). Already in 1971, famous post-Keynesian economist Joan Robinson (1971) pointed out the lack of correspondence between the assumptions of the new doctrine after Keynes and the unvarnished facts in reality:

> The new doctrine is now coming to a crisis. The first part of the doctrine—that the amount of investment is controlled by how much society wants to save—was discredited in the great slump. The second part, that the form of investment is controlled by the principle of maximizing the welfare of society, is being discredited by the awakening of public opinion to the persistence of poverty—even hunger—in the wealthiest nations, the decay of cities, the pollution of environment, the manipulation of demand by salesmanship, the vested interests in war, not to mention the still more shocking problems of the world outside the prosperous industrial economies. The complacency of neo-laissez faire cuts the economists off discussing the economic problems of today just as Say's Law cut them off discussing unemployment in the world slump. It seems that this second crisis, like the first, is due to the uncritical acceptance of the apologetic that seemed plausible (though it was never logical) in the nineteenth century. (Joan Robinson 1971, Introduction. pp. xiv–xv)

It seemed that the emergence of the economics of uncertainty and imperfect information in the 1970s was one step forward for filling the gap between the doctrine and the facts in reality. If Joan Robinson would have lived longer until 2000, then she would have found much interest in some other problems caused by nuclear power explosion and their serious aftereffects. The incentive compatibility problem paused by Hurwicz (1973), saving decisions under uncertainty by Sandmo (1970), behavior economics by Tversky and Kahneman (1974), the mathematical option problem of Black and Scholes (1973), and the complexity problem of Author (1994) were also intensively investigated in this exciting era.

[13]For details, see Akerlof (1984).

2.2.6 *The Uncertain Age as the Sixth Stage: The Return of Keynes and Knight and Beyond*

We are now in the Uncertainty Age as the sixth stage. It seems that all the old doctrines have been built on very shaky grounds, hoping for the arrival of new approaches. There are many people who eagerly look forward to the return of Keynes and/or Knight, the grand masters of the third stage. Alas, almost half a century has passed since their deaths. The simple return of the old masters would be no help! Probably, we need a new Keynes and/or a new Knight.

Quite recently, French economist Thomas Piketty (2013) has published a highly exciting book, first written in French and then immediately translated into English. It deals with the dynamics of wealth and income inequality covering a long span of the last 200 years. Piketty persuasively argues that we are now on the way back to the old-fashioned capitalism, in which the wealth and income inequalities are widening again and thus social and economic instabilities are also increasing. Since its publication, there have been many pros and cons for the book. Paul Krugman, Nobel prize winner, praised it very highly:

> It seems safe to say that Capital in the Twenty-First Century, the magnum opus of the French economist Thomas Piketty, will be the most important economics book of the year—and maybe the decade. (Krugman 2014, *New York Times*)

We are not certain whether and to what extent Krugman's appraisal of Piketty is correct. If we think of the happenings of big unexpected events such as Lehman shock (2008) and Fukushima nuclear disaster (2011), however, we must eagerly hope for the coming of new economic science. Piketty's new and ambitious analysis will perhaps be one of the most important books for many years to come.

2.3 J.M. Keynes and F.H. Knight on the Role of Uncertainty in Human Behavior

In view of the history of economic theory, there existed two outstanding superstars on uncertainty as distinct from risk. They were J.M. Keynes and F.H. Knight. Strangely enough, however, very few books and papers on Keynes versus Knight have been published so far.[14]

While Keynes and Knight were contemporaries, it seemed that their relations were rather strange, possibly being characterized as the alternation succession of separating and approaching. Their strange relations were chronologically stated in Table 2.4. Keeping in mind that their influences has remained strong and will continue to be so after their deaths, it would be quite convenient to divide those relations into the four phases: the first phase of separation (until 1890), the second

[14]Sakai (2015), written in Japanese, is one of notable exceptions. This chapter is regarded as its updated English version with complete alteration.

Table 2.4 Keynes versus Knight: their strangely intricate relations

Phase	Keynes (1883–1946)	Knight (1885–1972)
Phase 1	Born with a silver spoon	Born with a wooden spoon
Separating (~ 1890)	Colorful life at Cambridge, UK	Monotone life at Illinois, USA
Poles apart		
Phase 2	*Treatise on Probability* (21)	*Risk, Uncertainty and Profit* (21)
Approaching (1890–1930)	Took a middle position	Risk is measurable, but uncertainty is non-measurable
Research fields similar	Treacherous concept	
Phase 3	*The General Theory of Employment, Interest and Money (36)*	*Ethics of Competition (35)*
Separating again (1930–1980)	Macro with animal spirits	Micro, against macro
Macro vs. micro	Involuntary unemployment	Full employment at start
	Practical man	Academic man
Phase 4	Return of depression econ	Failure of capitalism again
Approaching again (1980~)	Lehman shock (08)	Economic gaps widening
Return of the masters	Second Keynes awaited	Second Knight awaited

phase of approaching (1899–1930), the third phase of separating again (1930–1980), and the fourth phase of approaching again (after 1980).

As for the first phase, Keynes and Knight were poles apart in origins. On the one hand, Keynes was born with a silver spoon in the old world; he spent his young days at a rich Victorian house in a peaceful Cambridge district in the Great British Empire. He spent a very colorful life until his untimely death in 1946, first as a university instructor, then as a high government officer, and sometimes as an art collector. On the other hand, Knight was born with a wooden spoon in the new world, beginning with unpromising roots in McLean County, Illinois, USA. He received general education at a small college in rural Tennessee. He later moved to Cornell University and wrote a Ph.D. thesis. It was in 1927 that he finally appointed Professor of Economics at the University of Chicago.

Although as stated above, the lives of Keynes and Knight were quite separated for both geographically and culturally, their research fields gradually approached around 1900 until 1930. In particular, the year of 1921 was recorded as a sort of miracle year for both of them: in this same year, Keynes wrote a well-written yet very difficult book *A Treatise on Probability* and Knight a rather incomprehensible and very difficult book *Risk, Uncertainty and Profit*.

Keynes was a man with many faces: a university instructor, a government officer, an art collector, a practical man, a romantic man, and the like. The following Byron-like poem written at the very end of his first book (1921) would show his unique view on probability.

O False and treacherous Probability,
Enemy of truth, and friend to wickednesse;
With whose bleare eyes Opinion learns to see
Truth's feeble party here, and barennesse. (Keynes 1921, p. 166)

According to the young Keynes, probability was double-edged, having dual meanings. For one thing, as was seen in the above poet, it might be a false and treacherous concept. For another, as his mathematical training at Cambridge told us, it could serve as a good guide to finding truth. Therefore, his position on probability was delicate and complicated; it seemed to lie somewhere between the subjective and objective theories. He thought that the concept of probability in social sciences was fundamentally different from the one in natural sciences. A more detailed discussion on this point was found in Sakai (2017).

Keynes's discussion did not stop here! Rather, he proceeded to go further to pick up a more challenging concept of uncertainty. According to his opinion, uncertainty was not only nonnumerical and noncomparable like probability but also a "very wild" concept including "animal spirits" or spontaneous optimism. He published a follow-up paper (1937) immediately after the *General Theory of Employment, Interest and Money* (1836), in which he clarified the concept of uncertainty:

> The sense in which I am using the term [*uncertainty*] is that in which the prospect of a European war is uncertain, or the 0price of copper and the rate of interest 20 years later hence are uncertain …… About these matters, there is no scientific basis on which to form any calculable probability whatever. We simply do not know. (Keynes 1937, p. 123)

In order to further develop his own idea of uncertainty and animal spirits, Keynes was bold enough to pick up very fashionable topics such as the so-called beauty contest conducted by British newspapers and the harsh rivalry between a British soldier Scott and a Norwegian adventurer Amundsen for the first reaching to the South Pole.

Independently of British scholar Keynes, American professor Knight also committed all his energies to scrutinize his own concept of risk and uncertainty. In his well-known book, Knight (1921) remarked:

> Uncertainty must be taken in a sense radically distinct from the familiar notion of Risk, from which is has never been properly separated. (Knight 1921, p. 19)

According to Knight, risk was a familiar notion in everyday life and was measurable in the sense that it could be described by a certain distribution function such as a normal distribution of Gauss. Both the mathematical probability of rolling the dice and finding "three" and the statistical probability of being involved in a critical traffic accident at a certain place belonged to the world of measurable risk. In contrast to risk, uncertainty was a fundamentally different concept in the sense that it was no longer measurable. "The distinction here is that there is no valid basis of any kind for classifying instances. This form of probability is involved in the greatest logical difficulties of all, and no very satisfactory discussion of it can be given" (Knight 1921, p. 225).

This non-measurable uncertainty was nothing but "true" uncertainty, thus being Knight's main theme of the famous 1921 book. It really constituted the core of the economics of Knight: it really served as his key concept for understanding the effectiveness and limitations of the market economy. Knight then deplored that such non-measurable uncertainty had been neglected thus far in economic theory. With the introduction of uncertainty into the real situation, its character must be completely changed. Then we see the emergence of a new type of the producer, called the entrepreneur, who had a forward-looking character in the unpredictable world, thus taking a bold action himself, which could result in an extra profit if his prediction was correct.

To sum up, around the miracle year of 1921, both Keynes and Knight energetically discussed on the role of non-measurable uncertainty in human behavior and the capitalist society. It was unfortunate, however, that their lives and works began to separate again. Two geniuses were seldom compatible with each other!

During the 1930s of Great Depression, Knight and Keynes were academically separating again. After all, Knight was the man of micro, but Keynes the man of macro. Micro is micro; macro is macro. Possibly, these two concepts were reconcilable to a certain degree, perhaps depending on a person in question. Knight belonged to the neoclassical world, however, in which macro was not duly accepted as an analytical concept. Indeed, in his critical paper, Knight (1937) remarked:

> I [Knight] must confess that the labor I have spent on *The General Theory of Employment, Interest, and Money* leaves me a feeling of keen disappointment. (Knight 1937; Emmet (ed.) 1999, Vol. 1, p. 201)

If we made use of the two comparisons of micro versus macro, and of certainty versus uncertainty, they we could classify all the economists into four groups. In Fig. 2.2, McKenzie represented the pair (micro, certainty), Marx the pair (macro, certainty), Keynes the pair (macro, uncertainty), and Knight the pair (micro, uncertainty). McKenzie and Keynes were diametrically opposite, and so were Marx and Knight. As McKenzie and Marx were partially opposed, so were Keynes and Knight. It is noted that academically partial opposition may emotionally yield more than

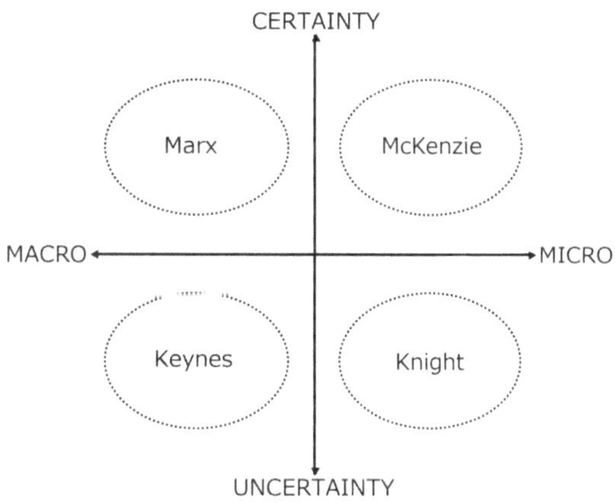

Fig. 2.2 McKenzie, Marx, Keynes, and Knight: How are they different?

partial disappointment, even very keen antagonism. After all, human beings are very emotional animals!

As Keynes noted, we are all dead in the long run. While the short life of Keynes ended in 1946, the long life of Knight finished in 1972. Since the year of 1980, especially after 2000, the academic wind has gradually changed its direction in favor of Keynes and Knight. We are now entering the fourth and final phase of approaching. The return of the two masters is eagerly called for in the academic world. In the cinema world, the man called *007* is alive twice. Likewise, Keynes and Knight seem to be immortal!

2.4 The Spirit of Geometry Versus the Spirit of Fineness: Final Remarks

In the above, we have outlined the history of the economics of risk and uncertainty, with special reference to J.M. Keynes and F.H. Knight. There are six stages of development for those 500 years: the Initial Age, the "B-A" Age, the "K-K" Age, "N-M" Age, "A-S" Age, and the Uncertain Age.

In our opinion, B. Pascal (1623–1662), who as a mathematical-philosophical genius made a spectacular showing in the Initial Age, seems to be still alive after 450 years of his death. He paid much attention to the critical difference between the two spirits: the spirit of geometry (or *esprit de géométrie*) and the spirit of fineness (or *esprit de finessee*). His famous Pensée (1656) should be regarded as a monumental book on the study of man. At its very beginning, he wrote:

> The difference between the spirit of geometry and the spirit of finesse—in the one, the principles are clear, but removed from ordinary use, so that it is difficult to turn one's spirit in that direction...... In the spirit of finesses, however, the principles are found in common use and before the eyes of everybody. One has only to look, and no effort is necessary, it is a question of good eyesight. But it must be good because the principles are so subtle and numerous that it is almost impossible to follow, thus tending to escape notice.[15]

Concerning with the spirit of Euclidean geometry, the principles are quite clear and can logically be derived on the basis of a set of axioms. People's mind, however, is usually non-mathematical, so that it is very difficult to turn one's mind in a mathematically rigorous direction. In contrast, as to the spirit of fineness, the principles are found in common use and can intuitively be understood by every man. They are so subtle and numerous that they tend to escape notice. Correspondingly, there are two kinds of intellect: the mathematical intellect and the intuitive intellect. The former has power and exactness in the sense that it can comprehend a great number of premises without confusing them. The latter can penetrate quickly

[15]Concerning this sentence, the English translation by Trotter (1910) seems to be less than perfect. In our opinion, the spirit of geometry should correspond to the original French expression *esprit de géométrie*, and the spirit of fineness *esprit de finessee*.

into the conclusions of premises without intermediate steps. Pascal stresses the necessity to have those two different kinds of intellect. He observes, however, that it is very rare in the real world that good mathematicians have good intuitive minds and vice versa.

It is worthy of notice that the difference between the spirit of geometry and the one of fineness may be quite applicable in modern times. In his best sellers, Richard Thaler (2008, 2015), who won the 2017 Nobel Prize in economic science, has energetically asserted that a distinction between two kinds of thinking must be kept in mind, one that is deductive and slow and another that is intuitive and slow. In a similar fashion, we should not mix up the following two concepts—*homo economicus* (or Econs in short) and *homo sapiens* (or Humans in short). Econs never make an important decision without checking with their deductive systems, thus being time consuming. Humans may sometimes rely on the rules of thumb, thus thinking and deciding fast. Needless to say, Econs, not Humans, appear in many economic textbooks. Thaler advocates the return of Humans in the world of economics. In passing, we note that Econs and Humans, respectively, correspond well to the Economic Man and the Total Man in our terminology aforementioned.

We are now in the age of uncertainty. Although so many theories and doctrines of risk and uncertainty have been accumulated so far, it seems that almost all of them are now getting behind the times, thus having less power of applicability than ever before. It seems that Keynes and Knight are rare exceptions and still alive even today.

The Age of Uncertainty—this was the very catchy phrase that was first invented and publicized by famous economist John K. Galbraith (1977). According to his opinion, we could contrast the great certainties in economic thought in the nineteenth century with the great uncertainty with which problems were faced in the twentieth century until the 1970s. "In the last century capitalists were certain of the success of capitalism, socialists of socialism, imperialists of colonialism, and the ruling classes knew they were meant to rule. Little of this certainty now survives. Given the dismaying complexity of the problems mankind now faces, it would surely be odd if it did" (Galbraith 1977, p. 7).

It seems the age of uncertainty has double meaning. First, it is the age in which the economics of risk and uncertainty is established and flourished: more exactly, it should be the age of uncertainty economics. Second, it is the age in which the existing economic ideas are uncertain and unreliable: it should be the age of uncertain economic thought. It is in this second meaning that Galbraith employed in his popular book and excited so many people.

Since Lehman shock (2008) and Fukushima nuclear crisis (2011), many people have had serious doubts about the foundation of the uncertainty economics per se. In other words, economic science per se is now in crisis. In order to get out of the crisis, new approaches and doctrines are urgently needed. Although the ideas of Keynes and Knight were once powerful and influential, they are now only has-beens; they are no longer almighty. In the twenty-first century, however, neither a Keynes nor a Knight has been in sight yet. At present, the new Keynes and the new Knight are urgently awaited. Where there is a solid will, there should be a good way out!

References

Akerlof GA (1970) The market for lemons: qualitative uncertainty and the market mechanism. Q J Econ 84:488–500
Akerlof GA (1984) An economic theorist's book of tales: essays that entertain the consequences of new assumptions in economic theory. Cambridge University Press, Cambridge
Allais M (1953) La comportement de l'homme rationnel devant le risque. Econometrica:503–546
Arrow KJ (1970) Essays in the theory of risk-bearing. North-Holland, Amsterdam
Author WB (1994) Increasing returns and the path dependence in the economy. University of Michigan Press, Michigan
Beck U (1986) Risikogesellschaft: Auf dem Weg in eine Andere Moderne (in German). Surbkamp Verlag, Frankfurt am Main. English translation by Ritter M (1992) Risk society: towards a new modernity. SAGE Publications, London.
Bell ET (1937) Men of mathematics. Simon and Schuster, New York
Bernoulli D (1738) Specimen Theoriae Novae de Mensura Sortes. Commentarii Academiae Scientiarum Imperiales Petropolitanae, (in Latin), Vol. 5. English translation by Sommer, L. (1954) Exposition of a new theory on the measurement of risk. Econometrica: 22-1
Black F, Scholes M (1973) The pricing of options and corporate liabilities. J Polit Econ 81:637–654
Borch KH (1968) The economics of uncertainty. Princeton University Press, Princeton
de Finetti M (1937) La prévision: ses lois logiques, sees sources subjectives. Annals de l'institut Henri Poincaré, 7, Paris
Emmett RB (ed) (1999) Selected essays by Frank H. Knight, Vol.1 & Vol. 2. University of Chicago Press, Chicago
Fellmann EA (1995) Leonhard Euler (in German). Rowohlt Yaschenbuch Verlag. English Translation by Gautschi et al (2007) Birkhäuer Verlag. Basel, Switzerland
Friedman M, Savage LJ (1948) The utility analysis of choices involving risk. J Polit Econ 56:279–304
Galbraith JK (1977) The age of uncertainty. Houghton, Mifflin
Galbraith JK (1987) Economics in perspective: a critical history, Houghton Mifflin
Greer WB (2000) Ethics and Uncertainty. Edward Elgers
Hicks JR (1969) A theory of economic history. Oxford University Press, Oxford
Hume D (1739) A treatise of human nature. Edinburgh
Hurwicz L (1973) The design of mechanisms for resource allocation. Am Econ Rev 63(2):1–30
Keynes JM (1921) A treatise on probability. Macmillan, London
Knight FH (1921) Risk, uncertainty and profit. Houghton Mifflin, Chicago
Krugman P (2014) The Piketty panic. New York Times, April 24
Leibnitz GW (1703) Correspondence between Leibnitz and Jac Bernoulli
Marx K (1867) Das Kapital (in German). London
Mizushima K (ed) (1995) Insurance culture: risk and the Japanese people (in Japanese). Chikura Publishing Company, Tokyo
Morgenstern O (1976) The collaboration between Oscar Morgenstern and John Von Neumann. J Econ Lit 14(3):805–816
Morishima M (1994) Modern economics as economic thought (in Japanese). Iwanami Publishing Company, Tokyo
Morishima M (1999) Will Japan collapse? (in Japanese). Iwanami Publishing Company, Tokyo
Nash JF (1951) Non-cooperative games. Ann Math 54:286–295
Negishi T (1989) History of economic theory. North-Holland, Amsterdam
Ogura E (1980) Ohmi merchants: a historical perspective (in Japanese). Nihon Keizai Newspaper Company, Tokyo
Pascal B (1656) Pensée (in French). Paris. English translation by Trotter WF (1910) Blaire Pascal's Pensée. Suzeteo Enterprises. Japanese translation by Matsunami S (1965) Kawade Shobo Shinsha Company, Tokyo

Pierce A (2008) The Queen asks why no one saw the credit crunch coming. The Telegraph: November 5, London
Piketty T (2013) Le capita *Capital in the* l au XXI siècle (in French). Paris, France. English translation by Goldhammer (2014) Capital in the twenty-first century. Harvard University Press
Posner R (2009) A failure of capitalism: the crisis of '08 and the descent into depression. Harvard University Press, Boston
Pratt JW (1964) Risk aversion in the small and in the large. Econometrica 32:122–136
Robinson J (1971) Economic heresies: some old-fashioned questions in economic theory. Basic Books Publishers, New York
Sakai Y (1982) The economics of uncertainty (in Japanese). Yuhikaku Publishing Company, Tokyo
Sakai Y (1985) The value of information in a simple duopoly model. J Econ Theory 36:36–54
Sakai Y (1990) The theory of oligopoly and information (in Japanese). Toyo Keizai Publishing Company, Tokyo
Sakai Y (1996) The economics of risk: information and society (in Japanese). Yuhikaku Publishing Company, Tokyo
Sakai Y (2010) Economic thought of risk and uncertainty (in Japanese). Minerva Publishing Company, Kyoto
Sakai Y (2015) Keynes versus knight: comparing their ideas on the "age of uncertainty" (in Japanese). Minerva Publishing Company, Kyoto
Sakai Y (2017) J.M. Keynes on probability versus F.H. Knight on uncertainty: reflections on the miracle year of 1921. Evol Inst Econ Rev 13(1):1–21
Sakai Y (2019) On the economics of risk and uncertainty: a historical perspective. Hikone Ronso, Shiga
Sandmo A (1970) The effect of uncertainty on saving decisions. Rev Econ Stud 37:353–360
Schumacher EF (1973) Small is beautiful: economics as if people mattered. Blond & Briggs, London
Selten R (1970) Preispolitik der Mehrproduktenuntermehmung in der statischen Theorie. Springer, Berlin
Shackle GLS (1938) Expectations, investment and income. School of Economics Press, London
Shackle GLS (1949) Expectation in economics. Cambridge University Press, Cambridge
Simon HA (1957) Models of man: social and rational. Wiley, New York
Skidelsky R (2009) Keynes: The return of the master. Public Affairs, New York
Smith A (1759) The theory of moral sentiments. London. Liberty Fund Edition by Raphael DD et al (eds) (1976) Oxford University Press
Smith A (1776) An inquiry into the nature and causes of the wealth of nations. The First Tuttle Edition by E. Cannan (ed) (1937). Random House, London
Soros G (1998) The crisis of global capitalism. Public Affairs, New York
Spence M (1973) Job market signaling. Q J Econ 87:355–374
Spence AM (1974) Market signaling. Harvard University Press, Cambridge, MA
Stigler GJ (1961) The economics of information. J Polit Econ 69:213–225
Stiglitz GJ (1975) The theory of 'screening', education, and the distribution of income. Am Econ Rev 65:283–300
Thaler R (2008) Nudge: improving decisions about health, wealth, and happiness. Yale University Press, New Haven
Taleb NN (2007) The black swan: the impact of the highly improbable. Random House, London
Thaler RH (2015) Misbehaving: the making of behavioral economics. Norton, New York
Tobin J (1958) Liquidity preference as behavior towards risk. Rev Econ Stud 25:65–86
Tversky A, Kahneman D (1974) Judgment under uncertainty: heuristics and biases. Science 185:19–34
Von Neumann J, Morgenstern O (1944) Game theory and economic behavior. Princeton University Press, Princeton

Chapter 3
J.M. Keynes on Probability Versus F.H. Knight on Uncertainty: Reflections on the Miracle Year of 1921

Abstract The purpose of this chapter is to discuss and compare the two giants in the history of economic thought, J.M. Keynes and F.H. Knight, with special reference to risk, probability, and uncertainty. It is in 1921 that both of them published apparently similar books on the economics of risk and uncertainty. While Knight's contribution on risk and uncertainty is now well recognized, Keynes' accomplishments on probability and uncertainty have been rather ignored in the shadow of his most famous book *The General Theory of Employment, Interest and Money* (1936). This chapter aims to focus on his earlier yet equally important book *A Treatise on Probability* (1921) and shed a new light on his outstanding ideas and everlasting influences on his later work including *The General Theory of Employment, Interest and Money*. It is really interesting to see how Keynes' concept of probability and uncertainty can be compared to Knight's distinction between a measurable risk and a non-measurable uncertainty. This paper also contains some new materials such as J.R. Hicks on decision and probability, thus intensively discussing how he has been influenced by the two predecessors, Keynes and Knight.

Keywords J.M. Keynes · F.H. Knight · J.R. Hicks · Risk · Probability · Uncertainty

3.1 1921 as a Miracle Year: An Introduction

There is no doubt that J.M. Keynes and F.H. Knight are two towering figures in the history of the economics of risk and uncertainty. Knight's contribution to risk and uncertainty is well-known to many economists: in fact, his book *Risk, Uncertainty and Profit* (1921) is now regarded as a classic in the economics profession. In contrast to this, Keynes' accomplishments on risk and uncertainty have been rather underestimated in the dark shadow of his most famous book *The General Theory of Employment, Interest and Money* (1936). The main purpose of this paper is to mend such an unfortunate tendency by focusing on his earlier yet equally important book *A*

This chapter is largely written on the basis of Sakai (2015, 2016).

Y. Sakai, *J.M. Keynes Versus F.H. Knight*, Evolutionary Economics and Social Complexity Science 18, https://doi.org/10.1007/978-981-13-8000-6_3

Treatise on Probability (1921). It is quite interesting to see that the two economic giants published apparently similar books on risk, probability, and uncertainty in the same year. Therefore, 1921 may be referred to as a sort of miracle year in the long history of economic thought.

The relation between Keynes and Knight, the two giants in the history of economic thought, is so delicate and complicated that cannot be described by a simple passage. It is true that they were contemporaries and lived through the two world wars, namely, the First World War (1914–1918) and the Second World War (1939–1945). It is noted, however, that they were poles apart in origins. Keynes (1883–1946) was born with a silver spoon in the UK: he spent his young days at a rich Victorian house, in a peaceful Cambridge district. During all his proactive career in the fields of academics and practical affairs, he could cheerfully return to this house, full of nice memories, and to his beloved parents. His roots were deep in Harvey road, which maintained the traditional values of the British society. He spent a very colorful life until his untimely death in 1946, first as a university instructor, then as a high government officer, and sometimes as an art collector. His academic accomplishments in monetary and macroeconomic theories were so novel and revolutionary that he was regarded by most people as the greatest economist in the twentieth century.

Unlike Keynes, Knight (1885–1972) was born with a wooden spoon in the USA: his career began from rather unpromising roots in Maclean County, Illinois. He was the eldest of 11 children, being raised by parents who strongly believed in Christian fundamentalism. He received general education at a small college in rural Tennessee and proceeded to the University of Tennessee. From there, he moved on to the Graduate School of Economics, Cornell University. His concentration and hard work resulted in a Ph.D. thesis entitled *A Theory of Business Profit*, written during the period from 1905 to 1915 and later published with some revisions in 1921 under the revised title *Risk, Uncertainty and Profit.* It was in 1927 that he was finally appointed Professor of Economics at the University of Chicago and continued to live there as the "Grandpa of Chicago" until he finished his long life in 1972.

In short, Keynes and Knight had very different backgrounds in many ways. First of all, comparison of these two men might be characterized as a silver spoon versus a wooden spoon. Or alternatively, they could be portrayed as an elite in the Old World versus an ordinary man in the New World or perhaps as a colorful "practical man" with many talents versus a colorless professor living quietly at the ivory tower. Considering such personal and educational differences between the two, it might be understandable to see that very few books and papers on Keynes versus Knight have ever been published in academic circles around the world. In this paper, however, I intend to break such an unfortunate tendency by carefully comparing the two great economists from an angle of probability and uncertainty.

The contents of this paper are as follows. Section 3.2 will focus on the way how Keynes has dealt with the concepts of probability and uncertainty. The exact meaning of probability and Keynes' strange chart of probability will carefully be discussed. Section 3.3 will attempt to compare Keynes and Knight in terms of risk, probability, and uncertainty. It will be shown that the figures of multiple rings are quite helpful for such a comparison. Section 3.4 will turn attention to J.R. Hicks, still another great economist in the twentieth century, who has regarded economics on the verges of both sciences and history. It will be seen that Hicks' approach is more or less influenced by Keynes and Knight. Some final remarks will be made in Sect. 3.5.

3.2 Keynes on Probability and Uncertainty

3.2.1 The Meaning of Probability

The concept of probability is ambiguous and unclear. It may change with persons, places, and the times. Besides, there are several words that are more or less similar to probability: risk, uncertainty, likelihood, ambiguity, complexity, and so on.

According to *Oxford Dictionary of English*, we can see the standard usage of probability as follows.

3.2.1.1 Probability

1. [noun] The quality or state of being probable: the extent to which something is likely to happen or be the case
2. [mathematics] The extent to which an event is likely to occur, measured by the ratio of the favorable cases to the whole number of cases possible

Probability has double meanings, (1) and (2). The first meaning is commonly used in everyday life. For instance, a man in the street may say that it is probable that it will rain tomorrow. The second meaning is more technical than the first and attached to a special meaning by a professional person such as a statistician or mathematician. For example, let us consider the game of rolling the dice. Then the probability of having one is 1/6 since there is only one favorable case (namely, one) and the whole number of cases possible is six (namely, 1, 2, 3, 4, 5, and 6). The first meaning is subjective and personal, whereas the second one is objective and scientific.

Keynes' position is delicate and complicated. It is not based on the second meaning of probability at all, but seems to be rather akin to the first one. On the one hand, his concept of probability is more general and comprehensive than it is adopted in the mathematical theory of probability. On the other hand, it is more academically and scientifically used than in everyday life.

He devoted more than 10 years of hard work to establish his own doctrine, which took a middle position between the subjective and objective theories of probability. The following poet written at the very end of his probability book (1921) is likely to show his unique opinion:

> O False and treacherous Probability,
> Enemy of truth, and friend to wickednesse:
> With whose bleare eyes Opinion learns to see,
> Truth's feeble party here, and barennesse. (Keynes 1921, p. 466)

This is an old, romantic Byron-like rhyming verse with classical wordings. According to the young Keynes, the notion of probability is double-edged, having dual meanings. For one thing, it may be a false and treacherous concept, even possibly becomes the enemy of truth. For another, it is a guide to truth in the sense that it plays the role of a feeble party on the truth-finding journey. In a sense, the concept of probability may be barren or fruitful. It depends: no one really knows in advance which one is applicable.[1]

To understand Keynes' position on probability and uncertainty, we find it very convenient to start with his charming chart of probability. A detailed discussion on the chart will be the aim of the next subsection.

3.2.2 Keynes' Strange Chart of Probability: An Attractive Partial-Order Network

In a long history of economic science, there are two different kinds of great books, nicely written and badly written books. In our opinion, Keynes' first masterpiece *A Treatise on Probability* (1921) is of the first kind, whereas his second one *The General Theory of Employment, Interest and Money* (1936) is of the second kind.

Keynes' earlier book is a well-organized, nicely written book, yet not easy to read. It looks like a high peak which waits its turn to be conquered by a well-trained climber. No matter how difficult to climb, there must be a guiding route for the climber to follow. In our opinion, such a route surely exists in its bulky and seemingly difficult book. As is seen in Fig. 3.1, it is featured by a very charming chart of partial network.

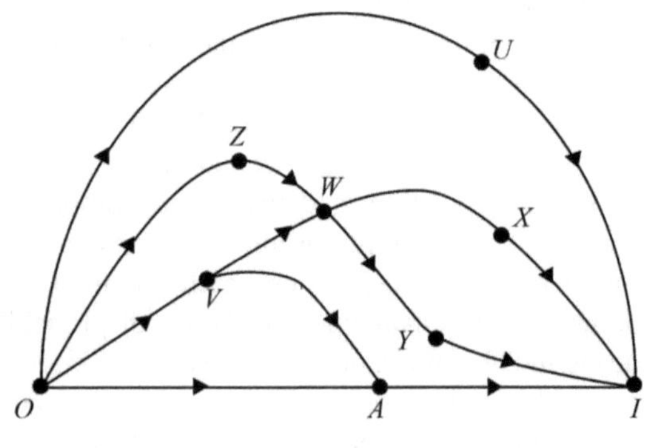

Fig. 3.1 Keynes' charming chart of probability: a partial-order network. The expression "*V* —▶—*A*" means that *A* is more probable than *V*. These arrows were newly introduced by the author and superimposed on the original chart of Keynes

[1]It is quite probable that Keynes' romantic poem aforementioned was influenced by Hume's view of human sentiments. See Hume (1739–1740). It is noted that the Keynes poem has almost completely been neglected until today, which may constitute a puzzle in the long history of the economic thought of risk and uncertainty. Also see Bateman et al. (2014), Biven (1989), Gillies (2000), Harrod (1951), Hicks (1977), Hirai et al. (2014), Ito (2011), Nasu (1995), Obata (2007, 2011), Sakai (1982, 1991,1996, 2006), Skidelsky (1983, 1992, 2000, 2009), The Royal Economic Society (1972).

Interestingly enough, Fig. 3.1 is depicted as a rather small figure in Keynes (1921), page 39. In order to make the partial-order property of his chart much clearer, we dare to superimpose many arrows (—▶—) on the original diagram. For example, the expression "*V* —▶— *A*" means that *A* is more probable than *V*. Fortunately, detailed explanations by Keynes himself are available and will be reproduced here:

> [The] properties are illustrated in the annexed diagram. *O* represents impossibility, *I* certainty, and *A* a numerically measurable probability intermediate between *O* and *I*; *U*, *V*, *W*, *X*, *Y*, *Z* are non-numerical probabilities, of which, however, *V* is less than the numerical probability *A*, and is also less than *W*, *X*, and *Y*. *X* and *Y* are both greater than *W*, and greater than *V*, but are not comparable with one another, or with *A*. *V* and *Z* are both less than *W*, *X*, and *Y*, but are not comparable with one another; *U* is not quantitatively comparable with any of the probabilities *V*, *W*, *X*, *Y*, *Z*. Probabilities which are numerically comparable will all belong to one series, and the path of this series, which we may call the numerical path or strand, will be represented by *OAI*. (Keynes 1921, p. 39)

As many people may remember, Frankenstein's dreadful monster in the SF movie was a creation of Dr. Frankenstein, a notorious German scientist. Likewise, Keynes' charming chart of probability was a creation of Mr. Keynes, a famous English economist. No sooner did we see this chart than we had a flash of inspiration. This must be the very essence of his concept of probability! It was so regrettable, however, that he failed

to provide any concrete illustration for the chart. Besides, it seems that almost all economists have been content themselves with its mere reproduction without going further. So, we have made up our mind to have the courage of escaping a blind alley toward a new open area.

In the following, we will attempt to provide the reader with one possible concrete illustration:

Point $O = 0\%$, or impossibility
Point $I = 100\%$, or certainty
Point $A =$ a numerically measurable probability between O and I, say 60%
Point $U =$ a non-numerical probability, or any unspecified point between O and I
Point $V =$ a non-numerical probability, which may be represented by an interval-valued probability, say 30%~40%
Point $W = 45\%$~65%
Point $X = 50\%$~80%
Point $Y = 45\%$~90%
Point $Z = 10\%$~65%

As the reader may notice, we have partially employed the concept of interval -valued probability $[\alpha,\beta]$, with the lower limit α and the upper limit β, which may be regarded as a natural extension of traditional, single-valued probability, α or β. In fact, any point on the path *OVA*, *OVW*, *OZW*, *WYI*, and *WXI* may correspond to a certain interval-valued probability. It is noted that Keynes himself developed such an upper-lower probabilistic interval approach to probability. In fact, he once remarked:

> The sphere of inexact numerical comparison is not quite so limited, Many probabilities, which are incapable of numerical measurement, can be placed nevertheless *between* numerical limits. And taking particular non-numerical probabilities as standards a great number of comparisons or approximate measurements become possible. If we can place a probability in order of magnitude with some standard probability, we can obtain its approximate measure by comparison. (Keynes 1921, p. 150)

How exactly we can understand this paragraph remains a mystery. Keynes himself considered and compared numerical and non-numerical probabilities and did exact and approximate measures. It is our belief that interval-valued probabilities of the form [α,β] can represent well Keynes' intention of inexact or approximate measures.[2]

Now, let us get back to Fig. 3.1. On the one hand, every point on the bottom line *OAI* is more certain than all other points in the chart, thereby it can be associated with a specific numerical probability. On the other hand, *U* on the uppermost half circle represents the most uncertain point: It is not quantitatively comparable with any other probability. In other words, it is not possible to represent *U* neither by an interval- valued probability nor by a single-valued probability.

The main results which have been derived so far are very important and will be summarized below.

1. Keynes' charming chart of probability is a collection of probability networks represented by partial ordering. For instance, the expression "*V*—▶—*A*," which is my own creation, means that "*A* is more probable than *V*." It is easy to see that such ordering is not a total ordering, but merely a partial ordering.
2. The area in which the traditional theory of probability is applicable is limited to the bottom line *OAI*. Every point on this path can be associated with a single-valued probability: for instance, *O* stands for 0%, *A* for 60%, and *I* for 100%. Therefore, any two points on the path are easily comparable with each other. In contrast, all the points off *OAI* are no longer quantifiable by a single value.
3. The path *OVWXI* indicates a path on which any two points are comparable by means of interval-valued probability. Note that *V* = [30%, 40%], *W* = [45%, 65%], and *X* = [50%, 80%]. To give a nice interpretation, let us suppose that a young girl who wishes to become a professional singer must enter a good school of music for very hard training. There are three schools available—School *V*, School *W*, and School *X*. The probabilities for admission to *V*, *W*, and *X* are, respectively, described by the intervals [30%, 40%], [45%, 65%], and [50%, 80%]. Apparently, getting into *X* is more probable than getting into *W*, which in turn is more probable than getting into *V*.
4. While there exists a path from *V* to *A*, there are no paths available from *W* to *A* and from *X* to *A*. Surely, 60% is more probable than [30%, 40%]. It is not correct to say, however, that 60% is more probable or less probable than [45%, 65%] or that 60% is numerically comparable to [50%, 80%].

---

[2]The role of interval-valued probability in Keynes' theory was intensively investigated by Brady (2004). Also see Sakai (2015, 2016).

5. The path *OZWYI* shows another possible ordering. It is fair to say that $Y = [45\%, 90\%]$ is more probable than $W = [45\%, 65\%]$, which in turn is more probable than $Z = [10\%, 65\%]$. However, comparison between W and $A = 60\%$ is not possible. Nor Z or X can be compared to A.

The job of comparing the three points *Y*, *W*, and *Z* may be a bit harder than before, requiring our wiser judgment based on common sense. Let me assume that the possibility of admission to School *Y* is greater than 45%, the one to *W* is somewhere between 45% and 65%, and the one to *Z* is less than 65%. Then it would be fairly reasonable to say that getting into School *Y* is more probable than *W*, which is in turn more probable than *Z*.

6. The most outer path OUI represents the most vague probability among any other path. Although it presumably lies somewhere between the impossibility point O and the certainty point I, its comparison with any other point in Keynes' chart constitutes a sort of "mission impossible."

In conclusion, Keynes' charming chart of probability looks like the unconquered, highest peak in the great land of Keynes. What we have attempted to do so far is nothing but the discovery of one possible route of mountain climbing. Probably, there would be alternative routes available, which requires further investigation.

3.2.3 Keynes' Theory of Induction: Reappraisal of Several Case Studies

This subsection will discuss Keynes' theory of induction. It is highly expected that reappraisal of several case studies gives us important clues for understanding the very unique features of the Keynes world.

In the following, let us discuss and shed a new light on a series of case studies, which were originally introduced by Keynes himself in *A Treatise on Probability* (1921) and in *the General Theory of Employment, Interest and Money* (1936).

3.2.3.1 [Case Study 1] Deciding for or Against an Umbrella

England is a country where the rain falls frequently and unexpectedly. Suppose that Mr. Smith is going to start out for a walk when the barometer is high but the clouds are black. The problem of interest is whether he should carry with him an umbrella in the expectation of rain. The possibility of rain may be small if the barometer is high, whereas it may not be so if the clouds are black. Therefore, if the barometer is high but the clouds are black, it is not always rational that one possibility should prevail over the other in his mind. It could be nonsense to numerically measure the probability of rain or even compare the likeliness of rain against non-rain It is really an arbitrary matter for Mr. Smith to decide for or against the umbrella. In case the weather report is available, it is likely to affect the probability of rain and his umbrella decision. According to Keynes, this simple case shows the essence and difficulty of probability.

Watching the weather forecast in the TV set, the weather man often says that probably it will rain tomorrow afternoon. The forecast is not perfect and may change whenever a new information becomes available. Keynes was a refined gentleman with many hobbies. In fact, he was not only interested in weather forecast but also in horseracing and beauty contest.

3.2.3.2 [Case Study 2] Breeding Racehorses: Recovering the Damages by Breach of a Contract

The contract at issue was that Cyllene, a racehorse owned by the defendant, should in the mating season of 1909 serve one of the plaintiff's mares. In the summer of 1908, however, the defendant sold Cyllene for £30,000 to go to South America without the consent of the plaintiff. The plaintiff claimed a sum equal to the average profit he had made through having a mare served by Cyllene during the past 4 years. During those 4 years, he had had four colts which had sold at £3300. Upon that basis his loss was estimated at £700.

Mr. Justice Jeff said that he was desirous to find some mode of legally making the defendant compensate the plaintiff; but the question of damages presented insurmountable difficulties. The estimate could only be based on a succession of contingencies. First of all, we had to assume that Cyllene would be alive and well, that the mare would be well bred and not barren, and that the foal would be born alive and healthy. Under such circumstances, he could only rely on the weighing of chances. Therefore, the damages must be a matter of speculation, but there may be some good reasons for compensation.

This second case teaches us that the concept of probability in social sciences is fundamentally different from the one in natural sciences since a series of human factors are working behind the scene. Keynes is interested in another interesting case, which arose out of an offer of the Beauty Prize sponsored by the *Daily Express*. The prize was to be a theatrical engagement to a handsome prince and, according to the press, the probability of subsequent marriage.

3.2.3.3 [Case Study 3] Assessing the Damages in the Court: The Beauty Contest Number One

Corresponding to the offer, 6000 photographs were submitted, and a certain number of them were to be selected and published in the newspaper in the following fashion. The UK was to be divided into many districts, and the photographs of the selected candidates living in each district were to be submitted to the readers of the paper in the district. The readers were to select by their votes those ladies whom they considered the most beautiful. Interestingly enough, a designated man named Mr. Hicks had the privilege to make personal appointments with the 50 ladies who obtained the greatest number of votes and to select 12 of them according to his taste and judgment.

The plaintiff, who came out the top candidate of a district, submitted the claim that she had not been given a reasonable opportunity to make an appointment; thereby she had lost of her chance of winning 1 of the 12 prizes and claimed damages accordingly. The jury found that the defendant had not given the plaintiff an reasonable opportunity of presenting herself for selection and assessed the damages at £100. The two questions then arose. Relative to what evidence should the probability be calculated? Was it numerically measurable in the first place? The attitude of Lord Justice was quite clear. The plaintiff had evidently suffered the damages, and justice required that she should be somehow compensated. It was equally evident; however, relative to the information available and also taking account of the arbiter's taste, it was not possible at all to exactly estimate the rate or amount of damages with a numerical value. But the final decision had to be given. Rough justice should be done: namely, the plaintiff's loss was estimated at 12/50 of the value of the prize.

According to Keynes, all the three cases were related to probability, but have not received serious considerations so far. By writing a book entitled *A Treatise on Probability*, he intended to mend such negligence, putting the things on the right track.

3.2.4 *Keynes on Uncertainty:* The General Theory of Employment, Interest and Money

As was seen in the case study 3 above, Keynes was deeply excited by the beauty contest and continued to consider its economic implications throughout his life. In his later book *The General Theory of Employment, Interest and Money* (1936), he picked up again a new version of the beauty contest in order to shed a new light on professional investment.

3.2.4.1 [Case Study 4] Thinking of the Investment Bubble: The Beauty Contest Number Two

According to Keynes, professional investment may be likened to those newspaper competitions in which the competitors are asked to pick up the six prettiest faces out of a hundred photographs. The prize is no longer getting a chance to date a handsome prince, but rather a handsome amount of money given to a beauty queen. Remarkably, such a prize is awarded to the competitor whose choice most nearly corresponds to the average preferences of the competitors as a whole. As a result, each competitor tends to pick up, not those faces which he himself finds prettiest, but those which he thinks likeliest to catch the fancy of other competitors. It is noted that all of the competitors are likely to look at the problem from the same viewpoint. Keynes remarked:

> It is not a case of choosing those which, to the best of one's judgment, are really the prettiest, nor even those which average opinion genuinely thinks the prettiest. We have reached the third degree where we devote our intelligence to anticipating what average pinion expects the average opinion to be. And there are some, I [Keynes] believe, who practice the fourth, fifth and higher degrees. (Keynes 1921, p. 156)

In the 1920s and 1930s when both *A Treatise on Probability* and *the General Theory of Employment, Interest and Money* were published, the British Empire constituted the largest empire on the earth: It was often called "the empire on which the sun never sets." One of the biggest event which excited the British people was the expedition to the South Pole, which then remained a virgin soil to the Empire.

3.2.4.2 [Case Study 5] Going on the South Pole Expedition: The Role of Animal Spirits

There was a strong sense of rivalry between the British team led by R.F. Scott and the Norwegian team led by R. Amundsen: Both teams wanted to be the first to reach the South Pole. When Scott reached the pole on 17 January 1921, he found that Amundsen had preceded him by mere 34 days and unfortunately died on the return journey from the pole.

Whether and to what extent Scott's expedition would be successful might be controversial even to him. What motivated him to engage in such an adventure could not be explained by a mathematical calculations, but rather depended on spontaneous optimism or what we may call "animal spirits." In this connection, Keynes remarked with great eloquence:

> Even apart from the instability due to speculation, there is the instability due to the characteristic of human nature that a large portion of our positive activities depend on spontaneous optimism rather than on a mathematical expectation, whether moral or hedonistic or economic. Most, probably, of our decisions to do something positive, the full consequences of which will be drawn out over many days to come, can only be taken as a result of animal spirits—of a spontaneous urge to action rather than inaction, and not as the outcome of a weighted average of quantitative benefits multiplied by quantitative probabilities. (Keynes 1936, p. 161)

To the best of our knowledge, Keynes was the first economist who employed the word "animal spirits" and discussed its economic consequences. As Keynes pointed out above, it is so important to make a distinction between the instability due to speculation and the instability due to human nature, or the nature of spontaneous optimism. While the first instability is related to mathematical expectation, or numerical probability, the second instability is connected with a sort of true uncertainty that is neither measurable nor comparable. We have to do something positive even under the second instability. According to Keynes, it is animal spirits that play a critical role under such circumstances. Individual initiative is only adequate when reasonable calculation is supplemented and supported by animal spirits, so that the thought of possible failure may effectively be put aside. According to Keynes, the roll of animal spirits in the working and performance of the market economy cannot be overemphasized.

3.3 Keynes Versus Knight: With Special Reference to Risk, Probability, and Uncertainty

3.3.1 Keynes on Probability and Uncertainty

We are in a position to compare Keynes and Knight from the viewpoint of risk, probability, and uncertainty. Their analyses look similar but are more or less different. In the following, we will show pictorially the similarities and differences between them.

The Keynes world of probability and uncertainty is well illustrated in Fig. 3.2. It constitutes a quadruple ring structure. The outer two rings are drawn by solid lines, but the inner rings by dotted lines. Whether the boundary lines are solid or dotted correspond to the degree of connectedness between the two separated areas.

The key concept of Keynes' *The General Theory of Employment, Interest and Money* (1936) is uncertainty, which is indicated by the most outer ring in Fig. 3.2. This is the field in which probabilities are neither numerical nor comparable. In the famous case of the beauty contest mentioned above, the factor which may play a critical role is not what each competitor thinks himself, but rather what he thinks likeliest to catch the fancy and rumors of the other competitors. The resulting situation would be a sort of bubble followed by another bubble. In the case of the competition of expedition to the South Pole between rival countries, the decision may depend on the aggressive character of an explorer rather than his mathematical expectation. In the dark shadow of uncertainty and fear, what makes a man go ahead without hesitation is no more than his animal spirits.

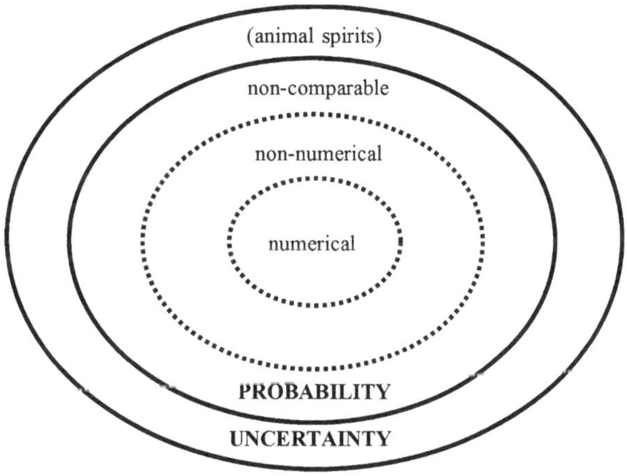

Fig. 3.2 Keynes on probability and uncertainty

The area lying the inside of the uncertainty ring represents the vast field of probability, which is thought of as the key concept in Keynes' *A Treatise on Probability* (1921). Probability may be small or large, depending on the degree of belief and/or evidence. If probability is small enough, it may be non-comparable. While interval-valued estimation may be feasible at this stage, single-valued estimation is not so. As probability gets larger and larger, it will become comparable, and gradually numerical. The core of the quadruple ring structure indicates the area where numerical representation is available: It is in this small area that the traditional probability analysis is effectively applicable.

Now, let us look at the matter from an opposite viewpoint. In other words, let us start from the center core and gradually move away toward the outer rings. As mentioned above, the core indicates the numerical area where risk in a narrow sense is present in the sense that some convenient concepts such as a probability density curve and a cumulative distribution curve can be employed. If we dare to enlarge the concept of "risk proper" by introducing the more realistic factors of "distortion" and "weight," then the "probability ring" in Fig. 3.2 will largely expand outward. It is interesting to note that such "distortion and weight factors" play a central role in modern theory of prospect which has been promoted by Kahneman and Tversky (1979).

Even if we get into a wider area of the rings, the concept of probability in a broad sense, whether it is based on point-valued or interval-valued, continues to be important. According to Keynes, the theory of probability should be logical because it is concerned with the degree of belief. More exactly, it is a sort of "common belief" which it is rational to have within a group in a given conditions. And it does not necessarily correspond to the actual beliefs of particular individuals, which may or may not be rational as can be seen in the famous beauty contest. The degree of belief thus defined cannot be fixed: It may change by acquisition of new information. In fact, it is rather common that a belief seems rather unlikely on the evidence at first hand, but becomes very probable on further information obtained.

Keynes thinks that uncertainty is radically different from probability. In sharp contrast to the latter, the former has nothing to with numerical representation. A person faces uncertainty when he walk around with no light at a dark night. Since the walking path is new and unknown to him, his experience does not help him much. What motivates him to walk ahead is his animal spirits or spontaneous optimism such that he can achieve something he has never seen before.

A year later than *The General Theory of Employment, Interest and Money* (1936), Keynes published a follow-up paper (1937) to clarify the concept of uncertainty:

> By 'uncertain' knowledge, let me explain, I do not mean merely to distinguish what is known for certain from what is only probable. The game of roulette is not subject, in this sense, to uncertainty; nor is the prospect of a Victory bond being drawn. Or, again, the expectation of life is only slightly uncertain. Even the weather is moderately uncertain. The sense in which I am using the term is that in which the prospect of a European war is uncertain, or the price of copper and the rate of interest twenty years later hence, or the obsolescence of a new invention, or the position of private wealth owners in the social system in 1970. About these matters there is no scientific basis on which to form any calculable probability whatever. We simply do not know. (Keynes 1937, pp. 113–114)

Keynes holds an unshakable belief that uncertainty is categorically different from probability: It is something more than that. The game of roulette is subject to the mathematical theory of probability, thereby does not belong to the world of uncertainty. So is a Victory bond because the prospect of returns remains within the anticipated range with an upper limit and a lower limit. The expectation of human life may change country to country, and time to time. Given a country and a year, however, a man's average life expectancy may easily be calculated by a life insurance company. A weatherman says that the probability of rain tomorrow is around 20%, so that the weather does not belong to true uncertainty, but rather to a wider range of probability. By contrast, once a war begins, a lot of uncertain things may happen. We do not know in advance how the war will proceed, nor are we in a position to know its economic consequences. The price of copper and the rate of interest may go up during the war, but the price of copper and the rate of interest 20 years later are beyond imagination. In respect to those and many other events, we have no scientific basis to calculate exact probability.

In recent years, the important role of animal spirits in the working of the market economy has drawn much attention in the economic circle. George Akerlof and Robert Shiller are influential American economists and have written their joint book *Animal Spirits* (2009). They remarked:

> To understand the economy then is to comprehend how it is driven by the animal spirits.Just as Adam Smith's invisible hand is the keynote of classical economics, Keynes's animal spirits are the keynote to a different view of the economy—a view that explains the underlying instability of capitalism. (Akerlof and Shiller 2009, Preface, p. ix)

According to Akerlof and Schiller, Keynes' animal spirits are the keynote to understanding the modern economy. They are really intermingled with uncertainty and imperfect knowledge. Its importance may be well compared to Adam Smith's individual hand as the keynote of the classical economy.

In short, we live in the world of probability and uncertainty. Without inquiry into these subjects, our economic science would not be complete. We will turn our attention to Knight, who was one of Keynes' contemporaries and did a great work on the field of risk and uncertainty.

3.3.2 *Knight on Risk and Uncertainty*

The question of much interest is how Knight discussed the concepts of risk and uncertainty. A related question is whether and to what extent his work differed from the work of Keynes.[3]

[3]For a detailed discussion on the economic thought of Knight, see Sakai (2010). Also see Emmett (1999a, b), Knight (1935).

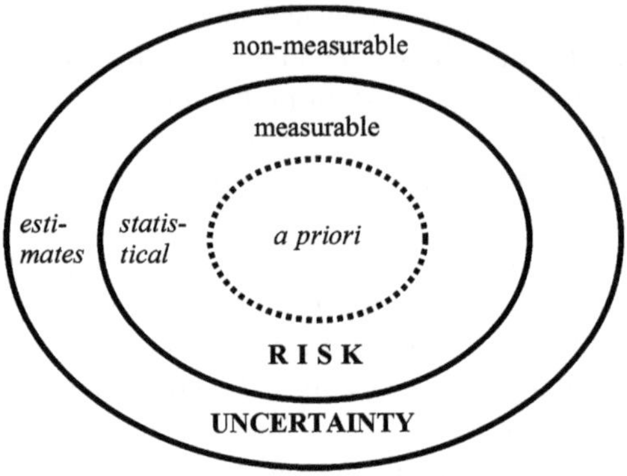

Fig. 3.3 Knight on risk and uncertainty

If we want to illustrate the world of Knight by the help of a figure, we may have a triple ring structure in Fig. 3.3. This new figure may be well compared to the quadruple ring structure of Keynes. While there were four rings for Keynes, there are now only three rings for Knight. Could such a decrease in the number of rings by one really make the systems of Keynes and Knight entirely different? Or alternatively, could we regard these two as essentially the same?

As is seen in Fig. 3.3, the most important ring of uncertainty is located in the most outer position. In the long history of economics, *Risk, Uncertainty and Profit* (1921) is presumably the first book whose title contains the word "uncertainty." It is so remarkable to see that the two terms, risk and uncertainty, are intentionally separated. In fact, Knight made the following remark:

> Uncertainty must be taken in a sense radically distinct from the familiar notion of risk, from which it has never been properly separated. The term 'risk,' as loosely used in everyday speech and in economic discussion, really covers two things which, functionally at least, in their causal relation to the phenomena of economic organization, are categorically different. (Knight 1921, p. 19)

Uncertainty must be radically distinct from risk. The two terms "risk" and "uncertainty" should be categorically different. Here Knight himself is using extremely strong expressions such as "radically distinct" and "categorically different." The question which would naturally arise is how these two are really different. In this connection, Knight remarked:

> A *measurable* uncertainty, or 'risk' proper, as we shall use the term, is so far different from an *unmeasurable* one that it is not in effect an uncertainty at all. We shall accordingly restrict the term "uncertainty" to cases of non-quantitative type. It is this 'true' uncertainty, and not risk, as has been argued, which forms the basis of a valid theory of profit and accounts for the divergence between actual and theoretical competition. (Knight 1921, p. 20)

According to Knight, uncertainty serves as the key concept for understanding the effectiveness and limitations of the market economy. There are two different kinds of uncertainties—*measurable* uncertainty and *non-measurable* (or *unmeasurable*) uncertainty. The problem of measurability is so important that he deliberately employs italics for the words "measurable" and "non-measurable." Measurable uncertainty is not in effect an uncertainty at all, but rather should be called "risk" proper. By contrast, non-measurable uncertainty is what he may call "true" uncertainty, thus being the main theme of his famous book *Risk, Profit and Uncertainty* (1921).

Knight thinks that there are three different types of probability situations. The first type is a priori probability and occupies the center core in the triple ring structure in Fig. 3.3. For instance, let us toss a coin. Then the probability that we get "one" is 1/6, a mathematically determined fraction. The second type is statistical probability, which correspond to a small ring or donut which encircles the core. A typical example of this type is provided by the proposition that the average life expectancy of a 50 years old man in Japan now is 30 years. These two types, a priori or statistical, belong to the same field of measurable risk. A more important concept is non-measurable uncertainty, which is shown by the outer ring encircling the inner ring of risk. Knight called this third type of probabilistic situation "estimates" or "judgments" and paid a special attention to it:

> The distinction here is that there is *no valid basis of any kind* for classifying instances. This form of probability is involved in the greatest logical difficulties of all, and no very satisfactory discussion of it can be given, but its distinction from the other types must be emphasized and some of its complicated relations indicated. (Knight 1921, p. 225)

Knight finds that estimates or judgments should not be perfect and are liable to err. Its distinction from a priori or statistical probability must strongly be pointed out. Indeed, it is meaningless to speak of either calculating probability a priori or of determining it empirically by studying a large number of instances. The essential fact is that the "instance" is so unique that there are not a sufficient number to form a scientific basis for any real probability. We simply do not know enough. We have to do our decisions on the basis of imperfect estimates or judgment, however. We are now subject to non-measurable uncertainty.

Knight continues to say that with the introduction of true uncertainty into the real economy, the latter's character is completely changed. Here we see the emergence of a new economic functionary, the entrepreneur, whose function is to do a new venture on the basis of a limited amount of knowledge. Such a venture itself may possess the nature of a gamble, involving a large proportion of unpredictable factors. The entrepreneur is categorically different from the conventional type of manager, who is supposed to do mere routine functions with no courage to do something new.

To sum up, Knight and Keynes are the two great economists newly introduced non-measurable uncertainty into economic science, and energetically discussed how it differs from measurable risk. So far so good. We have to recognize, however, that Knight is Knight, whereas Keynes is Keynes: There must be some differences between them. Those differences might look small in some situations but are really very large in the other situations.

Let us take a close look again at Figs. 3.1 and 3.2. Then a comparison of these two multiple ring structures may teach us that Knight and Keynes are different with respect to their views of probability and uncertainty in a delicate way. It is really remarkable to see that the "intermediate belt" of probability which plays a very important role in the world of Keynes is not present in the world of Knight. Knight really intended to do a direct comparison between risk and uncertainty without help of any type of "middle passage." Consequently, in contrast to Keynes, Knight found little interest in the distortions and weights of probability, interval-valued probability, and the like.

In the real world, the area in which uncertainty is measurable and the one where uncertainty is non-measurable cannot be so clearly divided. There should exist some gaps and/or overlaps between the two areas. It is in such a chaotic world that Keynes as a practical man preferred to live. Although he was born with a silver spoon, his "academic spoon" became very flexible as his age advanced and could sometimes be bent in many ways.

By contrast, Knight as an academic man used to live deep in an ivory tower throughout his entire life, whence he decided a clear-cut line between the measurable area and the non-measurable area. Whereas he was born with a wooden spoon, his "academic spoon" was strong and became even stronger as he got older.

In short, the relation between the "silver spoon" and the "wooden spoon" was too complex to be described by one word. These two "academic spoons" were so intermingled with each other that they created the complicated joint history of separation, approach, decoupling, and reunion.

3.4 Hicks on Decision and Probability: How Hicks Was Influenced by Keynes and Knight

3.4.1 Economics on the Edges of Both Sciences and History

In one of his later works *Causality in Economics* (1979), J. R. Hicks, who contributed so much to the development of economic theory, concentrated his attention on the difference between natural sciences and economics. In his opinion, economic knowledge is extremely imperfect. There are very few economic laws we can know with precision: Indeed, they are subject to errors and ambiguities, which would be regarded as intolerable by many natural scientists. Hicks remarked:

> Economics is a leading example of uncertain knowledge; it is knowledge, yet it is evidently uncertain. (Hicks 1979, p. 2)

So, he thinks that economics does not belong to the core of natural sciences, but rather is located at the edge of the sciences. Causality in economics is not as simple as one in natural sciences. The relation between cause and effect may not be one-to-one: In fact, one cause may have many effects, whereas one effect may have many causes. It would be the case that a certain degree of reciprocity or mutual causality exists between cause and effect. For instance, when a person makes a sales decision in the

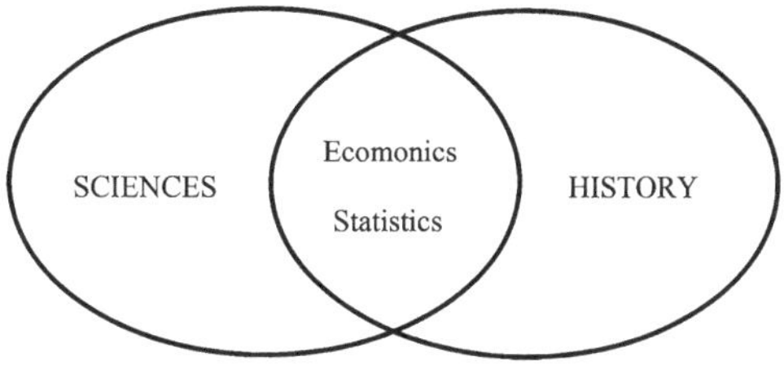

Fig. 3.4 Hicks' pluralistic view of economics and statistics

market, his decision may not be completely independent but is likely to be influenced by the pressure of the market.

The economist is concerned with the future as well as the past. Whereas the past provides him with his facts, he uses and processes those facts for future prediction. In this connection, the following sentences are quite interesting:

> Economics, if it is on the edge of sciences, is also on the edge of history; facing both ways, it is a key position. So a consideration of economics ... may throw light in both directions. (Hicks 1979, p. 4)

In our opinion, this is a very important point when we consider the place of economics in relation to sciences and to history. Hicks proceeds to think that the same key position is occupied by other social sciences, and presumably by statistics. They are all on the edge of sciences and on the edge of history. What we are saying may be more readily be understood if it is illustrated pictorially.

As is seen in Fig. 3.4, there are two overlapping rings, with an intersection area between them. The left ring and the right ring, respectively, indicate the field of sciences and the field of history. The intersection of the two fields shows the area in which both scientific and historical approaches are applicable. It is noted that such a pluralistic view was already pioneered by the two economists, Keynes and Knight. In particular, in the following, we will discuss more exactly why we must look at probability and statistics in both directions.

3.4.2 Decision and Probability

It should be remembered that Hicks once served as a president of Manchester Statistical Society, which was founded in 1833 as one of the earliest of such societies. As he noted, statistics used to mean social and economic statistics rather than mathematical statistics. Even Adolphe Quetelet (1796–1874), who began his career as a Belgian astronomer and mathematician, became very famous in his later years by introducing statistical methods to many social sciences including demography, sociology, and criminology.

Generally speaking, probability is regarded as the basis on which the field of statistics should be built. When we speak of statistics, it has a multiple meanings: Social scientists attach one meaning to it whereas natural scientists, another meaning. Such diversity of statistics may be a reasonable consequence of the wide range of views for probability.

It is conventional to say that there are two theories of probabilities. They are the frequency theory that starts with many data and is induction oriented, and the axiomatic theory that begins with many axioms and is deduction oriented. Most modern works on statistical mathematics tends to take the first frequency theory as their starting point.

There exists a third approach which lies somewhere between the frequency and axiomatic theories, however. According to Hicks, one of the leading proponents of this alternative approach has been Keynes in his *Treatise on Probability* (1921). This means that Hicks, who has praised Keynes as the greatest economist in the twentieth century, has also thought of Keynes as a great proponent of the alternative theory of probability. In fact, Hicks remarked:

> I have myself come to the view that the frequency theory, though it is thoroughly at home of the natural sciences, it is not wide enough for economics. Indeed on those points where Keynes and Jeffreys appear to differ, I generally find myself on the side of Keynes. (Hicks 1979, p. 105)

Regarding the theory of probability, Hicks generally find himself on the side of Keynes. As a good example, Hicks considered the question whether the European war would come to an end within a year. Surely, this was the probability which, in the particular year of 1944, most people would have assessed to be considerably high. It is quite clear, however, that it does not fall within the frequency definition since it is not a matter of trials which could frequently be repeated. Hicks was a very eloquent speaker on this point. Like Keynes (1921), Hicks was so eager to pick up the third kind of probability in economics.

> Investments are made, securities are bought and sold, on a judgment of probabilities. This is true of economic behavior; it is also true of economic theory. The probabilities of 'states of the world' that are formally used by economists, as for instance in portfolio theory, cannot be interpreted in terms of random experiments. Probability, in economics, must mean something wider. (Hicks 1979, p. 107)

The view that probability in economics must mean something wider clearly indicates the fundamental position of Hicks on the relation between economics and probability theory. This may more readily be understood if it is pictorially illustrated.

As is seen in Fig. 3.5, the Hicks world of probability and judgment consists of four rings. The inner three rings are related to a variety of probabilities, with the most outer ring being associated with uncertainty. More specifically, the smallest ring, namely, the center core, indicates the area in which probabilities are unquestionably numerical: they may be represented by specific distribution functions such as binomial and normal distribution functions. The larger ring covering the numerical core shows the field where probabilities are orderable (or comparable according to

Fig. 3.5 Hicks on probability and judgment

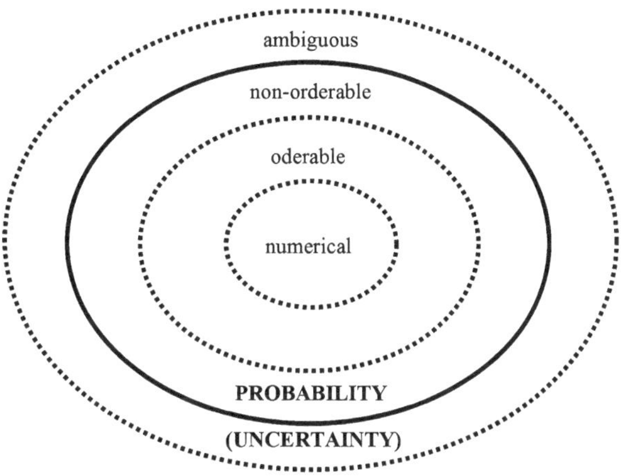

Keynes), but not expressible as numbers. The even bigger ring covering the orderable ring is the one in which they are neither orderable nor comparable.

Hicks maintains that in even the non-orderable ring, probability judgments can sometimes be made and that they can be rational since they could be improved by additional information. To sum up, the grand field of probability contains those three rings, namely, numerical, orderable, and non-orderable ones. By contrast, the most outer ring in the figure is associated with the area in which even probabilities are nonexistent and may be replaced by ambiguities or chaos.

Hicks did everything in his power to study many possible types of probabilities, so that he seemed to pay much less attention to uncertainty than both Keynes and Knight did. The young Hicks energetically investigated the modern utility theory, one of the cores of microeconomic theory, and discussed how and to what extent the ordinal utility differs from the cardinal utility. The ordinal utility is concerned with only orders, not with absolute levels, so that it must be a more general concept than the cardinal utility. It seems that there is a nice correspondence between probabilities and utilities: In fact, numerical and orderable probabilities, respectively, correspond to cardinal and ordinal utilities. Some preference orderings such lexicographic ones cannot be represented by any utility function. Likewise, there exist some probabilities which cannot be even ordered in a simple fashion. It is rather unfortunate that Hicks has found much less interest in the concept of true uncertainty or total ambiguities.[4]

[4]It is noted that Hicks (1979) has introduced the new idea of "gray zone," meaning that probabilities are clear and orderable outside the zone, but unclear inside. It remains an open question to see how the gray zone is related to the concept of interval-valued probability.

3.5 Beyond Keynes and Knight: Concluding Remarks

In the above, we have intensively discussed Keynes' theory of probability versus Knight's theory of uncertainty. In particular, we have focused on 1921 as a sort of miracle year, in which the two great books, *A Treatise on Probability* by Keynes and *Risk, Uncertainty and Profit* by Knight, were published. We believe that this was no accident at all, but rather marked the start of the coming age of uncertainty in a symbolic manner.

We are now in another age of uncertainty and complexity. In June 2009, the Lionel Robbins Lectures took place at the London School of Economics. Paul Krugman, a famed Nobel laureate, was then an invited speaker and impressed the audience by making the following speech:

> Most macroeconomics of the past 30 years was spectacularly useless at best, and positively harmful at worst. (Krugman 2009)

We are in general agreement with Krugman. And we would like to even add that most economic theories of the past 30 years, whether they are micro-oriented or macro-oriented, have been spectacularly useless at best, and positively harmful at worst.

According to John K. Galbraith (1977), the twentieth century may be characterized as the age of uncertainty. We would contrast the eminent certainties in economic thought in the nineteenth century with the great uncertainties in the twentieth century. In the nineteenth century capitalists were quite certain of the success of capitalism and socialists of the success of socialism. To our regret, however, little of this certainty survived in the twentieth century.[5]

We live now in the new twenty-first century. While the Cold War was ended with the fall of the socialist Soviet Union in 1991, the so-called Riemann Shock in 2008 gave a crushing blow to the USA and all other capitalist countries. Besides, a series of nuclear power plant accidents such as the Three Mile Island disaster (1979), the Chernobyl disaster (1986), and the Fukushima disaster (2011) recalled all the people of the existence of those dreadful risks which were far beyond human capacities. Surely, a great number of human and natural risks and uncertainties will be waiting for us.

As Joseph Stiglitz (2010), another Nobel prize winning economist, once remarked that a new economic paradigm would be strongly needed. There have existed many old economic paradigms so far. It seems, however, that almost all of them are either useless or even harmful, with some possible exceptions. What we have to do now is no less than the construction of a completely new economic paradigm.[6]

---

[5]See Galbraith (1977), Preface. Also see Morishima (1999), Piketty (2013), Soros (1998, 2008).

[6]See Stiglitz (2010). It is noted that a new approach based on socioeconomic physics is emerging in the academic circle. For a detailed discussion on this point, see Aoki, Aoyama, Aruka, Yoshikawa et al. (2011).

To carry such a task, we have to learn many new lessons from the old teachings of Keynes and Knight. We believe that the Keynes spirits are still alive and so are the Knight spirits. We need to have a new kind of animal spirits so that we may go beyond Keynes and Knight.

References

Akerlof GA, Shiller RJ (2009) Animal spirits: how human psychology drives the economy and why it matters for global capitalism. Princeton University Press, Princeton

Aoki M, Aoyama H, Aruka Y, Yoshikawa H et al (2011) Important 50 keywords in the new economic lectures : what is socio-economic physics all about? (in Japanese). Tosho Publishing Company, Tokyo

Aruka Y (2015) Evolutionary foundations of economic science: how can scientists study evolving economic doctrines from the last centuries? Springer Japan, Tokyo

Bateman BW, Hirai T, Marcuzzo M et al (2014) The return to Keynes. Tokyo University Press, Tokyo

Biven WC (1989) Who killed John Maynard Keynes ? Dow-Jones-Irwin, New York

Brady ME (2004) J.M. Keynes's theory of decision making, induction, and analogy. Xlibris Corporation, Illinois

Emmett RB (1999a) Selected essays by Frank H. Knight, Vol. 1: "What is Truth" in Economics. University of Chicago Press, Chicago

Emmett RB (1999b) Selected essays by Frank H. Knight, Vol. 2: laissez-faire: pro and con. University of Chicago Press, Chicago

Galbraith JK (1977) The age of uncertainty. Houghton Mifflin Company, Boston

Gillies D (2000) Philosophical theories of probability. Routledge, London

Harrod RF (1951) The life of John Maynard Keynes. Macmillan, London

Hicks JR (1977) Economic perspectives: further essays on money and growth. Oxford University Press, Oxford

Hicks JR (1979) Causality in economics. Basic Blackwell, Oxford

Hirai T et al (2014) Why Keynes is needed now: contemporary and global perspectives (in Japanese). Sakuhinsha Publishing Company, Tokyo

Hume D (1739–1740) A treatise of human nature: being an attempt to introduce the experimental method of reasoning into moral subjects. Oxford University Press, Oxford

Ito K (2011) The philosophy of Keynes (in Japanese). Iwanami Publishing Company, Tokyo

Kahneman D, Tversky A (1979) Prospect theory: an analysis of decision under risk. Econometrica 47:263–291

Keynes JM (1921) A treatise on probability. Macmillan, London

Keynes JM (1936) The general theory of employment, interest and money. Macmillan, London

Keynes, JM (1937) The general theory of employment. Quarterly Journal of Economics. pp. 109–123

Knight FH (1921) Risk, uncertainty and profit. University of Chicago Press, Chicago

Knight FH (1935) The ethics of competition. University of Chicago Press, Chicago

Krugman P (2009) The Lionel Robbins lectures. London School of Economics Press, London

Morishima M (1999) Why will Japan Collapse? (in Japanese). Iwanami Publishing Company, Tokyo

Nasu M (1995) Keynes as a practical man (in Japanese). Chuo-Koron Publishing Company, Tokyo

Obata J (2007) The thought of Keynes: the ethics of uncertainty and the policies of money and capital (in Japanese). Keio University Press, Tokyo

Obata J (2011) Hicks on time: a synthesis of the theory of money and capital and the theory of history (in Japanese). Keio University Press, Tokyo

Piketty T (2013) Le capital au XXI. siècle (in French), Paris. English Translation (2014): capital in the twenty-first century. Harvard University Press

Sakai Y (1982) The economics of uncertainty (in Japanese). Yuhikaku Publishing Company, Tokyo

Sakai Y (1991) Risk and information: toward new economics (in Japanese). Keiso Publishing Company, Tokyo

Sakai Y (1996) The economics of risk: information and culture (in Japanese). Yuhikaku Publishing Company, Tokyo

Sakai Y (2006) On risk society: a pluralistic view (in Japanese). Iwanami Publishing Company, Tokyo

Sakai Y (2010) The economic thought of risk and uncertainty (in Japanese). Minerva Publishing Company, Kyoto

Sakai Y (2015) Keynes versus Frank Knight: how the two economics giants dealt with 'the age of uncertainty' (in Japanese). Minerva Publishing Company, Kyoto

Sakai Y (2016) J.M. Keynes on probability versus F.H. Knight on uncertainty: reflections on the miracle year of 1921. Evol Inst Econ Rev 13(1):1–21

Skidelsky R (1983) John Maynard Keynes, Vol. 1: hopes betrayed, 1883–1920. Macmillan, London

Skidelsky R (1992) John Maynard Keynes, Vol. 2: the economist as saviour, 1920–1937. Macmillan, London

Skidelsky R (2000) John Maynard Keynes, Vol. 3: fighting for Britain, 1937–1946. Macmillan, London

Skidelsky R (2009) Keynes: the return of the Master. Public Affairs, New York

Stiglitz J (2010) Needed: a new economic paradigm. Financial Times, Friday, August 20

Soros G (1998) The crisis of global capitalism. Public Affairs, New York

Soros G (2008) The crash of 2008 and what it means: the new paradigm for financial markets. Public Affairs, New York

The Royal Economic Society (1972) The collected writings of John Maynard Keynes. Macmillan, London

Chapter 4
Daniel Ellsberg on J.M. Keynes and F.H. Knight: Risk, Ambiguity, and Uncertainty

Abstract This paper aims to focus on the life and work of Daniel Ellsberg, with an intensive discussion on its relation to J.M. Keynes and F.H. Knight, the two great pioneers of the economics of uncertainty. Ellsberg seems to be a man in paradox. When he was young, he was an outstanding researcher at Harvard University and the RAND Corporation; at the December Meeting of the Econometric Society in 1960, he presented his remarkable paper in which he successfully demonstrated what we may now call Ellsberg's paradox against the traditional expected theory a la Daniel Bernoulli and von Neumann. Although it was published with the title *Risk, Ambiguity and Decision* in the November issue of the *Quarterly Journal of Economics*, it was not paid due attention for a long time. It was partly because he was so preoccupied in the 1960s and onward by letting the general public know the Pentagon Papers that he could virtually have no time left to engage in purely academic activities. In the twenty-first century, however, the times have changed in favor of Ellsberg: we can see the dramatic return of interest in decision-making under ambiguity.

This chapter will first deal with uncertainties that are not risks. A focal point of discussion will be the similarity and difference between Keynes and Knight. Kenneth Arrow's skepticism about Knight on uncertainty will also be paid due attention. We will next turn to the concept of ambiguity that was first introduced by Ellsberg. This is really the main part of this chapter. Both the two-color problem and the three-color problem will systematically be examined by help of numerical representations. We will demonstrate many possible ways to solve the so-called Ellsberg paradox. Presumably, the Keynesian approach by means of interval-valued probabilities will be shown to be very simple and highly effective. In our opinion, the most amazing Ellsberg paradox lies in the fact that an accomplished economist specialized in risk aversion dared to make a personal choice to risk everything such as degrading his social status and putting him in prison for a long period. Surely, the intellectual legacy of Ellsberg seems to be an intriguing research in paradox.

Keywords Ellsberg · Keynes · Knight · Risk · Ambiguity · Uncertainty

---

This chapter is largely written on the basis of Sakai (2018, 2019a, b).

Y. Sakai, *J.M. Keynes Versus F.H. Knight*, Evolutionary Economics and Social Complexity Science 18, https://doi.org/10.1007/978-981-13-8000-6_4

4.1 Daniel Ellsberg as a "Man in Paradox": An Introduction

The main purpose of this paper is to focus on Daniel Ellsberg with an intensive discussion on how his life and work are related to his two predecessors, J.M. Keynes and F.H. Knight. It is in 1921 that Keynes and Knight published apparently similar books on the economics of risk and uncertainty (see Keynes (1921), Knight (1921)). Forty years later, Ellsberg (1961) published an important article on risk and ambiguity in the *Quarterly Journal of Economics.* Interestingly enough, in the following year of 1962, he completed his Ph.D. thesis in economics. Although this thesis, entitled *Risk, Ambiguity and Decision*, was a masterpiece, it remained nevertheless unaddressed for long in the academic world: in fact, only in 2001, it suddenly came out as an academic book and has been available to the general public since then. The long span between 1961 and 2001 may eloquently tell us his own turbulent years as the mastermind of the "Pentagon Papers" scandal in the 1970s and after: he was once called "the most dangerous man in America." It seems, however, that Ellsberg might live twice like the "007" in the popular spy movies. At present, his academic influence on the economics of risk and uncertainty is certainly stronger than ever before. So we believe that it is quite worthwhile to look closely into his life and work in special relation to Keynes and Knight.

In retrospect, Ellsberg seems to be a man in paradox. Although in 1952, he graduated in economics at Harvard University, a top academic institution in the USA, he dared to leave it immediately after graduation to serve a US Marine. In 1957, however, he came back to Harvard for his graduate studies, starting to work on decision-making under uncertainty, a new challenging field of investigation. During his graduate studies, he left Harvard again to join the RAND Corporation as a strategic analyst. In spite of his occupational status as a "practical man," he never gave up to pursue his academic career, and at the December Meeting of the Econometric Society in St. Louis in 1960, he presented his remarkable paper in which he successfully demonstrated what we may now call the Ellsberg paradox against the standard expected utility theory. Fortunately, it was published as part of a symposium on "Decision under Uncertainty" in November 1961 issue of the *Quarterly Journal of Economics*, a first-rate academic journal. Unfortunately, however, the issue per se was not paid a due attention for a long time. While 1 year later, namely, in 1962, he completed his thesis with an attractive title *Risk, Ambiguity and Decision*, it became almost forgotten until its publication as an academic book in 2001, almost 40 years later. Of course, there must be the reason for such overdue return of the master! In fact, he was a man of strong will and justice, being so preoccupied by letting the general public know the Pentagon Papers that he could virtually have no time left to participate in purely academic discussions. In his provocative book (2002), he remarked:

> So the question was, how could I now help to end this war [the Vietnam War], now that I was willing to go to prison. And within a few weeks the idea came to me of putting out the pentagon papers, which I thought put me to prison for the rest of my life. (Ellsberg 2002)

It is true that Ellsberg contributed to decision science by introducing the Ellsberg paradox into the academic profession. The more amazing Ellsberg paradox, however, lies in the fact that an accomplished economist specialized in the aversion of risk and uncertainty dared to make a personal choice to risk everything such as degrading his social status and putting him in prison for a long period. Surely, the intellectual legacy of Ellsberg seems to be an intriguing research in paradox.[1]

The remainder of this chapter is organized as follows. Section 4.2 will deal with uncertainties that are not risks. A focal point of discussion will be the similarity and difference between Keynes and Knight. Kenneth Arrow's skepticism about Knight on uncertainty will also be paid due attention. Section 4.3, the main part of this chapter, will turn to the concept of ambiguity that was first introduced by Ellsberg. The two-color problem and the three-color problem will systematically be examined by the help of numerical representations. Section 4.4 will tell us many alternative ways to solve the so-called Ellsberg paradox. Presumably, the Keynesian approach by means of interval-valued probabilities will be shown to be very simple and highly effective. Section 4.5 will make some final remarks.

4.2 Uncertainties that Are Not Risks

4.2.1 Keynes and Knight: Their Similar yet Different Views

In the light of the history of economic thought, J.M. Keynes and F.H. Knight stand out as the two superstars who have bravely introduced the concept of uncertainty into the main body of economic science and effectively demonstrated that uncertainty should categorically be different from risk. Let us briefly review their similar yet different views on risk and uncertainty.[2]

According to Robert Skidelsky, a famous biographer of J.M. Keynes, we have been living through one of the most drastic irregularities and collapses in the last 100 years. Our economic profession, however, has done "an exceptionally poor job in explaining it" (see Skidelsky (2009), Introduction, page xv). We have virtually little idea about how to stop a succession of economic depressions which might bear down on us for so many decades to come. So, Skidelsky concludes that it is high time to get back to J.M. Keynes, the economic master of the twentieth century.[3]

[1]In retrospect, the 1960s were truly turbulent years. While the Vietnam war was raging in Indochina, many young men and hippies in the USA and Japan were involved in social protest movements. So many scandals such as the Pentagon Papers scandal and the Watergate scandal took place, eventually leading to the resignation of Richard Nixon, the then American President.

[2]For details on Keynes versus Knight, see Sakai (2015, 2016). The writing of an English enlarged version is now in progress and will be finished in 2019. This book represents the English final version.

[3]Skidelsky has enthusiastically argued that "the economics of John Maynard Keynes is back in fashion. The guardian of free-market orthodoxy the *Wall Street Journal* devoted a full page spread to him on 8 January 2009. The reason is obvious. The global economy is slumping; 'stimulus

Keynes is the economist who takes uncertainty very seriously: the centerpiece of Keynes' theory is the existence of unavoidable uncertainty about the future. In a follow-up paper (1937) just after his main work (1936), he made his position on uncertainty quite clear:

> By 'uncertain' knowledge, let me explain, I do not mean merely to distinguish what is known for certain from what is only probable. The game of roulette is not subject, in this sense, to uncertainty; nor is the prospect of a Victory bond being drawn. Or, again, the expectation of life is only slightly uncertain. Even the weather is moderately uncertain. The sense in which I am using the term is that in which the prospect of a European war is uncertain, or the price of copper and the rate of interest twenty years later hence, or the obsolescence of a new invention, or the position of private wealth owners in the social system in 1970. About these matters, there is no scientific basis on which to form any calculable probability whatever. We simply do not know. (Keynes 1937, pp. 209–223)

Keynes makes a clear-cut distinction between risk and uncertainty. Risk can be described by a certain form of probability distribution. For an example, in regard to the game of roulette, the probability of winning or losing must be calculated in advance. For another, the life expectancy of Japanese female 60 years old as of 2017 is also calculable. In contrast to risk, uncertain events might take place all of a sudden: therefore, there should be no scientific basis on which to form any calculable probability at all. Presumably, unexpected events carrying huge impact, which is cleverly called "Black Swans" by Taleb (2007), might take place at any place at any time.

According to Keynes' observation, people are not only guided by mere pecuniary motives, they are also guided by more effective animal spirits or noneconomic motivations. In this connection, Keynes (1936) eloquently remarked:

> We are merely reminding ourselves that human decisions affecting the future, whether personal or political or economic, cannot depend on strict mathematical expectations, since the basis for making such calculations does not exist; and that it is our innate urge to activity which makes the wheels go around, our rational selves choosing between the alternatives as best we are able, calculating where we can, but often falling back for our motive on whim or sentiment or chance. (Keynes 1936, pp.162–163)

Keynes is a "practical man" with many faces. He spent a very colorful life throughout his career, first as a university instructor, then as a government officer and as a businessman, and sometimes as an art collector. He does not believe that human decisions cannot always depend strict mathematical calculations such as expected utility maximization. We often fall back for our motive on psychological factors including whim, sentiment, chance, and the like. We would like to say that the practical side of Keynes was somehow followed by Ellsberg, who left a prestigious university to get a practical job at the RAND corporation and was involved in the political "Pentagon Papers scandal" and a series of legal fights in court.

In their recent collaboration, G. A. Akerlof and R.J. Shiller (2009) have reminded us of the central position occupied by animal spirits in the economics of Keynes.

---

packages' are all the rage" (Skidelsky 2009, Preface, p. xi). It seems that we are now living in the second age of Keynes.

Keynes (1936) once remarked:

> [T]here is the instability due to the characteristic of human nature that a large proportion of our positive activities depend on spontaneous optimism rather than on a mathematical expectation, whether moral or hedonistic or economic. Most, probably, of our decisions to do something positive, the full consequences of which will be drawn out over many days to come, can only be taken as a result of animal spirits-of a spontaneous urge to action rather than inaction, and not as the outcome of a weighted average of quantitative benefits multiplied by quantitative probabilities. (Keynes 1936, p. 161)

Keynes has repeatedly stressed that if such animal spirits are dimmed and the spontaneous optimism falters and leave us depend on a mere mathematical expectation, then capitalist enterprises will fade and eventually die. According to Akerlof and Shiller (2009), the concept of animal spirits is not the forgotten lesson of the 1930s: it is still alive in the 2000s and even more lively in the 2010s. There are not a few people who optimistically believe that the Great Depression is merely the past tragedy of the twentieth century. We must bear in mind, however, that a repeat of the Great Depression is now a possibility since economists, the government, and the general public have in recent years grown more complacent than ever. As the saying goes, power will collapse, and absolute power will collapse absolutely! Likewise, over-expectation is destined to be self-destructive and will eventually collapse overly!

While Keynes was born with a silver spoon at Cambridge in the traditional British Empire, Knight was born with a wooden spoon in the countryside in the new superpower, namely, the USA. Although their birth places were quite apart, they could be regarded as contemporaries; strictly speaking, Knight was only 2 years younger than Keynes. Knight's novel idea of uncertainty is clearly seen in the following sentence:

> Uncertainty must be taken in a sense radically distinct from the familiar notion of Risk, from which it has never been properly separated. ...... It will appear that a *measurable* uncertainty, or 'risk' proper, as we shall use the term, is so far different from an *unmeasurable* one that it is not in effect an uncertainty at all. We shall accordingly restrict the term 'uncertainty' to cases of the non-quantitative type. It is this 'true' uncertainty, and not risk, as has been argued, which forms the basis of a valid theory of profit and accounts for the divergence between actual and theoretical competition. (Knight 1921, pp. 19–20)

The book of uncertainty written by Knight is one of the twentieth century's monumental book, firmly providing the theoretical basis of the market economy. Since the first edition was published in 1921 just after the First World War, the re-issue with a long preface came out during the Great Depression in 1933, and a reprint edition and another reprint one, respectively, followed in 1948 and in 1956 after the Second World War. Knight is a hard-boiled researcher, thereby persistently maintaining his original position on the role of uncertainty as distinct from risk during his long career. In fact, in the Preface for the Reprint of 1948, he remarked:

> No more elaborate theory of uncertainty would be offered. It is still my conviction that contingency or 'chance' is an un-analyzable fact of nature. ... Chance is more than human ignorance of causality which is 'really' absolute. No perfect probability class can be known as such. Perfect randomness cannot be defined, or its relation to "error" stated – nor to "freedom." For that, contingency seems to be a prerequisite, but freedom involves a mysterious something more, an act, in a unique sense, of "will." (Knight, 1957 edition, Preface, p. lxiii)

In spite of the fact that Knight and Keynes appeared to deal with very similar topics such as uncertainty and decision, their positions on the role of economic science looked considerably apart, and sometimes even antagonistic. In particular, Knight did not agree with Keynesian way of macroeconomic and monetary thinking. In his methodological paper on the role of principles in economics and politics, Knight (1951) criticized Keynes in very harsh words:

> The latest 'new economics,' and in my opinion rather the worst for fallacious doctrine and pernicious consequences, is that launched by the late John Maynard (Lord) Keynes, who for a decade succeeded in carrying economic thinking well back to the dark age, but of late this wave of the future has happily been passing. (Knight 1951; contained in *Selected Essays,* Vol. 1, pp.362–363.)

As the saying goes, dead men tell no tales. It must have been a sort of shocking surprise to the general public that in his presidential address delivered at the 63rd Annual Meeting at the American Economic Association, Chicago, 25 December 1950, Knight attacked the work of the late Keynes in a very ungentlemanly manner. We believe that if Keynes had been alive in 1951, he would surely have wanted to tell something. In retrospect, it would be grossly unfair to say that Keynes carried economic thinking well back to the dark age. More fairly speaking, Keynesian uncertainty is macro-oriented, and Knightian uncertainty is micro-oriented. Macro is macro, and micro is micro. To some fundamentals such as Knight, these two would never meet together. There are a group of more open-minded persons including the present author, however, who would say that macro and micro can stand together, implying that Keynesian and Knightian uncertainties are reconcilable. The question of integration of the two approaches, Keynesian and Knightian approaches, remains very important even today, requiring a further investigation in the future.

4.2.2 Arrow's Skepticism About Knight on Uncertainty

Kenneth J. Arrow is no doubt a superstar along with Paul A. Samuelson; their contributions to theoretical and welfare economics have been too vast and deep to be properly measured. It is this great Arrow who had serious doubts about Knight's distinction between risk and uncertainty. For instance, in one of his influential papers in *Econometrica*, Arrow (1951) once remarked:

> Knight denies that all types of risks can be described by probability statements. …… Knight's uncertainties seem to have surprisingly many of the properties of ordinary probabilities, and it is no clear how much is gained by the distinction. (Arrow 1951; contained in Arrow 1970, pp. 17–18)

Fairly speaking, Arrow was well-known as an open-minded and generous gentleman. So his uncharacteristic skepticism about Knight's distinction between risk and uncertainty must have been a shocking news to many economists. As mentioned above, Knight's fundamental position was that risk was measurable in the sense that it was describable by a certain distribution function but uncertainty was definitely not so. Therefore, Arrow shared the superficial view that Knightian uncertainties seemed to have so many properties of ordinary probabilities that the possible gain obtained by the distinction between risk and uncertainty was minimum. Here we can see the existence of a big gap between Knight and Arrow, which is the important point that has not been rather neglected in the literature.

In his characteristic fashion, Knight stubbornly defended his view in favor of uncertainty throughout his career. Let us remind of Knight's classification viewpoint by which three different types of probability situations should clearly be separated. First, we can argue a priori probability that is just logical or mathematical as can be exemplified by the probability of throwing a dice for "six," namely, the fraction 1/6. Second, we may refer to statistical probability such as the life expectancy of a person at a given point of time. These two probabilities are apparently measurable, thus being indicated by a certain probability distribution. Knight proceeds to point out the third and new type of probability, especially referred to estimates, which is neither mathematical nor empirical. Let us take a close look at the following sentence:

> The distinction here is that there is *no solid basis of any kind* for classifying instances. This form of probability is involved in the greatest logical difficulties of all, and no very satisfactory discussion of it can be given, but its distinction from the other types must be emphasized and some of its complicated relations indicated. (Knight 1921, p. 225)

Knight argues that estimates or judgments are liable to err, although the other two types of probability are completely free from any human mistakes. There should be no basis whatever of comparison for determining the probability of error in a judgment. He takes as an illustration a typical business decision. He eloquently continues his argument:

> The business man himself not merely forms the best estimate he can of the outcome of his action, but he is likely also to estimate the probability that his estimate is correct. The 'degree' of certainty or of confidence felt in the conclusion after it is reached cannot be ignored. For it is of the greatest practical significance. The action which follows upon an opinion depends as much upon the amount of confidence in that opinion as it does upon the favorableness of the opinion itself. The ultimate logic, or psychology, of these deliberations is obscure, a part of the scientifically unfathomable mystery of life and mind. We must simply fall back upon a 'capacity' in the intelligent animal to form more or less correct judgments about things, an intuitive sense of values. (Knight 1921, p. 227)

No doubt, the quotation aforementioned seems a bit too long. We do believe, however, that it deserves to do so. Knight emphasizes that the ultimate logic, or the psychology, of human action tends to be obscure, demonstrating a part of the scientifically unfathomable mystery of life and mind. We are no longer a scientifically logical super-machine, but rather the mere intelligent animal that is sometimes involved in the unfathomable mystery of life and mind. Presumably, it is in this psychological and even mysterious aspect of human life and mind that Arrow has mentioned his strong skepticism about Knight's view of uncertainty. In a sense, Knight is a philosophical man who takes account of non-reasonable aspect of human mind and behavior, whereas Arrow is a very reasonable man who tends to balance the cost and benefit of his action, thus under-evaluating the effect of psychology on economic behavior. Knight is very much concerned with following out the consequences of such higher form of uncertainty not susceptible to measurement. "It is this *true uncertainty* which by preventing the theoretically perfect outworking of the tendencies of competition gives the characteristic form of 'enterprise' to economic organization as a whole and accounts for the peculiar income of the entrepreneur" (Knight 1921, page. 232). Then he argues that the presence of true profit depends on true uncertainty in the estimation of the value of judgment.[4]

All in all, the existence and persistence of non-measurable uncertainty forms the core of the economic theory of Knight. Arrow's skepticism about Knight's concept of uncertainty cannot be accepted by Frank Knight and his followers.[5]

4.3 Ambiguity and Risk

4.3.1 Keynes on the "Two-Color Urn" Problem

It is said that 40 years after the Pentagon Papers scandal, Daniel Ellsberg remains a revel with a cause. Although Ellsberg has usually been associated with the historical scandal, we nevertheless must remember that he was once a first-rate researcher working for Harvard University and later for the RAND Corporation and that his academic prestige has come back rather quickly since academic interest in decision under ambiguity has gained a momentum in recent years.

As Levi (2001) lucidly explained, Daniel Ellsberg courageously challenged the traditional theory of rational decision based on the expected utility rule a la Bernoulli (1738). Ellsberg submitted his doctoral dissertation to the Economics Department of Harvard University in April 1962, within a year after he had published a highly academic paper "Risk, Ambiguity, and the Savage Axioms" in the *Quarterly Journal of Economics*. While the 1961 paper was a first-rate paper on decision-making under ambiguity, it was perhaps too academic to receive proper hearing. Besides, his dissertation had not been noticed for a long time as if it had been put in the black box. And eventually, it reappeared in the publishing circles in 2001 after nearly 40 sleeping years.

We would like to point out the fact that there has been a noticeable gap between the 1961 paper and the 1962 dissertation with respect to the place of Keynes and Knight in the world of Ellsberg. It would be quite worthwhile to fill in such a neglected gap so that we could more systematically discuss the relations among those three superstars, namely, Keynes, Knight, and Ellsberg.

As sharply pointed out by Zappia (2016) in quite recent times, it was the great Keynes himself who placed emphasis on the idea that in situations where

[4]For details of the economics of Knight, see Emmett (1999a, b) and Boyd (1997).

[5]Although Arrow described his strong skepticism about Knightian uncertainty, it would sound rather strange that Arrow's comment on Keynesian uncertainty was not so critical. In fact, in Arrow and Hahn (1971), Arrow was so kind to discuss the position of the Keynesian model in relation to general competitive model.

information was not so clear and rather vague, the traditional approach a la Bernoulli was zoomed to invalidity. It was a shocking truth that Ellsberg failed to refer to Keynes in the 1961 paper, but showed much respect to Keynes in the 1962 dissertation. Presumably, such nonsymmetrical treatment of Keynes by Ellsberg seemed to be mysterious to every conscientious reader.

As the saying goes, seeing is believing. Let us faithfully record the two-color urn problem originally provided by Keynes (1921):

> The typical case, in which there may be a *practical* connection between weight and probable error, may be illustrated by the two cases following of balls drawn from an urn. In each case we require the probability of a white ball; in the first case we know that the urn contains black and white in equal proportions; in the second case the proportion of each color is unknown, and each ball is as likely to be black as white. It is evident that in either case the probability of drawing a white ball is 1/2, but that the weight of the argument in favor of this conclusion is grater in the first case. (Keynes 1921, pp. 75–76)

The importance of the urn problem given by Keynes (1921) cannot be overstated since it represents a pioneering study on the new concept of ambiguity. We think that it is remarkable because of the following two reasons. First, it was presented and analyzed well ahead of Daniel Ellsberg (1961). Second, strangely enough, it was never referred to by Ellsberg. We believe that Ellsberg might have just overlooked it. Its graphical explanation is provided in Fig. 4.1. There are two cases to consider. In case I, the urn is supposed to contain black (B) and white (W) in equal proportions, namely, 50–50%. In case II, the proportion of B or W is quite ambiguous or totally unknown. We assume that in each case we bet on B to be underlined in the figure.

Clearly, this is a typical decision problem under ambiguity. Keynes himself has given the interpretation that the weight of the argument in favor of drawing W is greater in case I than in case II. Alternatively, Ellsberg would rather say that people prefer the

We draw balls from an urn. Then find the probability of drawing a white ball.

Case I (Bet on B): We know that the urn contains black (B) and white (W) in equal proportions.

30 30

B W

Case II (Bet on B): The proportion of each color is unknown.

60

B W

Keynes argues that the weight of the argument in favor of drawing W is greater in the first case than in the second case. Ellsberg would rather say that people prefer the numerically clear case I to the vague case II .

Fig. 4.1 Keynes on the urn problem: a pioneering study of ambiguity

numerically clear case I to the vague case II. In other words, in terms of modern terminology, we would say that the person who bets on B shows ambiguity aversion.

This two-color urn example tells us that the standard expected utility rule originated by Bernoulli is no longer valid. In fact, if we took advantage of the expected utility rule, the expected utilities of cases I and II could have led us to the same quantity as shown below:

$$EU(\mathrm{I}) = EU(\mathrm{II}) = (1/2)U(\mathrm{B}) + (1/2)U(\mathrm{W}). \tag{4.1}$$

It is recalled here that the indifference principle a la Keynes (1921) is adopted here, meaning that unknown proportions of each color can positively be interpreted as equal proportions, namely, half -and-half.

4.3.2 Ellsberg on the "Three-Color Urn" Problem

We are now in a position to carefully discuss the three-color urn problem originated in Ellsberg (1961, 1962). It is worth mentioning that the 1961 paper by Ellsberg began with the following conspicuous sentence:

> There are always been a good deal of skcpticism about the behavioral significance of Frank Knight's distinction between 'measurable uncertainty' or 'risk,' which may be represented by numerical probabilities, and 'unmeasurable uncertainty' which cannot. (Ellsberg 1961, p.643)

When Ellsberg was an active researcher in the 1960s, there was a good deal of skepticism about Knight's distinction between measurable risk and non-measurable uncertainty. Among those skeptical papers were Arrow's 1951 paper aforementioned. It was the young Ellsberg who intended to wipe out such unfair accusation against Knight and wanted to seriously discuss those uncertain prospects which are not risks. In so doing, he cleverly introduced the new concept "ambiguity" in his analytical framework. As will be seen below, ambiguity is neither ordinary risk nor wide-ranging uncertainty: it is an ingenious concept put somewhere between risk and uncertainty.

Seeing is believing! Let us revaluate Ellsberg's new approach to decision under ambiguity by means of a set of numerical illustrations. In particular, he considers the "three-color urn" problem which seems to be a masterly extension of Keynes' "two-color urn" problem to the three-color case. Take a close look at Fig. 2. Let us imagine an urn known to contain 30 red (R) balls and 60 black (B) and yellow (Y) balls, the latter in unknown proportions. One ball is to be drawn at random from the urn. First, compare a pair of gambles: Gamble I(Bet on R) and Gamble II (Bet on B). The question to ask is which gamble people prefer, Gamble I or II. Next, consider another pair of gambles: Gamble III (Bet on R or Y) and Gamble IV (Bet B or Y). According to Ellsberg's experiments, a very frequent pattern of response is as follows: Gamble I is preferred to II, but IV preferred to III.

	30	60	
	Red (R)	**Black (B)**	**Yellow (Y)**
Gamble I (Bet on R):	$100	$0	$0
Gamble II (Bet on B):	$0	$100	$0

	30	60	
	Red (R)	**Black (B)**	**Yellow (Y)**
Gamble III (Bet on R or Y):	$100	$0	$100
Gamble IV (Bet on B or Y):	$0	$100	$100

Fig. 4.2 Ellsberg's paradox: most people prefer Gamble I to II, but IV to III

The question is why such preference reversal occurs. People prefer I to II because they find the *sure* prize of $100 (with winning probability 1/3) more attractive than the *ambiguous* prize ranging from $0 to $100 (with winning probability 2/3). But they prefer IV to III since they feel the *sure* prize of $100 (with winning probability 2/3) more appealing to the *ambiguous* prize (with winning probability widely ranging from 1/3 to 1). In either choice, people indicates their preference for the *sure* prize over the *ambiguous* prize, demonstrating their attitude to ambiguity aversion.

Those examples shown in Fig. 4.2 will teach us that the standard expected utility principle is no longer valid here. In fact, if we apply the expected utility theory, the expected utility of Gamble I is calculated as follows:

$$EU(\mathrm{I}) = \mathrm{Prob}(\mathrm{R})U(100) + \mathrm{Prob}(\mathrm{B})U(0) + \mathrm{Prob}(\mathrm{Y})U(0). \tag{4.2}$$

Now if we assume that Prob(B) = ρ, we immediately have Prob(Y) = 1-ρ. Then Eq. (4.2) can be rewritten as follows:

$$EU(\mathrm{I}) = (1/3)U(100) + (\rho)U(0) + (1-\rho)U(0). \tag{4.3}$$

Without loss of generality, we can suppose that $U(100) = 1$ and $U(0) = 0$, a sort of normalization procedure. Then Eq. (36) is further simplified as follows:

$$EU(\mathrm{I}) = (1/3)(1) + (\rho)(0) + (1-\rho)(0) = 1/3. \tag{4.4}$$

In a similar fashion, we can compute the expected utility of Gamble II as follows:

$$\begin{aligned} EU(\mathrm{II}) &= \mathrm{Prob}(\mathrm{R})U(0) + \mathrm{Prob}(\mathrm{B})U(100) + \mathrm{Prob}(\mathrm{Y})U(0) \\ &= (1/3)(0) + (\rho)(1) + (1-\rho)(0) = \rho. \end{aligned} \tag{4.5}$$

Therefore, if Gamble I is preferred to II, then EU(I) must be greater than EU(II) by view of the expected utility theory. So taking account of Eqs. (4.3) and (4.5), this is equivalent to saying that 1/3 is greater than ρ. In other words, we have derived the following equivalent relation:

$$\text{I is preferred to II} \Leftrightarrow 1/3 > \rho. \tag{4.6}$$

Let us turn to comparison between Gambles III and IV. The expected utilities of those gambles are calculated as follows:

$$\begin{aligned} EU(\text{III}) &= \text{Prob(R)}U(100) + \text{Prob(B)}U(0) + \text{Prob(Y)}U(100) \\ &= (1/3)(1) + (\rho)(0) + (2/3 - \rho)(1) = 1 - \rho; \end{aligned} \tag{4.7}$$

$$\begin{aligned} EU(\text{IV}) &= \text{Prob(R)}U(0) + \text{Prob(B)}U(100) + \text{Prob(Y)}U(100) \\ &= (1/3)(0) + (\rho)(1) + (2/3 - \rho)(1) = 2/3. \end{aligned} \tag{4.8}$$

Hence, we find the following sequence of equivalent relations:

$$\begin{aligned} \text{IV is preferred to III} &\Leftrightarrow EU(\text{IV}) > EU(\text{III}) \\ &\Leftrightarrow 2/3 > 1 - \rho \\ &\Leftrightarrow \rho > 1/3. \end{aligned} \tag{4.9}$$

Apparently, the two equivalent relations (4.6) and (4.9) are not compatible! This is really the essence of the famous Ellsberg paradox. In order to resolve the paradox, the first thing we should do is to seek very nice ways to get rid of the traditional expected utility theory.

4.3.3 Alternative Ways to Resolve Ellsberg's Paradox

Generally speaking, any kind of paradox would be a challenge to any intellectual person. In historical perspective, there have been several attempts to solve Ellsberg's paradox. Although Ellsberg (1961, 1962/2001) himself attempted to propose his own solution, it is quite unfortunate that it has not been well-received and almost forgotten.

In our opinion, possibly the simplest solution is conceivable if Keynes' half-forgotten analysis of interval estimate technique is adopted here.[6]

Keynes once remarked:

> The sphere of inexact numerical comparison is not quite so limited. Many probabilities, which are incapable of numerical measurement, can be placed nevertheless *between* numerical limits. And by taking particular non-numerical probabilities as standards a great number of comparisons or approximate measurements become possible. (Keynes 1921, p.160)

[6]It is recalled that usefulness of the interval probability approach was later advocated by Hicks (1979), an outstanding Keynesian economist

Interval-valued probability, or simply interval probability, has not been a foreign idea to Keynes: and indeed, much interest has been revived by help of Brady (2004). As was seen above, Keynes argues that many probabilities, which are incapable of numerical measurement, can be placed nevertheless between numerical limits. Let us consider the interval probability of the form [α,β], with α and β being its lower and upper limits. If we take account of the "weight of argument" a la Keynes, the weight Wght(·) of the argument of the interval [α,β] should be less that the "point probability" Prob(·) of the mean (α + β)/2, so that we have

$$\mathrm{Wght}([\alpha,\beta]) < \mathrm{Prob}((\alpha+\beta)/2). \tag{4.10}$$

Besides, without loss of generality, let us assume again that $U(100) = 1$ and $U(0) = 0$. Then taking account of the interval probability argument, the weighted value of Gamble I is calculated as follows:

$$\begin{aligned} WV(\mathrm{I}) &= \mathrm{Wght(R)}U(100) + \mathrm{Wght(B\ or\ Y)}U(0) \\ &= \mathrm{Prob(R)}U(100) + \mathrm{Prob(B\ or\ Y)}U(0) \\ &= (1/3)(1) + (2/3)(0) = 1/3. \end{aligned} \tag{4.11}$$

In an analogous way, the weighted value of Gamble II is computed as follows:

$$\begin{aligned} WV(\mathrm{II}) &= \mathrm{Wght(R)}U(0) + \mathrm{Wght(B)}U(100) + \mathrm{Wght(Y)}U(0) \\ &= \mathrm{Prob(R)}U(0) + \mathrm{Wght}\ ([0,2/3])U(100) + \mathrm{Wght}\ ([0,2/3])U(0) \\ &= (1/3)(0) + \mathrm{Wght}\ ([0,2/3])(1) + \mathrm{Wght}\ ([0,2/3])(0) \\ &= \mathrm{Wght}([0,2/3]). \end{aligned} \tag{4.12}$$

Hence the assertion that Gamble I is preferred to II means that 1/3 is greater than Wght([0,2/3]), which tells us the gambler's "ambiguity aversion" a la Ellsberg. Summing up, we have thus obtained the following sequence of equivalent relations:

$$\begin{aligned} \text{I is preferred to II} &\Leftrightarrow WV(\mathrm{I}) > WV(\mathrm{II}) \\ &\Leftrightarrow 1/3 > \mathrm{Wght}([0,2/3]). \end{aligned} \tag{4.13}$$

Likewise, the weighted values of Gambles III and IV are computed as follows:

$$\begin{aligned} WV(\mathrm{III}) &= \mathrm{Wght(R)}U(100) + \mathrm{Wght(B)}U(0) + \mathrm{Wght(Y)}U(100) \\ &= \mathrm{Prob(R)}U(100) + \mathrm{Wght}([0,2/3)])U(0) + \mathrm{Wght}([0,2/3])U(100) \\ &= (1/3)(1) + \mathrm{Wght}([0,2/3])(0) + \mathrm{Wght}([0,2/3])(1) \\ &= 1/3 + \mathrm{Wght}([0,2/3]); \end{aligned} \tag{4.14}$$

$$\begin{aligned} WV(\text{IV}) &= \text{Wght}(\text{R})U(0) + \text{Wght}(\text{B or Y})U(100) \\ &= \text{Prob}(\text{R})U(0) + \text{Prob}(\text{B or Y})U(100) \\ &= (1/3)(0) + (2/3)(1) = 2/3. \end{aligned} \tag{4.15}$$

Therefore we can obtain the following sequence of equivalent relations:

$$\begin{aligned} \text{IV is preferred to III} &\Leftrightarrow WV(\text{IV}) > WV(\text{III}) \\ &\Leftrightarrow 2/3 > 1/3 + \text{Wght}([0, 2/3]) \\ &\Leftrightarrow 1/3 > \text{Wght}([0, 2/3]). \end{aligned} \tag{4.16}$$

Very remarkably, this equivalent relation (4.16) is exactly as the same as the one (4.13). There exist no contradictions whatever if people prefer I to II but IV to III. Thus Ellsberg's paradox is now successfully resolved!

Although we think that the interval probability approach aforementioned is simple and powerful enough, it is also true that there has recently emerged mathematically minded people who have taken a more ambitious and sophisticated approach to resolution of Ellsberg's paradox. Nishimura and Ozaki (2017), both ambitious Japanese mathematical economists, are among those people who have dared to make full use of Choquet integral and other highly advanced mathematical tools.

Following Nishimura and Ozaki, let us define the set function $\Theta(\cdot)$—especially named "probability capacity function"—as is indicated in Fig. 4.3. In view of the set of three colors, $\Sigma = \{\text{R,B,Y}\}$, let us think of the following set of subsets of Σ as the domain of the function Θ:

$$\begin{aligned} \text{The domain of } \Theta &= 2^{\Sigma} \\ &= \{\phi, \{\text{R}\}, \{\text{B}\}, \{\text{Y}\}, \{\text{R, B}\}, \{\text{R, Y}\}, \{\text{B, Y}\}, \{\text{R, B, Y}\}\} \end{aligned} \tag{4.17}$$

Thus Θ is a set-to-point mapping from the domain indicated by (4.17) into the range given by the unit interval [0,1] such that $\Theta(\varphi) = 0$, $\Theta(\{\text{R}\}) = 1/9$, $\Theta(\{\text{B}\}) = 1/9$, $\Theta(\{\text{Y}\}) = 1/9$, $\Theta(\{\text{R,B}\}) = 4/9$, $\Theta(\{\text{R,Y}\}) = 4/9$, $\Theta(\{\text{B,Y}\}) = 2/3$, and $\Theta(\{\text{R,B, Y}))= 1$. It is noted here that in contrast to probability function $\text{Prob}(\cdot)$, the newly defined capacity function $\Theta(\cdot)$ does not satisfy the additivity property: for instance, $\Theta(\{\text{R}\}) + \Theta(\{\text{B}\}) = 2/9 < 4/9 = \Theta(\{\text{R,B}\})$. The Choquet expected utilities of Gambles I and II above are calculated as follows:

$$\begin{aligned} CEU(\text{I}) &= \Theta(\{\text{R}\})U(100) + \Theta(\{\text{B, Y}\})U(0) \\ &= (1/3)(1) + (2/3)(0) = 1/3; \end{aligned} \tag{4.18}$$

$$\begin{aligned} CEU(\text{II}) &= \Theta(\{\text{R}\})U(0) + \Theta(\{\text{B}\})U(100) + \Theta(\text{Y})U(0) \\ &= (1/3)(0) + (1/9)(1) + (1/9)(0) = 1/9. \end{aligned} \tag{4.19}$$

Fig. 4.3 Ellsberg's paradox reconsidered: a highly mathematical approach by means of the Choquet expected utility

Domain	Set function Θ	Range
φ	——————→	Θ(φ) = 0
{R}	——————→	Θ({R}) = 1/9
{B}	——————→	Θ({B}) = 1/9
{Y}	——————→	Θ({W})= 1/9
{R,B}	——————→	Θ({R,B})= 4/9
{R.Y}	——————→	Θ({R,W})= 4/9
{B,Y}	——————→	Θ({B,W})= 2/3
{R,B,Y}	——————→	Θ({R,B,Y}) = 1

According to the Choquet expected utility, the assertion that I is preferred to II means that *CEU*(I) is greater than *CEU*(II). This must be true since 1/3 is surely greater than 1/9. Likewise, the Choquet expected utilities of Gamble III and IV are computed as follows:

$$\begin{aligned} CEU(\mathrm{III}) &= \Theta(\{R\})U(100) + \Theta(\{B\})U(0) + \Theta(\{Y\})U(100) \\ &= (1/3)(1) + (1/9)(0) + (1/9)(1) = 1/3 + 1/9; \end{aligned} \tag{4.20}$$

$$\begin{aligned} CEU(\mathrm{IV}) &= \Theta(\{R\})U(0) + \Theta(\{B, Y\})U(100) \\ &= (1/3)(0) + (2/3)(1) = 2/3. \end{aligned} \tag{4.21}$$

Consequently, the assertion that IV is preferred to III is equivalent to saying that as is expected, 2/3 is greater than the sum of 1/3 and 1/9. Thus, relying on the Choquet expected utility theory, Nishimura and Ozaki have found their own way to solve Ellsberg's paradox.

As common sense experience tell us, there are surely many routes available to climb the mountaintop! One simple and reasonable route is the interval probability approach which was originally promoted by Keynes himself but later almost forgotten until it was rediscovered by Brady (2004). Another mathematically sophisticated route would be the Choquet expected utility approach which was initially taken on the base of Choquet integral and recently developed by Nishimura and Ozaki (2017) for resolution of Ellsberg's paradox.[7]

---

[7]Gustave Choquet (1915–2006) is a contemporary French mathematician. His contributions include work in functional analysis, potential theory, and measure theory. He is well-known for creating Choquet integral and Choquet theory. Choquet integral may be regarded as an extension of Lebesgue integral, which was created by Henri-Léon Lebesgue (1875–1941), another famed French mathematician. Although Choquet integral per se belongs to a highly advanced branch of mathematics, it has recently been applied to economic theory by Schmeidler (1989), Gilboa and Schmeidler (1989), and Nishimura and Ozaki (2017). We have bear in mind, however, that there should be an insurmountable trade-off between intuitive simplicity and mathematical complexity. For a detailed review of Nishimura and Ozaki (2017), see Sakai (2019a).

We would like to stick to the common sense principle "the simpler, the better." Hopefully, a simpler approach could appeal to a wider range of audience.

4.4 Econs Versus Humans: Concluding Remarks

In the above, we have intensively discussed the life and work of Daniel Ellsberg, with special reference to J.M. Keynes and F.H. Knight, the two superstars in the economics of uncertainty. As repeatedly mentioned, Ellsberg seems to be a man in paradox. Although he was the first man who pointed out Ellsberg's paradox in the world of ambiguity, his academic results were destined to be forgotten because of his involvement in the political Pentagon Papers scandal. He is immortal, however; he will constantly be shining in the twenty-first century.

In the light of economic history, we think that behind Ellsberg's personal struggle, there lies the academic struggle between "Econs" and "Humans." According to Richard H. Thaler (2015), a respected representative of our Rochester graduates, many standard models tend to use a fictional creature called homo economicus, or simply Econs. Econs are a sort of "rational fools" a la Amartia Sen (1987) in the sense that they rationally choose goods by optimizing their utilities and have always rational expectations about market equilibriums. Although the traditional expected utility model is an extension of the standard rational model to the world of risk and uncertainty, its basic structure remains the same as before. In our opinion, a more mathematically sophisticated model using Choquet integral seems to essentially rely on the assumption of Econs.

In contrast, Humans are just human beings—homo sapiens. Compared with fictional Econs, Humans do a lot of misbehaving, implying that economic models lead to a lot of bad predictions. Humans are supposed to have a lot of nonrational feelings such as envy, hatred, optimism, pessimism, sympathy, compassion, and the like. In the world where many Humans live, the traditional economic theory is far from satisfactory. We need to establish a more comprehensive model of human behavior including a variety of complicated psychologies. For instance, a nice bridge between economic theory and economic psychology must urgently be built.

In the above, we have sometimes introduced highly mathematical tools. It is recalled that Albert Einstein (1879–1955), probably the greatest scientist of the twentieth century, once talked about his own philosophy of science:

> I have little patience with scientists who take a board of wood, look for its thinnest part, and drill a great number of holes where drilling is easy. (Albert Einstein, quoted by Phillip Frank 1949)

In the real world, we are exposed to various temptations for easy-going lives. So, it would be a sad fact that we have a tendency to drill a great number of holes on a board of wood where drilling is rather easy. However, we have to take a very broad view of the wood without looking at only small trees. We are really Humans rather than Econs! In order to further develop decision-making under ambiguity, it is necessary to have the second Ellsberg or like in not a distant future.

References

Akerlof GA, Shiller RJ (2009) Animal spirits: how human psychology drives the economy, and why it matters for global capitalism. Princeton University Press, Princeton

Arrow KJ (1951) Alternative approaches to theory of choice in risk-taking situations. Econometrica 19:404–437. Contained in Arrow (1970), Chapter 1

Arrow KJ (1970) Essays in the theory of risk-bearing. North Holland, Amsterdam

Arrow KJ, Hahn EH (1971) General competitive analysis. Holden-Day, San Francisco

Bernoulli D (1738) Specimen theorie novae de mensura sortis (in Latin). *Commentarii Academiae* Scientiarum Imperialis Petropolitanae (Papers of the Imperial Science Sciences in Petersburg) 1:175–195. English Translation by Sommer L (1954) Exposition of a new theory of the measurement of risk. Econometrica: 22, 23–36

Boyd R (1997) Knight FH, 1935, The ethics of competition: a new introduction to the transaction edition. Transaction Publishers, New Brunswick/London

Brady ME (2004) J.M. Keynes' theory of decision making, induction, and analogy: the role of interval valued probability in his approach. Xlibris Corporation, Bloomington

Ellsberg D (1961) Risk, ambiguity and the Savage axioms. Q J Econ 75(4):643–669

Ellsberg D (1962/2001) Risk, ambiguity and decision. Routledge, London/New York

Ellsberg D (2002). Secrets: a memoir of Vietnam and the Pentagon papers

Emmett RB (1999a) Selected essays by Frank H. Knight, volume one. University of Chicago Press, Chicago

Emmett RB (1999b) Selected essays by Frank H. Knight, volume two. University of Chicago Press, Chicago

Frank P (1949) Einstein's philosophy of science. Rev Mod Phys:21–23

Gilboa I, Schmeidler D (1989) Maxmin expected utility with non-unique prior. J Math Econ 18:141–153

Hicks JR (1979) Causality in economics. Basic Blackell, Oxford

Keynes JM (1921) A treatise on probability. Macmillan, London

Keynes JM (1936) The general theory of employment, interest and money. Macmillan, London

Keynes JM (1937) The general theory of employment. Q J Econ 51(2):209–223

Knight FH (1921) Risk, uncertainty and profit. University of Chicago Press, Chicago

Knight FH (1951) The role of principles in economics and politics. Am Econ Rev 41:1–29

Levi I (2001) Introduction to risk, ambiguity and decision. Contained in the new edition of Ellsberg (2001), pp ix–xxxvii

Nishimura GK, Ozaki H (2017) Economics of pessimism and optimism: theory of Knightian uncertainty and its applications. Springer, Tokyo

Sakai Y (2015) J.M. Keynes versus F.H. Knight (in Japanese). Minerva Publishing Company, Kyoto

Sakai Y (2016) J.M. Keynes on probability versus F.H. Knight on uncertainty: reflections on the miracle year of 1921. Evol Inst Econ Rev 13(1):1–21

Sakai Y (2018) Daniel Ellsberg on J.M. Keynes and F.H. Knight: risk, ambiguity and uncertainty. CRR Discussion Paper No. A-31, Shiga University, Japan, pp 1–21

Sakai Y (2019a) Economics of pessimism and optimism: theory of Knightian uncertainty and its applications, Kiyohiko G. Nishimura and Hiroyuki Ozaki, Springer Japan (2017). J Econ Psychol 72:51–53

Sakai Y (2019b) Daniel Ellsberg on J.M. Keynes and F.H. Knight: Risk, ambiguity and uncertainty. Evolutionary and Institutional Economics Review, forthcoming

Schmeidler D (1989) Subjective probability and expected utility without additivity. Econometrica 57:571–587

Sen A (1987) On ethics and economics. Blackwell Publishing

Skidelsky R (2009) Keynes: the return of the master. Public Affairs, New York

Taleb N (2007) The black swan: the impact of the highly improbable. Allen Lane, New York

Thaler RH (2015) Misbehaving: The making of behavioral economics. Norton, New York

Zappia C (2016) Daniel Ellsberg and the validation of normative propositions. Œconomia (6–1):57–79

Part II
Market and Application

Chapter 5
Involuntary Unemployment Versus "Involuntary Employment": J.M. Keynes and Beyond

Abstract This chapter is concerned with the important question of how and to what extent great economists such as J.M. Keynes, F. H. Knight, J.R. Hicks, P. A. Samuelson, Y. Takata, and M. Morishima have been intermingled with each other. Our discussion focuses on the two key concepts in the labor market—involuntary unemployment and "involuntary employment." On the one hand, there are so many persons in the street who are willing to work at the existing wages but cannot find jobs because of a shortage of the effective demand as a whole. This is clearly the issue of involuntary unemployment, which has been energetically tackled by J. M. Keynes and his followers since the 1930s. On the other hand, since the 1990s, there also have emerged so many people who must work unwillingly for their survivals at the minimal level of wages. This is a new issue of "involuntary employment" or "non-regular workers," which has recently been investigated by Nobuaki Takahashi, a rising Japanese economist. Although the Takahashi approach is an attractive one, it nevertheless seems to remain at the embryo stage, thus requiring further developments in many ways. The second Keynes would urgently be needed.

Keywords J.M. Keynes · Involuntary unemployment · N. Takahashi · Involuntary employment · Non-regular workers · N. Okishio · Y. Takata

5.1 J.M. Keynes, F.H. Knight, and Y. Takata: An Introduction

One day when I myself felt tired of writing some essays, I happened to find a rather old book in the corner of the bookcase of my study. The book, entitled *Keynes' General Theory: Reports of Three Decades*, was published in 1964. It also contained my personal signature printed on the back cover, "Yasuhiro Sakai, University of Rochester, April 1970." This book was a collection of very important papers which comprehensively reported the impact of The General Theory of Employment,

This paper is a revised version of Sakai (2018a, b).

Y. Sakai, *J.M. Keynes Versus F.H. Knight*, Evolutionary Economics and Social Complexity Science 18, https://doi.org/10.1007/978-981-13-8000-6_5

Interest and Money for the period between 1936 and 1966. More than four decades have passed since then. As the saying goes, time and tide wait for no man![1]

In the light of the history of economic thought, back in the 1930s, John Maynard Keynes (1936) wrote a monumental work of economics, entitled *The General Theory of Employment, Interest and Money*. How and to what degree this book influenced the academic circle at the time of publication, by and large, seemed to be dependent on the age of economists. According to Samuelson (1946), contained in Lekachman (1964), there existed two dividing lines of ages: the age of 35 and the one of 50:

> The General Theory caught most economists under the age of thirty-five with the unexpected virulence of a disease first attacking and decimating an isolated tribe of the sea islanders Economists beyond fifty turned out to be quite immune to the ailment. With time, most economists in-between began to run the fever, often without knowing or admitting their condition. (Samuelson 1946, p. 315)

In 1936, Keynes himself was 53 years old because he was born in 1883. Remarkably, both Joseph Schumpeter and Yasuma Takata were born in the same year as Keynes. If we followed the Samuelson doctrine aforementioned, both of them should have been quite immune to the "Keynesian ailment." It was well-known that Schumpeter had thought Keynes as one of his greatest rivals from his youthful days. Although Takata distinguished himself as a great social scientist in Japan and the East, it was quite unfortunate that he was kept rather unknown in the West until Michio Morishima, once Takata's disciple, helped to publish some English translations of Takata's great books on sociology and economics. In his important yet non-translated book, Takata (1950) once remarked:

> [T]his book aimed to state my own theory of power economics for which, as a critic of the Keynes doctrine, I [Takata] have continuously put all my energy for those thirty years. . . .. . . Although Keynes and I were born in the same year and have done research in the same field, namely social sciences, the opinions of the two persons should not be the same. How and to what extent my theory is different from his must be a very interesting question to ask. Which will be the correct theory of economics, Keynes or Takata? Let the future history decide it! This is my true motive of writing this book. (Takata 1950, Preface, p. 1)

Martin Bronfenbrenner, who was once my teacher at Kobe University, had great respect for Takata and even called him "Marshall of Japan." As the reader will see, it is one of my intentions of writing this book to reexamine the question how and to what extent Keynes and Takata differ from each other with respect to the problem of unemployment, one of the key issues in modern times.

Another related topic would be the relationship between Keynes and Knight. Frank H. Knight was born just 2 years later than Keynes and made an outstanding contribution to the same field as Keynes, that is, the economics of risk and uncertainty. When The General Theory of Employment, Interest and Money was published in 1936, Knight was 51 years old, thus a bit over 50. In spite of, or perhaps because of, almost the same age and almost the same research area, there appeared a clear divergence of their views on the unemployment problem. Why and how their opinions became different will be another topic to be explored in this

[1]For details, see Lekachman (1964).

paper. In this regard, it is worthy to note that Knight (1937) carefully read The General Theory of Employment, Interest and Money just after its publication, leaving the following criticism of Keynes:

> I [Knight] must confess that the labor I have spent on *The General Theory of Employment, Interest, and Money* leaves me with a feeling of keen disappointment. (Knight 1937, p. 167; Emmett (ed.), 1999, p. 366)

Knight's word "keen disappointment" was a very strong expression to demonstrate his spiteful criticism after reading the book. The degree to which Knight was disappointed was also well-described by P. A. Samuelson, who went to Chicago at 16 in 1931 and received his B.A. before going to Harvard for his Ph.D. In the New Yorker, Columnist John Cassidy (2009) wrote a very instructive interview article with Samuelson, which was later reproduced by Tyler Durden (2012) in Zero Hedge with a more attractive title. According to the article, "Knight really thought Keynes was the devil," Samuelson recalled. "Knight didn't believe in God, but he knew a devil when he saw one." He insisted that the old economic system—the neoclassical one—worked pretty well, except in the Great Depression." It seems that Keynes and Knight are like oil and water: Keynes likes macro, but Knight likes micro. On the surface, they are both fond of risk and uncertainty. At the bottom of their thoughts, however, they look fundamentally incompatible.

In contrast to Knight as a difficult person to please, Takata (1950, 1995) has never revealed such bad feeling but rather broadmindedly praised Keynes in the following fashion.

> Keynes is no doubt a big star of economics in the first half of the 20th century. His shining place in the academia will never be shaken no matter who will appear in the latter half. . . . . . Why has his fame spread out in the 20th century? It is because his achievements has been so revolutionary, and even destructively effective. (Takata (1950, 1995), p. 1)

How and to what extent great economists such as Keynes, Knight, Hicks, Samuelson, Takata, and Morishima have been intermingled with each other would surely be a very challenging question to ask. Presumably, this paper would represent a small yet important attempt for seeking the correct answer.

The contents of this paper is as follows. In Sect. 5.2, we will carefully reexamine the concept of involuntary unemployment that was first employed by Keynes in the 1930s and later have given rise to a heated controversy. We will especially pick up the two great economists, Takata and Knight, and aim to discuss how and to what extent they differ from Keynes in modern perspective. In Sect. 5.3, the concept of "nonvoluntary employment" rather than the one of voluntary unemployment will be introduced in line with the original work of Nobuaki Takahashi, a rising Japanese economist. The former concept is very important in modern Japan since the existence of non-regular workers who are forced to work for bare survival against their wills is becoming more conspicuous every year. Concluding remarks will be made in the Sect. 5.4.

5.2 Involuntary Unemployment a la Keynes

5.2.1 A Very Terribly Written Book of Macroeconomics

According to J. M. Keynes, the fundamental facts of the capitalist economy lies in massive unemployment and the inequality of income and wealth. In fact, Keynes (1936) lamented with a strong expression:

> The outstanding faults of the economic society in which we live are its failure to provide for full employment and its arbitrary and inequitable distribution of wealth and incomes. (Keynes 1936, p. 372)

When Keynes was writing The General Theory of Employment, Interest and Money, he was constantly annoyed by his long struggle of escape habitual modes of thought and expressions. The difficulties lay in finding the best way to get rid of the old ideas which ramified into every corner of our minds. Surely, as the saying goes, old customs die hard. The cost of replacing the old ideas by the new ones would sometimes make the burden too heavy for Keynes. As a result, his final work, namely, The General Theory of Employment, Interest and Money, became one of the most difficult books in the history of economic thought. In this connection, it is quite interesting to record what Richard Kahn once told Hirofumi Uzawa after reading it:

> Mr. Uzawa, this may sound strange to you. I honestly tell you, however, that only in the last year (namely, 1978), I finally read the General Theory to the very last page. Then I found it a very terribly written book. I could not understand at all what it really intended to inform the reader about. (Uzawa 1984, p.15)

Keynes was well-known as the master of English writing before The General Theory of Employment, Interest and Money. Such a fame, however, was completely reduced to ashes after its publication. Although the difficulty of the book has not changed a bit from the past, it is worthwhile that the men living in the twenty-first century have to make every possible effort to understand it. When I myself attempted to read it though after long absence, I found some key lessons to reach on the top of "Mt. General Theory." First of all, we have to reconfirm the lesson that macro is macro and should not be regarded as the simple sum of micros: any attempt to seek the micro foundations of macro must be an exercise in futility. Second, we have to come back to the original text in a humble manner, thus ignoring the unnecessary "noises" or complexities of later developments. Then we will immediately find that, in the world of Keynes, unemployment is a macroeconomic concept rather than a microeconomic one; it is the outcome of aggregate decisions in a collective sense, not the simple sum of outcomes of individual decisions.

In this connection, it is recalled that John Kenneth Galbraith (1987) once remarked:

> Keynes was a lucid and resourceful master of English prose, as were Smith, Bentham, Malthus, the two Mills, Marshall and Veblen. ...... The General Theory of Employment, Interest and Money, however, is a complex, ill-organized and sometimes obscure work, as Keynes himself recognized, noting that the general public, 'though welcome at the debate, are only eavesdroppers' at this necessarily technical effort to persuade his fellow economists. Very few people outside the field of professional economics have ever accepted Keynes's invitation to listen. (Galbraith 1987, p. 232)

I would like to add that Galbraith himself was a lucid and resourceful master of English prose. Interestingly enough, such an eloquent writer acknowledged that The General Theory of Employment, Interest and Money was "a complex, ill-organized, and sometimes obscure book." He was very fair to say, however, that the central ideas were not so troublesome but even very lucid and unequivocal. As he clearly noticed, Keynes's main interest was centered around the question of how the level of output and employment was determined. In order to conquer an academically high mountain named The General Theory of Employment, Interest and Money, we have to make every possible effort to find a very effective route leading us to the peak. As the saying goes, where there is a will, there is a way.

5.2.2 The Original Framework: The Aggregate Supply and the Aggregate Demand

First of all, we should remember that Keynes (1936) was a specialist book that was chiefly addressed to his fellow economists, thereby being hardly intelligible to the general public. Second, Chapter 1 per se was named a very challenging name "The General Theory of Employment, Interest and Money," meaning that the existing neoclassical theories including Pigou (1933) were regarded by Keynes as merely special theories.

After critically discussing the postulates of the neoclassical economics in Chapter 2, Keynes boldly attempted to introduce his own ideas and concepts in Chapter 3, in which he gave a brief summary of his unique theory of employment and unemployment. In our opinion, the following sentence is of the utmost importance for us to comprehend the essence of Keynes's theory.

> [T]he volume of employment in equilibrium depends on (i) the aggregate supply function,φ, (ii) the propensity to consume,χ, and (iii) the volume of investment, D_2 , This is the essence of the General Theory of Employment. (Keynes 1936, p. 29)

Then the following question would come to our mind right away. What is the aggregate function all about? Very strange enough, the properties of the aggregate supply function had not been thoroughly investigated until Nobuo Okishio (1956) wrote a technical yet excellent paper in an obscure Japanese journal but then, unfortunately, doomed to leave out of memory again by an explosion of works on the more fashionable topic of IS and LM functions. In this paper, we attempt to let the old story of aggregate supply-aggregate demand come to life again, thus reexamining the problem of employment and unemployment from a new angle. We can learn new lessons from old teachings![2]

Following the original work of Keynes (1936), let Z be the aggregate supply price of the output from employing N men. We may call the relationship between Z and N,

[2]Nobuo Okishio was one of my respected teachers at Kobe University. It was quite unfortunate that almost all of his works were written in Japanese.

namely, $Z = \varphi(N)$, the aggregate supply function. Let D be the proceeds that entrepreneurs expect to receive from the employment of N men. We can call the relationship between D and N, i.e., $D = f(N)$, the aggregate demand function. Then the volume of employment is provided by the point of intersection between the aggregate supply function and the aggregate demand function. The value of D at the point of $f(N)$, where it is intersected by$\varphi(N)$, is named by Keynes the effective demand. Keynes claims that this is the substance of his book *The General Theory of Employment, Interest and Money* (1936).

According to Keynes, the effective demand, namely, D, is the sum of the two quantities, D_1 and D_2. Here, D_1 represents the amount which the community is expected to spend on consumption and D_2 the amount which it is expected to devote new investment. Keynes assumes that D_1 is a function of N, which we may write $\chi(N)$, depending on the propensity to consume. In contrast to D_1, D_2 is supposed to be an independent variable since it may increase or decrease rather independently of N. Summing up, we may have the following relations:

$$Z = \phi(N) \tag{5.1}$$

$$D = f(N) = \chi(N) + D_2 \tag{5.2}$$

By carefully looking at equations (5.1) and (5.2), we may reach the following conclusion. The equilibrium volume of N at which Z and D are equal depends on the three factors: namely, φ, χ, and D_2. Needless to say, this is the very essence of Keynes's theory of employment.

Graphically speaking, the aggregate supply function $Z(N)$ and the aggregate demand function $D(N)$ are depicted in Fig. 5.1. As has been lucidly pointed out by Okishio (1956), the function $Z(N)$ must be an increasing and convex function, whereas the function $D(N)$ must be an increasing and concave function. Note that the distinction between convex and concave curves is of the most importance. The point of intersection Q^* stands for the equilibrium of the Keynes system, and N^*

Fig. 5.1 The aggregate supply and aggregate demand functions

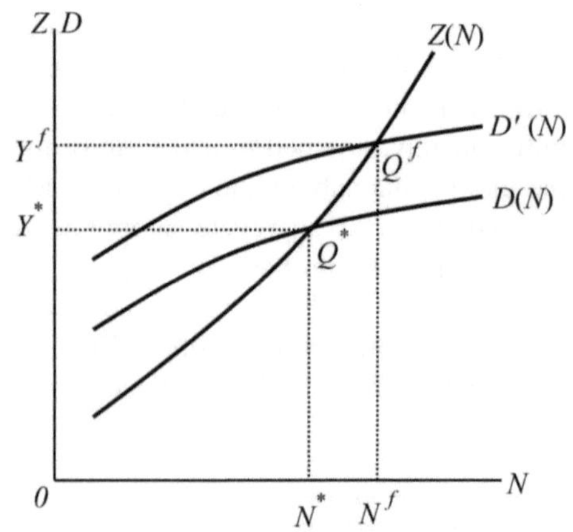

and Y^*, respectively, show the equilibrium volume of employment and the one of the aggregate output so that $Y^* = Z^* = D^*$.

Let as suppose that the point of full employment is denoted by N^f. Then we will easily see in Fig. 5.1 that the two points N^* and N^f should not be identical. Expectedly, N^* is less than N^f, meaning that we are in an underemployment equilibrium. By the same token, on the vertical axis, Y^* is less than Y^f so that the aggregate production is operating at less than full capacity. In the history of economic thought, only a limited number of economists have been brave enough to point out the non-equivalence of N^* and N^f. Karl Marx (1867), a famous or infamous socialist who has written *Das Kapital*, was a remarkable exception. It is J.M. Keynes that represented another outstanding exception among non-socialists.

More than 60 years ago, Okishio (1956) took great pains to mathematically derive the aggregate supply function from the microeconomic basis and to rigorously discuss its interesting properties. He led a rather solitary life in the Land of the Rising Sun, being isolated from the Land of the Union Jack and the Land of the Stars and Stripes; indeed, his outstanding works have been relatively unknown until Michio Morishima, his close friend, energetically introduced Okishio's accomplishments to foreign countries in a small yet influential book, *Marx's Economics*. Since Okishio's mathematical derivation of the aggregate supply function was so complicated to follow, we are content here to attempt more elementary derivation by help of a simple figure.[3]

To this end, let us denote the aggregate production function by $F(N)$. It is usually assumed to be increasing and concave, so that $F'(N) > 0$ and $F''(N) < 0$. The vertical axis measures the aggregate supply price of the output from employing N, whence $Z = p\,F(N)$. Corresponding to three possible supply prices, p^1, p^2, and p^3, we have three possible concave curves, $p^1\,F(N)$, $p^2\,F(N)$, and $p^3\,F(N)$. Since the aggregate profit can be written as $\Pi = p\,F(N) - w\,N - C^o$ where C^o denotes the fixed cost, its maximization with respect to w results in the following equation:

$$p\,F'(N) = w, \tag{5.3}$$

which would teach us that even at the aggregate level, the price of the marginal product of labor is supposed to be equal to wages. Presumably, we could interpret Eq. (5.3) as the "aggregate version" of the marginal productivity doctrine. This is just one possible interpretation, being subject to critical investigation. In the light of economic thought, there has been serious controversies regarding the existence of the aggregate production function per se. Whether and to what degree Keynes himself would agree with such an interpretation would remain a hard nut to crack.

Equation 5.3 enables us to obtain the three equilibrium points Q^1, Q^2, and Q^3 as shown in Fig. 5.2. By combining these three points and possibly many more equilibrium points, we are able to find an increasing and convex curve Z(N), which is indicated by a bold dotted curve in the figure. This Z(N) is what we have strongly wanted to derive, the aggregate supply function. People might call it

[3]For a detailed derivation, see Okishio (1956) and Niino-Okishio (1957).

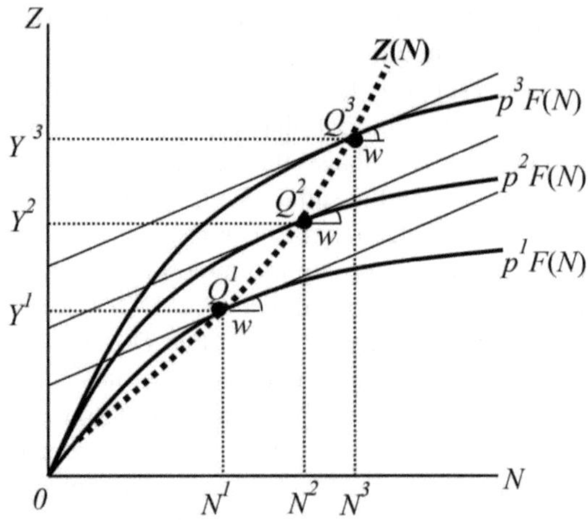

Fig. 5.2 A graphical derivation of the aggregate supply function

Keynes's favorite "macro tool" or possibly his unwanted "macro enigma," depending on the degree and direction of his taste for Keynes's theory.

By boldly introducing the new concepts of the aggregate supply and aggregate demand functions into his new book The General Theory of Employment, Interest and Money, Keynes intended to escape from the old modes of thought and expression. New wine had to be put into new bottles! One of such old modes was well represented by the neoclassical doctrine, which could be expressed in the following Say's law: "supply creates its own demand."

If we restate such a law within the new framework a la Keynes, we can say that "the aggregate demand price of output as a whole is equal to its aggregate supply price for all volumes of output" (Keynes (1936), p. 26). In short, $f(N)$ and $\varphi(N)$ are equal for all values of N, namely for all levels of output and employment; in other words, these two functions are identical, or $f(\mathrm{N}) \equiv \varphi(N)$. Consequently, in the neoclassical world, there should be no obstacle to full employment. By completely denying Say's law, Keynes thus succeeded in getting out of the old world toward the new one.

5.2.3 Involuntary Unemployment: A New Concept in the Labor Market

In writing a new book, Keynes courageously called it "*The General Theory of Employment, Interest and Money*" with a definite article "The," placing his emphasis on the word "General." He never wanted to employ a more modest name "A Theory of Employment" with an indefinite article "A." The object of such a highly motivated title was to contrast the unique character of his new theory with that of the existing neoclassical theory including Ricardo, J.S. Mill, Marshall, Pigou (1933), and possibly Knight. According to his argument, the postulates of the neoclassical theory are applicable only to the very special case of full employment, and not the general case which allows for an arbitrary number of unemployed workers.

There is fundamentally a methodological issue between Keynes and Knight. Keynes analysis started with the presence of unemployment and then discussed how to adopt new policy measures to eliminate unwanted obstacles to the return to full employment. In contrast, Knight remained to live in the old neoclassical world: he thought that the other way around should be the correct one: i.e., full employment was regarded as the most usual state of affairs. Unlike Keynes, we should not assume unemployment first, but instead start our discussion with full employment, and then explain how unfortunate situations with no jobs could occur. To sum up, the question of where we should start our discussion, either at the situation of unemployment or at the one of full employment, was the turning point in our argument. The two giants, Keynes and Knight, adopted just the opposite ways of thinking.

In what follows, let us carefully discuss how Keynes introduced his new concept of "involuntary unemployment" in the labor market. In plain English, involuntary unemployment occurs when a person is willing to work but cannot find his job: he is unwillingly out of the job market. Note that involuntary unemployment must be different from "voluntary unemployment," where workers intentionally choose not to work. The former is also distinguished from frictional unemployment, where certain degrees of mismatches between job offers and seekers take place because of geographical, seasonal, informational reasons, or whatever.

The neoclassical view of the labor market is simple and straightforward. The labor market is depicted in Fig. 5.3, where the horizontal axis measures the amount of employment, N, and the vertical axis the real wage rate, R ($= w/p$). According to Keynes, the neoclassical doctrine is based on the two fundamental postulates:

(1) The real wage rate is equal to the marginal product of labor, namely, $R = w/p = F'(N)$.
(2) The utility of the real wage when a given amount of labor is employed is equal to the marginal disutility or pain of that amount of employment.

In the light of postulate (1), it would be an easy job to find that an increasing R results in a decreasing N, so that the labor demand curve DD must be decreasing. Similarly, by virtue of postulate (2), we could show that an increasing N corresponds to an increasing R; whence the labor supply curve SS must be increasing. The intersection point Q^* of the two curves, DD and SS, shows the equilibrium of the labor market in which the labor demand and supply are just equal. The equilibrium amount of employment and the equilibrium rate of real wage are, respectively, indicated by N^* and R^*. In such a perfect world, there should emerge no unemployment at all.

The question of critical importance is whether or not the equilibrium point Q^* guarantees the ideal state of full employment in the labor market. Let us denote the equilibrium amount of full employment and its corresponding rate of real wage by N^f and R^f, respectively. Such a situation would occur in Fig. 5.3 when the labor demand curve from shift upward from DD to $D'D'$ and the new equilibrium point shift upward from Q^* to Q'. If this is the case, then we would find N^f less than N^* and Y^f less than Y^*, meaning that a undesirable situation with jobless persons would

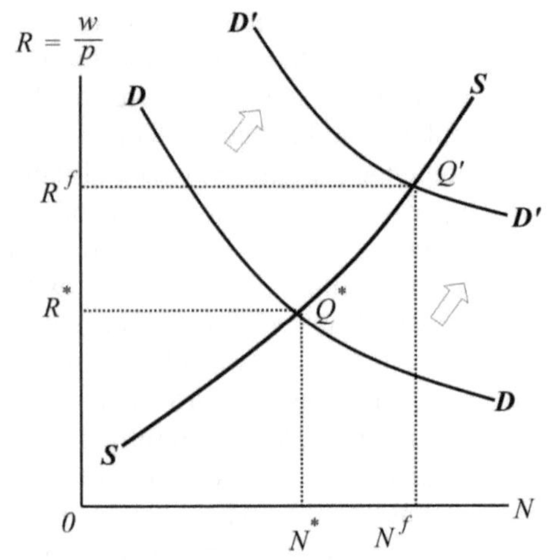

Fig. 5.3 Is involuntary unemployment a real phenomenon?

occur. Not all the persons who are willing to work cannot find their jobs. More exactly, the line segment $N^* N^f$ on the horizontal axis measures the amount of involuntary unemployment.

The important question to ask at this point is why we have entered the miserable world of involuntary unemployment. According to Keynes, the answer should be unmistakably clear: it is because of the lack of aggregate demand which in turn is caused by the insufficient amount of consumption or investment as a whole. Otherwise, the labor demand curve could be pushed up from DD to $D'D'$ and correspondingly the equilibrium point from Q^* to Q^f.

In the academic world, there are a group of liberal economists who have the strong desire to understand the meaning of involuntary unemployment and its policy implications. For example, Shapiro and Stiglitz (1985) remarked:

> To us, involuntary unemployment is a real and important phenomenon with grave consequences that needs to be explained and understood. (Shapiro and Stiglitz 1985, p. 1217)

In contrast, there exist another group of conservative economists who do not believe that involuntary unemployment in its true sense really exists, thus having serious doubts about its relevance to the core of economic theory. In this regard, Robert Lucas (1978), a famous market fundamentalist, once remarked:

> [T]here is an involuntary element in all unemployment in the sense that no one chooses bad luck over good; there is also a voluntary element in all unemployment, in the sense that, however miserable one’s current work options, one can always choose to accept them. …… the unemployed worker at any time can always find some job at once. (Lucas 1978, p. 354)

Lucas has the strong belief that unemployment must be voluntary rather than involuntary. It is true that a certain jobless worker could desperately accept any job if he neglects human right and dignity. We must remember, however, that a person should not be a “working machine”; if he wants to work at a shop or factory, then he must find a good reason for staying there as a human being.

We could also think that the labor market operates like a social institution in which both employers and employees as flesh-and-blood persons meet together and make some form of labor contracts between them. Remarkably, Yasuma Takata, a very famous Japanese social scientist, applied his unique power theory to the labor market, thus shedding new light on involuntary unemployment. This and related topics will carefully be discussed in the following subsection.

5.2.4 Takata on Keynes: Another Look at Involuntary Unemployment

Yasuma Takata (1883–1972), a contemporary of J.M. Keynes (1883–1946) and J. A. Schumpeter (1883–1950), was a person with plenty of striking characters, namely, cool head, warm heart, and strong will. In his young days, he found much interest in the problems of social reform and race discrimination, which in his later years helped to stimulate his own dualistic view and brilliantly multifaceted life. He was not only a world famous sociologist and a first-class economist but also a highly talented poet. He distinguished himself as a great educator who succeeded in establishing the world -famous Socioeconomic Institute at Osaka University, which collected a group of young and ambitious scholars including the young Morishima and the young Nikaido.[4]

In contrast to the neoclassical tradition, Takata thought that Robinson Crusoe, who survived a shipwreck and spent a rational and economical life for years on an isolated island, was no more than the imaginary creation of Daniel Defoe (1719), thereby having no qualification at all for a typical person to be modeled in economics.

According to Takata, a person engaged in trading does not only seek for more utility, but also he or she possesses a strong desire for more power. Such desire for seeking power is most clearly present in the labor market. Because the labor market is of human and social character, the concepts of justice and moral must also be involved. The real wage rate for different works are not so freely determined by supply-demand interactions as are traditionally supposed by neoclassical economists, but the absolute money wage per se should demonstrate the worker's true desire for maintaining or raising pride or prestige.

It is in this sense that Takata believed that Keynes's new approach to the working of the labor market became somehow close to Takata's one. We will show their analytic similarity by help of a new figure, namely, Fig. 5.4. Note that the real wage rate is the ratio of money wage rate to the price level; i.e., $R = w/p$. This figure distinguishes itself from the last figure in the sense that the vertical axis does not measure R any more but rather w. As both Takata and Keynes strongly believed, the

[4]See Takata (1950, 1995) and Morishima (1994, 1998). Also see Klein (1950), Pierce (2008) and Sawyer and Spencer (2006).

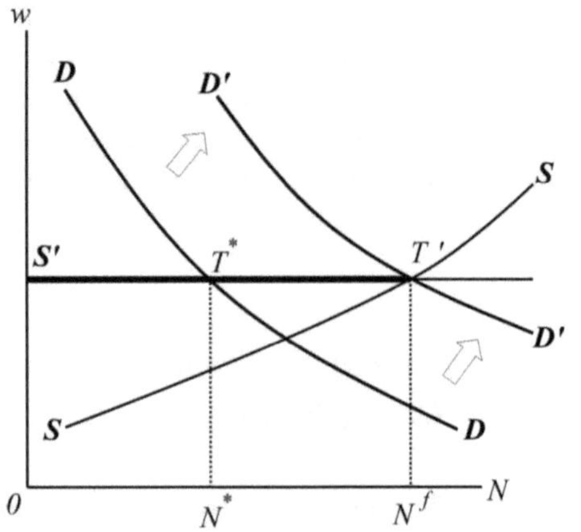

Fig. 5.4 Strong resistance to cut in money wages: Takata's interpretation of involuntary unemployment

difference between *R* and *w* is of critical importance with relation to the origin and persistence of involuntary unemployment. To take an example, a person may demonstrate strong resistance against a 5% cut in his or her money wage, even though his or her degree of resistance might be rather weak when the price level increases by 5%. Mathematically speaking, these two effects should be the same in terms of real wage rate. In reality, however, the person in question is most likely to prefer the price rise to the money wage fall. This is certainly because the level of money wage per se may indicate the degree of his status in the society; indeed, a cut in w, not a rise in p, would represent a downfall in his pride or prestige. In this connection, Keynes (1936) once remarked:

> In fact, a movement by employers to revise money-wage bargains downward will be much more strongly resisted than a gradual and automatic lowering of real wages as a result of rising price. (Keynes 1936, p. 264)

Keynes already recognized strong resistance by workers against a money wage cut in a modern democratic society. It is in this sense that Keynes became very close to Takata, who as a strong promoter of sociological power theory was brave enough to go even beyond Keynes.

Let us look back at Fig. 5.4. Then we see that the vertical axis measures the money wages, *w*, not the real wages, $R = w/p$. In our opinion, such an assumption looks very congruent with the Keynesian spirits. The upward-sloped curve *SS* associates employment, *N*, with money wage, *w*. This is not the aggregate supply curve we want to discuss here, however. We are instead eager to pay special attention to the kinked curve S' T^* T' S which consists of the two parts: the horizontal part S' T^* T' and the increasing and concave part T' S. The first horizontal (bold-faced) part represents the absolute level of money wage to be desired by the workers; indeed, as was wisely asserted by Keynes himself, any movement by the employers to revise the level downward would strongly be resisted by the workers.

Let the aggregate demand curve be denoted by *DD*. Then surely, its intersection T^* with the kinked curve S' T^* T' S would stand for the equilibrium under question.

Note that N^* indicates the amount of underemployment. Note that N^* must be less than N^f, the amount of full employment, which is attainable only if the aggregate demand moves upward from DD to $D'D'$.

In the above we have shown that when the aggregate demand is deficient, there is underemployment of labor: there are workers unemployed who would be willing to work at the existing level of money wage. As the aggregate demand rises, however, aggregate employment increases correspondingly. The above is by and large the essence of Keynes-Takata theory of employment and unemployment. Power really matters!

It is remarkable to see that in their later years, both J.R. Hicks (1989) and Robert M. Solow (1990) came close to Takata. As Morishima (1994) remarked, Takata's power theory is still alive today. We can learn new lessons from old teachings!

5.3 "Involuntary Employment": Another New Concept Beyond Keynes

5.3.1 Depression Economics: Old and New

Most people in the world, especially in the USA, remember the 1930s as the most terrified and most tragic years in the twentieth century. In 1935, just 1 year before the publication of The General Theory of Employment, Interest and Money, J.M. Keynes (1936) recognized the serious failure of the capitalist system as a whole. This is now what we could call "Old Depression Economics."

Around 20% of the American labor force was unemployed, and real gross national product still remained under the level of 1929. As Galbraith (1987) correctly recalled, to none of those horrible events could the neoclassical economics correctly respond. In spite of the fact that so many people in the street could not find jobs, they were by and large regarded as being voluntary unemployed. The depression economics of Keynes seemed to offer us the only one solution which could solve the serious problem of mass unemployment in the capitalist society.

And so many years have past since then. And so many events have happened between the 1930s and the 1990s—the Second World War, the Cold War, the Fall of the Berlin Wall, the Collapse of the Soviet Union, the Iraq War, and the like. It seemed that the capitalist economy was the final and indisputable winner of the Cold War. As a result, on appearance, so many people have enjoyed high economic growth and great prosperity, almost forgetting the curse of the old depression economics a la Keynes.

As the saying goes, however, history repeats itself. The "Economic Tower of Babel" is destined to collapse. Already in the late 1990s, a respectable group of Asian economies including Japan, India, and China experienced an economic slump which bore a striking resemblance to the Great Depression. In his new edition, Paul

Krugman (2008), a winner of the Nobel prize in economics and one of the most influential economists today, published a very interesting book entitled *The Return of Depression Economics and the Crisis of 2008*. Indeed, he remarked:

> [A]s this new edition goes to press, much of the world, very much including the United States, is grapping with a financial and economic crisis that bears even more resemblance to the Great Depression then the Asian troubles of the 1990s. (Krugman 2008, p. 4)

This is what we would like to call "New Depression Economics." As Krugman and other prominent economists have noticed, "Depression Economics" has never been dead and now is safely and triumphantly returned to the academic profession. In his new book, Robert Skidelsky (2009), Keynes's well-known biographer, has declared that after so many years, Keynes is still alive and fundamentally all right. It seems that we live in the Second Age of Keynes, which is similar to, yet must be different from, the First Age of Keynes. A simple reproduction of the Old Keynes would not work well. We need the New Keynes who goes beyond the Old Keynes, presumably giving us new useful sets of guides for solving much more complicated problems of unemployment and economic inequality than ever before.

5.3.2 Unhappy Workers Dispatched by Outside Agencies

I have a habit of getting up rather early, exactly at 6:30, every morning and enjoying reading several daily newspapers from the top page through the last one. One cold winter morning, I had a serious shock by reading the following complaint against social injustice by Mr. Taro Tanaka, who was one of the now popular non-regular workers in contemporary Japan:

> I am a non-regular employees who unwillingly have to work under only five year agency contracts. I would like to let you know that my yearly income is merely two million yen, around half of the pay of a regular worker. Because of such a low income, I remain unmarried, having no choice other than living with my old parents. I wonder whether and how I am able to get out of such a hopeless situation. I want to die without losing my human dignity.[5]

We could call Mr. Tanaka one of the modern working poor or even one of the modern "wage slaves." Keynes has paid special attention to those people who are willing to work at the existing pay but cannot find their jobs. Clearly, Mr. Tanaka is not such an involuntarily unemployed person. Judging by appearance, he has a job but is unwillingly working under unfair working conditions such as extremely low pay, no guarantee for promotion, and no permanent contract. In substance, he might be called an "involuntarily employed person" or a sort of "wage slave" in a modern society.

[5]Mr. Tanaka's complaint or similar accusations can be heard everywhere and every day in Japanese newspapers today. Japan is no longer an ideal class-less society!

As discussed above, Keynes (1936) has shown that when the aggregate demand is deficient, there emerges underemployment of labor in the sense that there are men unemployed who would be wiling to work at less than the existing real wage. As a result, as the aggregate demand increases by means of a rise in investment or consumption, employment as a whole is expected to increase. This is certainly the problem of involuntary employment which was energetically discussed by Keynes in the 1930s.

Eighty years have passed since then. We are now in the 2010s. Presumably, the depression economics a la Keynes has returned to a certain degree. We would like to say, however, that that was the past; things seem to be a bit different today. Looking at the Japanese data today, there are so many men including Mr. Tanaka aforementioned, whose jobs are neither regular nor wanted. There should be a clear-cut distinction between the regular and non-regular workers, which has been rather ignored even by Keynes himself. Non-regular workers are those who are dispatched by an outside agency in order to work less than full time for a limited duration (at most for 5 years). In contrast, regular workers are those who work full time under permanent contracts with their companies. Although regular workers enjoy benefits such as bonuses, housing, training, and lifetime employment, non-regular members might get as little as half of the pay for the same work, with no bonuses and no fringe benefits.

We have been informed that in the past 20 years or so, the number of non-regular workers has grown to one-third of all workers (young and old, male and female included) and even to 40% of all young workers. Seeing is believing! So let us take a look at the recent data that shows the significant pay gaps between regular and non-regular workers in Japan today. In Fig. 5.5, the horizontal axis measures the age of each person (from 25 years old to 50 years old) and the vertical axis the monthly pay of that person (on the basis of thousand yen). Note that this is not the original figure per se but an intentionally simplified version for the purpose of easily grasping the whole picture.[6]

By looking at the figure, we can learn several lessons. First of all, the pay gaps between regular and non-regular workers are significant and persistent for all the age groups. Second, those gaps are rather small at the young age of 25 years old, but tend to gradually widen as the age of a worker advances. Third, the gaps are the greatest at the age of 50 years (in fact, regular workers can earn twice as big as non-regular workers) , and stays the same until the retirement age of 60 years old. It seems that Japan is now a sort of "class society" in which the regular worker class and the non-regular one are firmly divided. Once a man gets a small job with a temporary labor contract, he will almost probably be trapped in a series of unhappy jobs until his retirement. Although there is a strong will, there is perhaps no way out! Around 30 years ago, Japan was highly praised as the "All the Middle Class Society for One Hundred Million People" all over the world. This is no longer correct any more. As the saying goes, nothing is certain in this world.

[6]For rigorous empirical approaches to the 2014 employment structure and the 2016 wages structure in the Japanese society, see Japan Ministry of Welfare and Labor (2015, 2016).

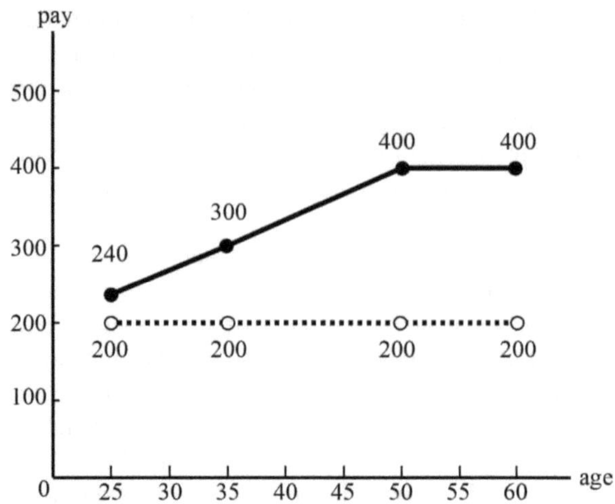

Fig. 5.5 The pay gaps between regular and non-regular workers: Japan pay statistics 2016 on monthly basis (thousand yen)

5.3.3 N. Takahashi's New Approach to "Involuntary Employment": Looking Beyond Keynes

More than 80 years ago (exactly in 1936), J.M. Keynes published the *General Theory of Employment, Interest and Money*. This was no doubt the greatest book of economics ever written in the twentieth century. As the saying goes, time and tide wait for no man!

We now live in the twenty-first century that appears to be the Uncertain Age in which everything in the future is uncertain and unpredictable. Although so many things have happened between the 1930s and the 2010, it seems that the depression economics a la Keynes has returned. As they say that the "007" in the movie is alive twice, Keynes is destined to be alive more than twice.

If we look at the Japanese labor data today, we are surprised to see that there are so many men and women whose jobs are neither regular nor wanted. The Japanese society that was once proud of its economic superpower with no definite classes is now entering into a new sort of "class society." In fact, it is divided into two classes—the upper class of regular workers and the lower class of non-regular workers. This seems to be the new phenomenon even Keynes has ever imagined. Regular workers are those who work full time under permanent contract with their companies. They can enjoy a variety of fringe benefits such as summer and winter bonuses, housing subsidies, and sport facilities. In contrast to this, non-regular workers work on part-time basis (at most 5 years and without fringe benefits) under temporary agency contracts. Presumably, their pays are as little as half as those of regular workers.

It is under such circumstances that Nobuhiko Takahashi, one of rising liberal economists in contemporary Japan, boldly introduced the new concept "involuntary employment" into economic theory. In his small yet ambitious

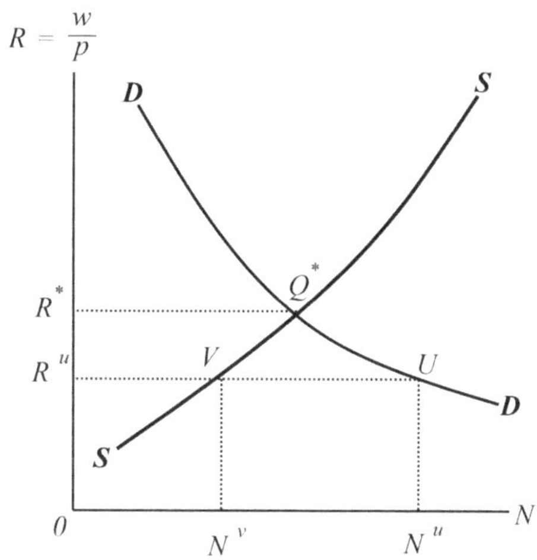

Fig. 5.6 Takahashi on "involuntary employment": Is there no resistance to pay cut?

book, Takahashi (2012) has wanted to show that the severe crisis of the Japanese economy today resides neither in deflation nor in accumulated financial deficit but rather in involuntary employment. Here, the word "involuntary employment," which has newly been invented by him, is supposed to mean the severe state of employment in which, as typically exemplified by the working poor and the men who work overtime till late, the employees are forced to work against their wills: indeed, their working pains presumably far exceed their earned wages. In what follows, let us attempt to explain his ideas of involuntary employment by help of a figure.

In Fig. 5.6, it is noted that the vertical axis measures real wages, $R = w/p$, rather than money wages, w. The equilibrium in labor market is indicated by the intersection point Q^* , of the two curves, namely, the upward-sloped labor supply curve SS and the downward-sloped labor demand curve DD. Needless to say, the equilibrium amount of wages is indicated by R^*. This R^* is supposed to show the wages for fortunate regular workers, not the one for unfortunate non-regular workers.

As mentioned above, we now live in a sort of "class society." Like airplane passengers, there are two distinct classes within the workers—the "first-class workers" and the "second-class workers," with no intermediate "business-class workers" being present. The second-class workers or non-regular workers are not hired by the firm they are actually working at but merely dispatched to the job from an outside human-allocation agency. From the very nature of things, the power of humble non-regular employees are much weaker than the one of upper-seated employers. Consequently, as is seen in Fig. 5.6, there emerges a double wages structure, the upper level R^* and the lower level R^u. While the regular members earn their wages as much as R^*, the non-regular members are forced to accept the minimal wages R^u. There the difference between the points U and V or equivalently the one between N^u and N^v is supposed to measure the amount of "involuntary employment" or more plainly "unwanted employment."

If the labor market under question is depicted in Fig. 5.6, we have to face a sort of "labor discrimination." At this point, the question which might naturally arise in our head is why and how long such a discrimination can continue. This would really be a rather easy question but very hard to answer!

In our opinion, there are by and large two different points of views conceivable—economical and sociological. According to the first economical point of view, the efficiency or productivity differs from person to person: the regular workers work more efficiently than the non-regular workers; hence the former is entitled to earn definitely more than the latter. In reality, this is sometimes only partly true, and not true at all in most of the cases. To take an example from university instructors, the teaching and research capability differences between permanent members and nonpermanent members are by and large minimal; whence there would be no justification whatever for overly preferential treatment for regular members with tenures. It would almost always be the case that non-regular members such as temporary or part-time instructors without tenures are simply underpaid; they earn much less pay than they really deserve.

Those economic considerations point out to seek sociological point of view. In particular, Takata's power theory may work again here! The place of regular workers in a modern society has been historically high, and their powers are guaranteed by strong labor unions. In contrast, non-regular workers are not well-organized and less respected by other members of the society; consequently, they could little resistance against pay cut. Notwithstanding those power theoretic interpretations, we need to do much further inquiry. As the saying goes, steady dripping may wear away stone!

5.4 The Impact of Piketty's New Book: Concluding Remarks

Quite recently, Thomas Piketty (2013), a rising French economist, published a very exciting book entitled *Le capital au XXIe siècle*. Its English translation *Capital in the Twenty-First Century* published a year later immediately became a best seller all over the world. This title per se seems to remind us of the return of Karl Marx (1867), who published a very sensational book entitled Das Kapital more than 140 years ago.

Upon the publication of Piketty's new book, Paul Krugman quickly wrote the book review in the New York Times:

> It seems safe to say that Capital in the Twenty-First Century, the magnum opus of the French economist Thomas Piketty, will be the most important economic book of the year—and maybe of the decade. Piketty, arguably the world's leading expert on income and wealth inequality, does more than document the growing concentration of income in the hands of a small economic elite. (Krugman 2014)

Piketty's new book is a timely and well-written book. By and large, it has been so well received by the general public as well as the economics profession. Why has it been so popular all over the world? In our opinion, the key to answering this question resides in the old and new remark by Keynes (1936): the outstanding faults of the economic society in which we live are its failure to provide for full employment and its arbitrary and inequitable distribution of wealth and incomes.

According to Keynes, there are two critical problems we have to solve in the capitalist economy, i.e., unemployment and income inequality. We think that the first problem has been thoroughly investigated by Keynes himself. The key concept he has employed is the one of "involuntary unemployment": there are so many persons in the street, who are willing to work at the existing wages but cannot find jobs because of a shortage of the effective demand as a whole. It would be safe to say, however, that Keynes's attempt to solve the second problem has not been so successful. Only in the recent times, Piketty, acting as the modern Keynes, has bravely tackled the leftover problem of inequality of income and wealth with a smashing success.

If we carefully look at the Japanese economy today, we have to point out that a new and old phenomenon "involuntary employment" has been emerged, and its importance is getting greater and greater every year. There are simply so many people in the street who have to work unwillingly at the minimal level of wages. The gaps between regular and non-regular workers are so wide and persistent that the people fell as if they lived in a sort of class society. Although Takahashi's analysis of involuntarily employed workers seems to be less than perfect, we would think that it is in the right direction, requiring further investigation in the future.

In their challenging book, Lindbeck and Snower (1988) have developed the new insider-outsider theory of employment and unemployment. Whereas the "insiders" are the incumbent employees whose jobs are protected by labor turnover costs, the "outsiders" are those who are not employed and have no solid protection at all. In our opinion, although the Lindbeck-Snower theory looks attractive, it cannot give an effective tool to analyze the miserable states of the non-regular workers. It is noted that both regular and non-regular workers may be regarded as insiders; they rather belong to distinct classes of insiders—"upper-class insiders" and "lower-class insiders." Besides, unfortunately, the barriers between those two classes are great and almost insurmountable.

Now, we live in the New Age of Uncertainty. We believe that there remain so many important problems unsolved. And time seems to fly so fast. We need another Keynes and also another Piketty.

References

Cassidy J (2009) Postscript: Paul Samuelson. The New Yorker, December 14

Durden T (2012) On Samuelson: 'Frank Knight was the devil' and other insights. Zero Hedge, December 16

Emmett RB (ed) (1999) Selected essays by Frank H. Knight, volume one, 'what is truth' in economics? University of Chicago Press, Chicago

Galbraith JK (1987) A history of economics: the past as the present. Hamish Hamilton, London

Hicks JR (1989) A market theory of money. Oxford University Press, Oxford

Japan Ministry of Welfare and Labor (2015) The 2014 employment structure: statistical research (in Japanese). Japan Government Printing Bureau, Tokyo

Japan Ministry of Welfare and Labor (2016) The 2016 wages structure: statistical research (in Japanese). Japan Government Printing Bureau, Tokyo

Keynes JM (1936) The general theory of employment, interest and money. Macmillan, London

Klein LR (1950) The Keynesian revolution. Macmillan, London

Knight FR (1937) Unemployment and Mr. Keynes' revolution in economic theory. Canadian Journal of Economics and Political Science. Canadian Economic Society. Also contained in Emmett, RB (ed) (1999), pp 345–371

Krugman P (2008) The return of depression economics and the crisis of 2008. Penguin Books, Ltd, London

Krugman P (2014) The Piketty Panic. The New York Times, Opinion, April 24, 2014

Lekachman R (ed) (1964) Keynes' general theory: reports of three decades. St. Martin's Press, New York

Lindbeck A, Snower D (1988) Insider-outsider theory of employment and unemployment. MIT press, Boston

Lucas RE (1978) Unemployment policy. Am Econ Rev 68(2):353–357

Marx, K. (1867) Das Kapital, volume I. Later published by Marx-Engels-Lenin Institut, 1932

Morishima M (1994) Modern economics as economic thought (in Japanese). Iwanami Publishing Company, Tokyo

Morishima M (ed) (1998) Joseph A. Schumpeter and Yasuma Takata: power or pure economics? Macmillan, London

Niino K, Okishio N (1957) The economics of Keynes (in Japanese). Sanichi Publishing Company, Kyoto

Okishio N (1956) On the aggregate supply function (in Japanese). Kobe Univ Res Annu 2:1–25

Pierce A (2008) The queen asks why no one saw the credit crunch coming. The Telegraph, 5 November

Pigou AC (1933) Theory of unemployment. Macmillan, London

Piketty T (2013) Le capital au XXI siècle. Editions du Seuil, Paris. English Translation by Goldhammer A (2014) Capital in the twenty-first century. Harvard University Press

Sakai Y (2018a) Involuntary unemployment versus "involuntary employment", CRR Discussion Paper A-20. Shiga University, Japan

Sakai Y (2018b) Involuntary unemployment versus "involuntary employment": J.M. Keynes and beyond. The Hikone Ronso 417:48–64

Samuelson PA (1946) The general theory. Econometrica, 14. Also contained in Lekachman R (ed) (1964) pp 315–331

Sawyer M, Spencer D (2006) On the definition on involuntary unemployment. Harvard University Discussion Paper

Shapiro C, Stiglitz JE (1985) Can unemployment be involuntary?: reply. Am Econ Rev 75 (5):1215–1217

Skidelsky R (2009) Keynes: the return of the master. Public Affairs, New York

Solow RM (1990) The labor market as a social institution. Basic Blackwell, Cambridge, MA

Takahashi N (2012) Old teachings of Keynes: their implications on shaky Japan today (in Japanese). NHK Publications, Tokyo

Takata T (1950) Critical essays on Keynes: from the viewpoint of power theory (in Japanese). Yuhikaku Publishing Company, Kyoto

Takata Y (1995) Power theory of economics. Macmillan, London

Uzawa H (1984) A reexamination of Keynes' *General Theory* (in Japanese). Iwanami Publishers, Tokyo

Chapter 6
Frank H. Knight on Uncertainty and Profit: Manager Versus Entrepreneur

Abstract This chapter aims to carefully discuss how Frank H. Knight, the "Grand Old Man" of Chicago, dealt with uncertainty and profit, with special reference to manager versus entrepreneur. Frankly speaking, Knight was a sort of man in paradox, having a dualistic view and adopting an eclectic approach. In order to shed a new light on his life and work, we first argue that there possibly exist some traces of the great Knight in the words and deeds of Martin Bronfenbrenner, once one of Knight's students at Chicago. Then we focus on the distinction between risk and uncertainty. According to Knight, non-measurable uncertainty must radically be different from measurable risk: only uncertainty, but not risk, enables the entrepreneur to acquire true profit as its reward. In contrast to the manager who are doing just routine jobs every day, the entrepreneur dares to engage in new venturous activities, thus playing the central figure of the capitalist system. We live in the new age of uncertainty. The second Knight is urgently needed.

Keywords Frank H. Knight · Martin Bronfenbrenner · Risk · Uncertainty · Entrepreneur · Profit · Capitalist system

6.1 M. Bronfenbrenner as "Prof. Sharp Tongue": Some Traces of F.H. Knight

Speaking of myself, I have known Prof. Martin Bronfenbrenner (1914–1997) for more than 50 years, first as a student, later as a colleague, and always as an intimate friend. Whenever I met with him on university campuses, on city streets, or in private houses, he was fond of teaching me and even himself and of course always criticizing the academic and world affairs. Long time ago, when I was a graduate student at Kobe University, Japan, my fellow classmates were fond of calling him "Prof. Sharp Tongue" because he was so famous of being an eloquent speaker with sharp tongue. Listening to his ironic expressions and even cynical remarks, I myself

This chapter is largely based on Sakai (2019).

Y. Sakai, *J.M. Keynes Versus F.H. Knight*, Evolutionary Economics and Social Complexity Science 18, https://doi.org/10.1007/978-981-13-8000-6_6

wondered if I could probably see some traces of his own teachers at Chicago. Needless to say, Frank H. Knight was among those great teachers.

Any kind of tradition, whether it is good or bad, is likely to be handed down from generation to generation. Although I myself have never had an opportunity to personally speak to Knight, I would like to say that I possibly observed some traces of his unique way of thinking in the words and deeds of Bronfenbrenner, one of his bright students at Chicago. So when I happened to check the term "Frank H. Knight, 1885–1971" at Google, Wikipedia, it was really a happy surprise to find the following interesting sentence[1]:

> Knight failed to acquire any followers and failed to build up a distinct "school of thought" around himself. We can see *some* traces of his perspective in the work of Kenneth E. Boulding, Martin Bronfenbrenner, James Buchanan and George J. Stigler, but they can hardly be called "Knightian" in any meaningful sense.

It should be noticed that the delicate expression "*some* traces of Knight's perspective" with the word "*some* "emphasized in italics is carefully employed here. Presumably, it would be almost "a mission impossible" to find *all* the traces of his perspective in the work of other scholars. It is my bold mission, however, to trace *some, but not all,* traces of the perspective of Knight in the work of Bronfenbrenner.

In historical perspective, Frank H. Knight was Martin Bronfenbrenner's great teacher and Bronfenbrenner my great teacher. So it would be no wonder that the dualistic view and critical eyes in the work of Knight had more or less handed down to Bronfenbrenner and eventually even to me. I still recall that Bronfenbrenner's personal letter to the late Dr. Shigeo Minabe, my very close friend in the USA and Japan, contained the following honorable ending with his own personal signature:

> "Bronf Von Brenner," followed by the Japanese red stamp "Baka," meaning "Fool" in English. Interestingly enough, this had dispelled all my doubts on the question of why he used to say that not a few Japanese professors were not "full professors" but only "fool professors." According to his twisted usage of expressions, "a fool professor" never meant "a fool" in its literary sense but rather "a cool professor" or "a respected professor." It is because Bronfenbrenner as a gentleman with such pride was so self-effacing that he was preferred to be called himself "a fool," alias " a highly respected gentleman." In the same letter aforementioned, he kindly gave the following advice to Minabe, "You should do as I say, but not as I do." As the saying goes, saying is one thing, but doing is another![2]

---

[1]Speaking of myself, for the period 1968–1975, I was first a graduate student at the University of Rochester and later an assistant professor at the University of Pittsburgh, where I taught economic theory and mathematical economics for both undergraduate and graduate students. Since Knight passed away in 1970, I could possibly have met with him sometime in the period 1968–1970, but alas, I could not. I had instead the golden opportunities at both universities in which I talked with so many Chicago graduates including the late Sherwin Rosen and the late Walter Oi. Dr. Robert Thaler, a Nobel laureate and now a distinguished professor at Chicago, was once one of my earnest classmates at Rochester.

[2]Similar personal episodes of Bronfenbrenner were recorded by Goodwin (1998). Bronfenbrenner arrived at Chicago in 1934 and stayed there until 1938. According to Goodwin, Bronfenbrenner described Knight as a little man with a toothbrush mustache, a squeaky voice, and a quirk of wrinkling up the lower half of his face while propounding defiance of the universe. When I talked with Bronfenbrenner, I felt that he had some traces of Knight, his mentor: indeed, he had strong defiance of the universe, especially harsh criticism of academism in the USA and Japan.

I remember how Bronfenbrenner managed to take care of his class at Kobe University in 1965. The graduate course he taught us was named "Income Distribution Theory." The course was conducted in English, which was a rather extraordinary practice in Japan in the 1960s. To make his teaching more accessible to Japanese students, he used to come to the classroom 1 h earlier than the regular schedule. Taking advantage of such extra hour, he usually draw six or seven fancy-looking figures filling in a big blackboard. We graduate students were astonished by his skill of making use of so many colored chalks including red, yellow, blue, green, brown, and white. This was the reason why Bronfenbrenner acquired another honorable nickname "Professor Rainbow" from attentive Japanese students.

His income distribution lecture at Kobe turned out to be so successful that its whole contents together were put in a single academic book entitled *Income Distribution Theory* in 1971. Interestingly enough, this was the year when I myself served as an ambitious assistant professor at Pittsburgh, exactly the birthplace of Bronfenbrenner. According to Harry G. Johnson who kindly wrote *Forward* to this book, Bronfenbrenner (1971) was a very brilliant book in the sense that this was then the only book available that ranged—and ranged authoritatively—over the whole field of distribution theory. Bronfenbrenner himself, however, seemed to have his own unique opinion that clearly showed his distinguishing features. In fact, at the very opening page, he strongly declared that "this book was dedicated to [his] brilliant failures." Of course, this book was not "the product of complete failures" at all but rather more objectively "the product of *brilliant successes.*" But, alas, he was not a straightforward person in any sense but strangely a bit self-effacing person. In fact, in writing *Preface,* he appeared very modest as usual and even apologetic to the prospective reader:

> This is an old-fashioned income distribution book.... What makes the book old-fashioned is, primarily, the content of "reformation and restatement," which also makes it long. Some sections may sound like a minor Mozart essaying rock and roll. (Bronfenbrenner 1971, Preface, p. xi)

In the light of economics history, any book which is often called "a great book" must contain to a certain extent the old-fashioned part of reformation and restatement. As Johnson (1971) noted, "knowledge is painful to acquire and too easy to forget: and in a busy and bustling profession, it is too easy to be fascinated by each new wave as it rolls in and to overlook the fact that the tide is ebbing out (or flowing in as the case may be) (p. ix)." I am in general agreement with Johnson's opinion that in the distribution book written by Bronfenbrenner, there must exist some new waves that appear to be rather small but is likely to grow larger as time goes by. At this point, it is recalled that the great classic *Risk, Uncertainty, and Profit* (1921) written by Knight, one of Bronfenbrenner's teachers at Chicago, characteristically begins with the following very modest *Preface*:

> There is little that is fundamentally new in this book. It represents an attempt to state the essential principles of the conventional economic doctrine more accurately, and to show their implications more clearly, than has previously been done. That is, its object is refinement, not reconstruction. (Knight 1921, Preface, p. ix)

Frank H. Knight seemed to be a man in paradox. According to Paul A. Samuelson, "this book is certainly a classic. Time has not made it obsolete." George J. Stigler has convinced that "the volume is clearly one of the half-dozen classics in economic theory to appear in the U.S. in the first half-century." So, in the light of those fine appraisals by Samuelson and Stigler, it should be almost impossible to agree with the modest man Knight's own assessment that "there is little that is fundamentally new in this book." This sounded like "a bad joke."

We would like to point out here that Martin Bronfenbrenner was no doubt a rhetorical successor of his master, Frank H. Knight. According to my teacher's teacher Knight, his uncertainty book (1921) represented the mere restatement of the conventional economic doctrine in a more accurate and more clear fashion than ever before. Strangely echoing such modest statement, my own teacher Bronfenbrenner argued that his distribution book (1971) was nothing more than the refinement and restatement of the old-fashioned economic theory. Therefore, it would be safe to say that we clearly see some traces of the perspective of the great Knight in the words and deeds of Bronfenbrenner.[3]

So far, concerning introductory remarks, we have shed new light to the relation between Bronfenbrenner and Knight. The contents of the remainder of this chapter are as follows. Section 6.2 aims to argue that contrary to Knight's apparent modesty, there have been so many new ideas in his uncertainty book. The point of discussion is how he has succeeded in separating the two concepts, measurable risk and non-measurable uncertainty. Then Sect. 6.3 will deal with his unique idea for the role of an entrepreneur distinct from a manager. He passionately will discuss that only an entrepreneur, but not a manager, is entitled to acquire net profit as the reward for "uncertainty seeking." Section 6.4 will be kept for final remarks.

6.2 Risk, Uncertainty, and Profit: Knight's Theory of Trinity

6.2.1 How Uncertainty Is Radically Distinct from Risk

Knight's lifework *Risk, Uncertainty, and Profit* (1921) per se seemed to be a book in paradox. Although he modestly said that there was little that was fundamentally new in this book, he nevertheless did not forget to add the following prideful sentence:

[3]Bronfenbrenner(1971) used his own rhetoric to express gratitude to his wife Teruko Okuaki Bronfenbrenner for her consistent support: "every married man's wife improves his professional acumen, his scholarship, his mathematics, his statistics, his English, or at least his typing. Or it seems. Teruko Okuaki Bronfenbrenner, however, is not singularly competent in any of those respects. My main reason for thanking her is that she has been a better-than-average psychiatric nurse. Need I say more? (Preface, page xiii). Shigeo Minabe constantly served as Bronfenbrenner's research assistant at Kobe and other places, thereby being called "a real gem" by Bronfenbrenner. It is recalled that Michiko Minabe, the wife of Shige Minabe, has been an excellent professional nurse in New Zealand, the USA, and Japan. Also see Patinkin (1973).

> The particular technical contribution to the theory of free enterprise which this essay purports to make is a fuller and more careful examination of the role of the entrepreneur or enterpriser, the recognized "central figure" of the system, and of the forces which fix the remuneration of his special function. (Knight 1921, Preface, p. xi)

Knight certainly had the conviction that this book contributed a great deal to understanding the working and performance of the free enterprise system and the critical role played by the entrepreneur as an adventurer. He has repeatedly stressed that uncertainty must be taken radically distinct from the more familiar notion of risk. The essential point is that "risk" usually means a quantity susceptible of measurement, while "uncertainly" is not so. In other words, whereas risk is measurable in the sense that it can be described by a certain distribution function such as the normal distribution, Pareto distribution, and the like, uncertainty is neither measurable nor quantifiable.[4]

He wrote the following memorable remark:

> It is this "true" uncertainty, and not risk, which forms the basis of a valid theory of profit and accounts for the divergence between actual and theoretical competition. (Knight 1971, p. 20)

We are not quite sure of how and to what extent "actual competition" differs from "theoretical competition." According to my slightly bold guessing, actual competition or the competition as is seen in the real world is definitely much more aggressive and even destructive than theoretical competition or the competition imagined by the traditional theorists in their brains. In fact, Knight wisely observed the following fact:

> The writer [namely, Knight himself] is strongly of the opinion that business as a whole suffers a loss. The main facts in the psychology of the case are familiar.... The behavior of men in lotteries and gambling games is the most striking fact. Adam Smith pointed out the tendency of human nature to exaggerate the value of a small chance winning. (Knight 1921, p. 365)

From the viewpoint of "theoretical competition," it would be utterly unthinkable to find that the whole business may suffer a loss: the amount of aggregate profit would gradually decrease as competition becomes harder and harder and eventually reaches the terminal point of zero profit, namely, the theoretically ideal state of perfect competition. The critical Knight was in no mood to stop thinking at this stage. He rather proceeded to go beyond, thereby carefully observing the reality of cut-throat.

competition or the probability of the cruel form of "actual competition," in which the aggregate profit would possibly go under zero profit. As the great Adam Smith once observed, human being has a tendency to overestimate the small chance of

---

[4]Frank H. Knight's main work *Risk, Uncertainty, and Profit* (1921) was a "Jugendarbeit" or a "masterpiece" in the old sense, by which an apprentice qualified for admission to the gild in old days. This first edition was reissued in 1933 during the Great Depression, reprinted in 1948 after the Second World War and reprinted again in 1957 after the Korean War. Thus Knight's masterpiece seems to be immortal and will survive well in the twenty-first century.

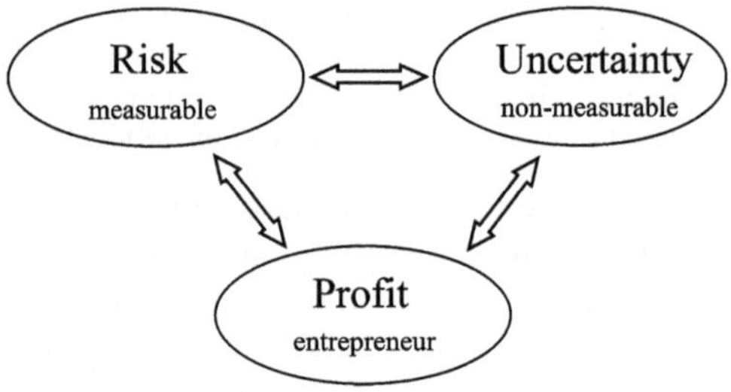

Fig. 6.1 Risk, uncertainty, and profit: Knight's trinity

winnings, thus unintentionally resulting in a loss as a whole. As human history tells us, human being could foolishly engage in such a large scale of war that there would eventually no winners left, with the tragic result of total destruction.

Summing up, the trinity of "risk, uncertainty, and profit" constitutes the keystone of the grand system of Frank H. Knight (1921). Fig. 6.1 clearly depicts such an interesting structure.

6.2.2 *Three Types of Probability Situations*

Knight argues that it is quite convenient to separate the following three types of probability situations. They are as follows: (1) a priori probability, (2) statistical probability, and (3) estimates or judgments. Let us attempt to discuss what they are all about and how they differ in characteristics.

6.2.2.1 A Priori Probability

This is really mathematical or purely theoretical probability. The most simple example for this case is given by the probability of rolling one dice for the number six, namely, the fraction 1/6. Another good example is provided by the probability pf rolling two dices for the sum of seven. Its answer must be 6/36 or 1/6 since there are mathematically 6 possible combinations (namely, 1 + 6, 2 + 5, 3 + 4, 4 + 3, 5 + 2, 6 + 1) out of 36 conceivable combinations (namely, $6 \times 6 = 36$). The whole picture of combinations and probabilities may be depicted in Table 6.1.

We may arbitrarily increase the number of rolling dices. For instance, if we roll three dices, then we easily obtain the following sequence of fractions:

1/216, 3/216, 6/216, 10/216, 15/216, 21/216, 25/216. 27/216
27/216, 25/216, 21/216, 15/216, 10/216, 6/216, 3/216, 1/216.

Table 6.1 Rolling two dices: a statistical probability

The sum of two numbers	Possible combinations of two numbers	Number of combinations	Probability
2	1 + 1	1	1/36
3	2 + 1, 1 + 2	2	2/36
4	3 + 1, 2 + 2, 1 + 3	3	3/36
5	4 + 1, 3 + 2, 2 + 3, 1 + 4	4	4/36
6	5 + 1, 4 + 2, 3 + 3, 2 + 4, 1 + 5	5	5/36
7	6 + 1, 5 + 2, 4 + 3, 3 + 4, 2 + 5, 1 + 6	6	6/36
8	6 + 2, 5 + 3, 4 + 4, 3 + 5, 2 + 6	5	5/36
9	6 + 3, 5 + 4, 4 + 5, 3 + 6	4	4/36
10	6 + 4, 5 + 5, 4 + 6	3	3/36
11	6 + 5, 5 + 6	2	2/36
12	6 + 6	1	1/36

As is clearly seen, those theoretical probabilities together are expected to produce a symmetric distribution diagram. There may exist, however, a variety of nonsymmetrical distribution diagrams, which are more commonly seen in daily life than symmetrical ones.

6.2.2.2 Statistical Probability

This is neither mathematically nor theoretically determined but merely empirically evaluated. Its evaluation is also done on the solid basis.

One of the best examples is given by what we may call life expectancy. Strictly speaking, life expectancy is defined as the average number of years a person born in a certain country is expected to live if mortality rates at each age are assumed to remain steady in the future. Table 6.2 indicates the life expectancy at birth for both sexes, females and males in selected countries in the world. As is seen in the table, it varies a great deal from country to country. As of 2015, Japan as a developed country has the highest expectancy: on average, the Japanese female is expected to live for 86.8 years and the Japanese male 80.5 years. Sierra Leone is a developing country in which the life expectancy is considerably low: only 50.1 years for both sexes, 50.8 years for male, and 49.3 years for male.

Another example of statistical probability is provided by road traffic-related death rate. As is seen in Table 6.3, there are large disparities in this rate from country to country. As you can see, the UK and Japan are among the most safe countries. To take an example, in Japan in 2015, the road fatalities per 100 thousand persons is 4.7, implying that 47 persons out of one million are destined to be killed by various traffic accidents.

Both a priori probability and statistical probability have one important thing in common because they both are related to measurable risk in the sense that they can

Table 6.2 Life expectancy at birth: world selected list (2015)

Country	Both sexes	Female	Male
Japan	83.7	86.8	80.5
United Kingdom	81.2	83.0	79.4
United States	79.3	81.6	76.9
China	76.1	77.6	74.6
India	68.3	69.9	66.9
Nigeria	54.5	55.6	53.4
Sierra Leone	50.1	50.8	49.3

Source: The World Health Organization (WHO 2015)

Table 6.3 Traffic-related death rate: comparison of selected countries (2013)

Country	Road fatalities per 100 thousand	Road fatalities per 100 thousand
Japan	4.7	6.5
United Kingdom	2.9	5.1
United States	10.6	12.9
China	18.8	104.5
India	16.6	130.1
Nigeria	20.5	615.4
Sierra Leone	Not available	Not available

Source: World Health Organization (WHO 2013)

be described by specific distribution functions. There is another sort of probability, however, which is not measurable at all. It is this third kind of probability that should be our next topic to pick up.

6.2.2.3 Estimates or Judgments

In relation to estimates or judgments, Knight has attracted our special attention to the distinction between measurable risk and non-measurable uncertainty in the following way:

> The distinction here is that there is *no solid basis of any kind* for classifying instances. This form of probability is involved in the greatest logical difficulties of all, and no satisfactory discussion of it can be given, but its distinction from the other types must be emphasized and some of its complicated relations indicated. (Knight 1921, p. 225)

Concerning the above sentence, the expression “no solid basis of any kind” should be of the greatest importance since it tells us the clear distinction between theoretical and empirical probabilities on the one hand and estimates and judgments on the other hand. Undoubtedly, both theoretical and empirical probabilities have solid scientific basis, thus making no errors or no imperfections whatever. In contrast to those two cases, the third case of “estimates or judgments are ‘liable’ to err” (Knight 1921, p. 225). Human beings often make mistakes in every daily life. For example, every baseball player is liable to err: an infield or outfield player may fail to catch a ball, whereas a batter may fail to hit hard enough. Although the baseball game is usually played on some basis of pitching or hitting records, the baseball statistics is not so solid as the life expectancy or traffic-related death rate aforementioned.

Knight is eager to make estimates/judgments radically different from ordinary kinds of theoretical/empirical probabilities. At this point, he has also written the following remark:

> The theoretical difference between the probability connected with an estimates and that involved in such phenomenon as are dealt with by insurance is of the greatest importance, and is clearly discernable in nearly any instance of the exercise of judgment. (Knight 1921, p. 226)

In reality, we observe a variety of insurance including life insurance, traffic accident insurance, and fire insurance. Life expectancy and traffic accidents are subject to reliable information and solid calculation, so that they are almost always insurable. According to Knight, however, there are other kinds of probabilities connected with human estimates and imperfect judgments, which are in no way subject to insurance.

Joseph A. Schumpeter (1878–1950) is the great economist who was born in Austria and later immigrated to the USA, working for Harvard University until his death. He highly appreciated Knight for making the solid distinction between measurable risk and non-measurable uncertainty. His massive book *History of Economic Analysis* (1954) was posthumously came out in the publishing world. It is really worthwhile to record his remark on the work of Knight:

> To Professor Knight we owe, in the first place, a very useful emphasis upon the distinction between insurable risks and non-insurable uncertainty; and, in the second place, a profit theory that linked this non-insurable uncertainty on the one hand to rapid economic change—which, barring extra-economic disturbances, is the main source of this uncertainty—and on the other to differences in business ability which are much more obviously relevant to the explanation of profits and losses in condition of rapid change than would be otherwise. He thereby achieved a synthesis that is not open to the main objection against the ordinary type of risk theories. (Knight 1921, p. 894)

I myself stand squarely behind Schumpeter. Knight's distinction between insurable risk and non-insurable uncertainty is so important that it has contributed a great deal to the history of economic analysis. I would like to point out, however, the historical fact that this distinction has not been supported by all the economists. For instance, Kenneth Joseph Arrow (1921–2017), when he was young, expressed his serious doubts in a straightforward way:

> In brief, Knight's uncertainties seem to have surprisingly many of the properties of ordinary probabilities, and it is not clear how much is gained by the distinction. (Arrow 1951, p. 18)

I am not quite sure that Arrow in the 1970s and hereafter is academically what he was in the 1950s. As the saying goes, time flies like an arrow. I would like to believe, however, that he has somewhat outgrown from his younger days: even after his death in 2017, he remains admired all over the world as a very outstanding economist in the theory of risk and uncertainty.

6.3 Enterprise and Profit

6.3.1 The Effects of Uncertainty on the Organization

We are now in a position to carefully consider the effects of uncertainty on the form of organization of economic life. The best method seems to take up a society in which uncertainty is absent, then introduce uncertainty, and ascertain what changes will take place in its structure.

With uncertainty entirely absent, every person possessing perfect knowledge of the situation, there would be no occasion for responsible management and control of productive activity. The flow of raw materials and productive services through productive processes to the consumer would be entirely automatic. It is true that there might be managers, superintendents, and the like for the purpose of coordinating the activities of individuals. Under conditions of perfect knowledge and full certainty, however, such functionaries could be regarded as mere workers, performing purely routine functions, without responsibility of any sort, on a level with men engaged in just mechanical operations.

Now let us introduce uncertainty into the business organization and ascertain what changes will take place in its working and performance. Knight (1921) becomes a very eloquent speaker at this stage:

> With the introduction of uncertainty—the fact of ignorance and necessity of acting upon opinion rather than knowledge—into this Eden-like situation, its character is completely changed. With uncertainty absent, man's energies are devoted altogether to doing things; and it is doubtful whether intelligence itself would exist in such a situation; in a world so built that perfect knowledge was theoretically possible, it seems likely that all organic readjustments would become mechanical, all organisms automata. With uncertainty present, doing things, the actual execution of activity, becomes in a real sense a secondary part of life; the primary problem or function is deciding what to do and how to do it. (Knight 1921, p. 208)

Knight skillfully compares the society without uncertainty and the one in the presence of uncertainty. With uncertainty absent, people are supposed to live the Eden-like situation in which persons are just doing the same things as before and the organizations are mechanical like automata. Knight doubts that even human intelligence itself would cease to exist.[5]

With uncertainty present, those situations must change dramatically. While doing works routinely becomes a secondary part of people's life, deciding intentionally what to do and how to do it would be thought of as the primary problem. Then the internal organization is no longer a matter of indifference or a mechanical detail. Centralization of determination and controlling function is now

[5]Arrow (1951, 1970) seemed to react rather harshly against such strong opinion of Knight. So Arrow once remarked: "[A]ccording to Professor Frank Knight, even human consciousness itself would disappear in the absence of uncertainty" (Arrow 1970, page 1). In retrospect, the two giants, Knight and Arrow, seem to be considerably emotional at this stage, thus showing that both are just human beings, but not automata.

imperative. A very important change in this direction resides in the tendency of the groups themselves to specialize, finding the greatest managerial capacity and placing them in charge of the group work. With the specialization of function goes also a differentiation of reward. The produce of society is now divided into two kinds of income. The first kind is contractual income or *rent* and the second one residual income or *profit*. The question which might occur to our mind is who is the person acquiring the first income and who is the man being entitled to obtain the second one.

6.3.2 Manager Versus Entrepreneur

When uncertainty is absent, the duties of managers at business organization would be of a routine character, thus being not significantly different from those of any other operatives; they would be just like other ordinary workers, and their incomes are wages like other wages. When the managerial function comes to require the exercise of judgment, however, the business situation would change dramatically. Then the judgment by the management is liable to make an error, and the manager in charge ought to have responsibility for the correctness of the opinion. In a sense, "the nature of the function is revolutionized; the manager becomes an entrepreneur" (Knight 1921, p. 276).

We must keep in mind that the entrepreneur's income is not determined but rather may be regarded as *residual* in the sense that it is what is left after the others are determined. In other words, "the entrepreneur's income is not fixed but consists of whatever remains over after the fixed incomes are paid" (Knight 1921, p. 280). The presence of true profit, therefore, depends on an absolute uncertainty in estimating the value of judgment or on the absence of the requisite organization for combining a sufficient number of instances to secure certainty through consolidation.

In conclusion, Knight (1921) has left us the following impressive sentence:

> The only "risk" which leads to a profit is a unique uncertainty resulting from an exercise of ultimate responsibility which in its unique nature cannot be insured nor capitalized nor salaried. Profit arises out of the inherent, absolute unpredictability of things, out of the sheer brute fact that the results of human activity cannot be anticipated and then only in so far as even a probability calculation in regard to them is impossible and meaningless. (Knight 1921, pp. 310–311)

By carefully reading the above sentence, we strongly feel Knight's passion for true uncertainty or absolute unpredictability of things that may serve as the source of true profit distinct from ordinary rent. Knight was a man with many faces. He was truly a man in paradox.

6.4 Bronfenbrenner on "the Chicago School": Final Remarks

It is generally agreed that Frank H. Knight is one of the superstars in the history of economic thought. Today, his distinction between risk and uncertainty seems to be a common knowledge among all the economists in the world.

Although Knight used to be called the "Grand Old Man" of Chicago, it is worth mentioning that he managed to remain an outsider in his own kingdom. It is fair to say that he failed to build up an exclusive "school of thought" around himself. As we have repeatedly mentioned in the above, however, we are able to find some important traces in his thought in the work of Martin Bronfenbrenner. Of course, Knight is Knight, and Bronfenbrenner is Bronfenbrenner. Although there are some important interactions between them, the ideological foundations seem to be a bit apart. For example, while Knight has constantly opposed Keynesian macro policies of market intervention, Bronfenbrenner sometime called himself "Bastard Keynesian." We do see, however, that those two economists are not mathematically oriented but find much interest in much wider area such as philosophy, history, religion, policies, and real-world problems. In short, they are men of dualistic views, with sharp tongue and sarcastic remarks.[6]

There remains an important question of whether and to what extent the "Chicago School of Economics" has ever existed. As far as we can see, there are opposing views on this matter. On the one hand, Laurence Miller, Jr. (1962) claims that the Chicago School represents a subject of legitimate professional interest. In historical perspective, in the 1930s, 1940s, and 1950s, so many eminent economists such as Frank Knight and Jacob Viner were doing outstanding research in theories and applications. And in the 1970s, 1980s, and hereafter, Chicago has produced so many leading theorists including Milton Friedman and George Stigler. Although Milnor has been brave to propose several elements as defining the "Chicago economists," alas, his proposal has not gained full endorsement from George Stigler himself (1962). We should not forget the presence of Paul Douglas, Oscar Lange, and Martin Bronfenbrenner, who were all independent, bastard Keynesian or liberal-oriented economists.

Martin Bronfenbrenner (1962) caught a golden opportunity to say his unique opinion on the "Chicago School." In his famous or infamous paper, he characteristically declared his strong position against the existence of such school:

> I [namely, Bronfenbrenner] never heard of any "Chicago School" until I left Chicago. I thought of my teachers and my older fellow students as good economists, not as members of a sect of cult or clique. Shortly after leaving the Midway, however, I encountered the term full force. It was usually used pejoratively, especially when I was included in the membership. On the banks of Lake Mendora, for example, "the Chicago School" meant Pangoloss

[6]While the life and work of Frank H. Knight was systematically reviewed by Patinkin (1973) and later by Boyd (1997), the accomplishment of Bronfenbrenner, one of Knight's student, was carefully evaluated by Goodwin (1998). Also see Schumpeter (1954) and Emmett (1999).

plus Crandgrind, with touches of Peachum, Torquemada, and the Marquis de Sade thrown in as “insulter’s surplus.” (Bronfenbrenner 1962, p. 72)

Here, Martin Bronfenbrenner’s sharp tongue was so apparent, requiring no further explanation. Especially, the use of the word “Marquis de Sade” was amazingly provocative. I believe that he was more or less influenced by the works and deeds of his mentor, Frank H. Knight. Unfortunately, the relation between Knight and Bronfenbrenner has not been fully investigated so far. I strongly believe, however, that it should be brought to more light, requiring still further investigation.

References

Arrow KJ (1951) Alternative approaches to the theory of choice in risk-taking situations. Econometrica 19:404–437. Also contained in Arrow (1970), Chapter 1

Arrow KJ (1970) Essays in theory of risk-bearing. American Elsevier, North-Holland

Boyd R (1997) Frank H. Knight, the ethics of competition: introduction to the transaction edition. Transaction Publishers, New York

Bronfenbrenner M (1962) Observations on the “Chicago School(s)”. J Polit Econ 5:72–75

Emmett RB (ed) (1999) Selected essays by Frank H. Knight, volume one: introduction. University of Chicago Press, Chicago

Goodwin CD (1998) Martin Bronfenbrenner, 1914–1997. Econ J 108(451):1775–1780

Knight FH (1921) Risk, uncertainty and profit. University of Chicago Press, Chicago

Miller L Jr (1962) On the “Chicago school of economics”. J Polit Econ 70:64–69

Patinkin D (1973) Frank Knight as teacher. Am Econ Rev 63(5):787–810

Sakai Y (2019) F.H. Knight on risk, uncertainty and profit. Center for Risk Research, Shiga University, Discussion Paper No. A-28

Schumpeter JA (1954) History of economic analysis. Allen & Unwin Publishers, London

Stigler GJ (1962) Comment [on the Chicago school]. J Polit Econ 70:70–71

WHO (2013) World health statistics 2013. World Health Organization

WHO (2015) World health statistics 2015. World Health Organization

Chapter 7
Frank H. Knight on Market Thinking: Reflections on the Logic and Ethics of the Capitalist Economy

Abstract The purpose of this paper is to shed a new light on the working and performance of the market economy from a pluralistic viewpoint. To this end, we first pay attention to the general equilibrium theory a la L.W. McKenzie, K. J. Arrow, and G. Debreu. Whereas this theory seems to be established on the foundation of solid logic and advanced mathematics, the existence of special ethics and ideology behind the scenes should not be forgotten. We next reexamine the thought of Frank H. Knight, who has raised a strong objection against glorification of the market economy.

In the late 1960s, I was a graduate student at the University of Rochester. I still recall the touching moment when Professor McKenzie, finally succeeding after a long struggle to prove the existence of a competitive economy by help of a mathematical theorem of fixed point, posed a bit in a class and said quietly, "It's so beautiful!". The world was then in the midst of the Cold War and divided into the two powerful blocs, the socialist bloc dominated by the Soviet Union and the capitalist bloc led by the USA. McKenzie's complacent whispering sounded like the victory declaration of capitalism over socialism.

Around 40 years have passed since then. It seems that the "academic Cold War" between Marxian economics and modern economics is now over. At the same time, the ethics and ideology of general equilibrium looks surely fading away although it is not completely vanished. It is our regret, however, that the new, synthetic social science which can replace the existing dogmatic doctrines is not in sight yet. A completely new approach like a second Knight or a second Keynes would urgently be needed.

Keywords Knight · Market thinking · L. McKenzie · Fixed point theorem · General equilibrium

This paper is a completely revised English version of Sakai (2014), Chapter 6.

Y. Sakai, *J.M. Keynes Versus F.H. Knight*, Evolutionary Economics and Social Complexity Science 18, https://doi.org/10.1007/978-981-13-8000-6_7

7.1 What Money Can and Cannot Buy: An Introduction

This chapter aims to shed a new light on the working and performance of the market economy from a pluralistic viewpoint a la Knight. The problem of much interest is whether and to what extent we can persuasively discuss the efficiency and limitations of the economy without reference to equity and justice. The contents of this paper are as follows. In Sect. 7.2, we will outline the solid framework of general equilibrium theory which was strongly promoted by McKenzie, Arrow, and Debreu and point out the unique ethics and ideology lying its background. In Sect. 7.3, we will turn to the reassessment of Knight's strong objections against the market fundamentalism. To escape from mathematical jungles, we will make use of graphical illustrations as much as possible. We sincerely hope that our visual and intuitive way of presentation will work out beautifully. Section 7.4 will turn to Knight's objections against the capitalist economy. And final remarks will be made in Sect. 7.5.

7.1.1 Michael Sandel on the Moral Limits of Markets

For every man in the street, it is so important to distinguish between what money can buy and what money cannot buy. These two things are clearly different and should not be confused. It seems very strange to see, however, that there are many modern economists who tend to forget the differences, thus simply applying the logic of buying and selling to the whole aspects of life.

Michael Sandel is a famous professor of political philosophy at Harvard University. His famous "Justice" course has been the first Harvard course made freely available online and on television.[1]

In a very popular book, Sandel (2012) once remarked:

> As the cold war ended, markets and market thinking enjoyed unrivaled prestige, understandably so. No other mechanism for organizing the production and distribution of goods had proved as successful as generating affluence and prosperity. And yet, even as growing number of countries around the world embraced market mechanisms in the operation of their economies, something else was happening. Market values were coming to play a greater and greater role in social life. Economics was becoming an imperial domain. Today, the logic of buying and selling no longer applies to material goods alone but increasingly governs the whole of life. It is time to ask whether we want to live this way. (Sandel 2012, pp.5–6)

Presumably, almost every man who has common sense and conscience would have to agree with Sandel. Market values were likely to play a greater and greater

[1]Sandel's Harvard course was also easily available on Japanese television. Its style was so appealing and influential that it was nicknamed "Sandel's exciting lecture." It seems that his emphasis on justice and equity impressed very much those Japanese economics students who were tired of repeated talk on money and efficiency.

role in every aspect of human life. Although economics was once regarded as a dismal science, it experienced a great transformation through mathematical rigor and big data analysis: some people dared to call economics "the queen of social sciences."

Let us recall the 1950s and the 1960s when the general equilibrium theory was firmly established by the three eminent economists, Lionel W. McKenzie (1919–2010), Kenneth J. Arrow (1921–2017), and Gerard Debreu (1921–2004). Interestingly enough, if we collect the initials of these economists, we would form the catch word MAD. Therefore, some cynical persons might say that we then lived in the MAD Age or perhaps another name of the Golden Age. We would like to investigate how mad or how powerful the general equilibrium way of thinking once was and also discuss how and to what degree it continues to be so even today.

7.1.2 Gary Becker on the Economics of Marriage

Gary S. Becker (1930–2014) was a Nobel-winning scholar of economics and sociology. He was working for the University of Chicago and greatly contributed to raising the good (and possibly bad) reputations of the Chicago School in modern times. He was a famed scholar of remarkable impact beyond the academic world.

His way of thinking was extremely money-oriented. According to him, any rational person must make his/her decision-making on the basis of monetary benefits and losses. Any standard microeconomic text taught us that any consumer maximized his/her utility subject to the budget constraint and any producer, the net profits as revenues minus costs. In a sense, so far so good. Consumers and producers could be regarded as typical subjects of economics in conventional economics.

Becker proceeded to go beyond the traditional domain of economics. For instance, he extended his analysis to what people usually thought of as noneconomic problems such as marriage and crime. Although such an extension might look rather brave and challenging, it could possibly be overextension or even a long way off the mark.

In a very interesting book, Becker (1976) once remarked:

> According to the economic approach, a person decides to marry when the utility expected from marriage exceeds that expected from remaining or additional search for a more suitable mate. Similarly, a married person terminates his (or her) marriage when the utility anticipated from becoming single or marring someone exceeds the loss in utility from separation, including losses due to physical separation from one's children, division of joint assets, legal fees, and so forth. Since many persons are looking for mates, a *market* in marriages can be said to exist. (Becker, 1976, p. 10)

When I myself was about to leave the USA after my stay there for 8 years, I happened to encounter Becker's article mentioned above. In fact, Bill, one of my American friends in Pittsburgh, strongly recommended to read it and sincerely wished to hear my personal reply. To tell the truth, the article sounded to me a thunderbolt from a clear sky. Although I got married with a lovely girl a year before, any kind of pecuniary calculations over benefits and losses never crossed to my mind. In short, my marriage had nothing to do with the Becker way of market thinking. Besides, the change of my place of employment from an American university to a Japanese university resulted in a reduction of my yearly income by half. I was then in a mood to accept it: I did this because of my family obligation to old parents living in the land of the Rising Sun. It may be fair to say that Becker's market-oriented solution to the marriage problem constituted merely one of possible many solutions conceivable. I do think, however, that the young Sakai's noneconomic solution was another possible solution in a cultural/historical perspective.

7.1.3 F. H. Knight Versus M. Friedman: H. Uzawa's Remark

Hirofumi Uzawa (1928–2015) was one of the most famous economists in postwar Japan: he was once working for the University of Chicago before he came back to the University of Tokyo, Japan. In a very popular book, Uzawa (2013) once made a very important remark in Japanese. Although it was a bit long sentence, let us attempt to write its English translation down below:

> In the 1950s and the 1960s, the central figure of the so-called Chicago School was Friedman, with a supportive role being played by Hayek. In contrast, Knight thoroughly condemned the atomic bombing by the U.S. over Hiroshima and Nagasaki in 1945 for the worst crime ever committed by mankind. Knight gave serious thought to the problem of competition and ethics: he was really an outstanding economist. In my opinion, Knight was entirely different from what people loosely called the Chicago School.
>
> What I particular want to mention is the fact that Knight kindly adopted as his daughter the young girl who had lost her parents by the Hiroshima atomic bombing. He was so nice to her that he used to take her to Uzawa's house. Besides, one of his sons became a professor at the Institute of Low Temperature Science, Hokkaido University, Japan. Knight was really such a man of warm heart as well as a man of high morals. . . .. . .
>
> Friedman and his circle continued to devote themselves to moneymaking. As Knight seemed to think that this was not the right thing to do, he once said to many colleagues around him, 'It is true that Milton Friedman and George Stigler finished their doctoral dissertations under my direction. I would like to say, however, that their recent behaviors were too much for me. So I would rather like to declare that they are no longer my students'. This was presumably a sort of the declaration of expulsion. I can recall that he was then an old man over 80 years, yet such a good and wonderful person. (Uzawa 2013, pp. 35–36)

Uzawa's remark aforementioned clearly indicates a striking difference between Knight and Friedman from an ethical point of view. Concerning the relationship between the logic and ethics of the market economy, Knight was very cautions against falling into the trap of the market logic first and nothing else: in fact, he emphasized that ethics and social philosophy should play a critical role in protecting from possibly devastating consequences of excessive competition. Contrary to such teachings of his mentor, Friedman became a strong believer in "market fundamentalism without ethics." It would not be fair to say that Knight and Friedman belonged to the same school of economic thought, namely, the Chicago School. Alternatively, we could say that Knight early led the original Chicago School and Friedman later modified the morals of the school in a different direction.

7.2 The Ethics and Ideology of General Equilibrium Theory

7.2.1 The Life and Work of "Professor Fixed Point"

In the 1960s, the campuses of many Japanese universities and colleges were so noisy: there were so many political gatherings and strike activities. Many students dared to go out of the university campuses, thus shouting political slogans and engaging in street demonstrations. In short, Japanese universities were no longer good places for study and research. So some of the active youth wanted to go abroad and could continue to do their graduate studies. I myself was one of those ambitious students, thus applying for admission of graduate schools at American universities. Very fortunately, in 1968, I was admitted to the Graduate School of Economics, the University of Rochester.

There was a very prominent professor at the Rochester economics faculty, who was mainly responsible for the establishment of the outstanding graduate program in economics. The name of that famous professor was Lionel W. McKenzie. He was one of those pioneers who together with Kenneth Arrow and Gerard Debreu succeeded in introducing advanced mathematics such as differential topology into economics. One of his favorable mathematical tools was the fixed point theorem which was established by great mathematicians including L.E.J. Brouwer (1881–1996) and Shizuo Kakutani (1911–2004). So it would be quite natural to see that McKenzie was nicknamed "Professor Fixed Point."[2]

The way in which McKenzie taught general equilibrium theory at Rochester was legendary. Every time, he distributed to a selected group of graduate students his

[2]Interestingly enough, we can point out a sort of McKenzie-Hicks-Samuelson connection. McKenzie once dared to go to Oxford, and his supervisor was J. R. Hicks, the famed author of Hicks (1939, 2nd ed. 1946). Although McKenzie wrote a draft of a thesis, it was unfortunately a rather unfinished product, so that he had to be satisfied with the less prestigious degree of B. Litt. When McKenzie was visiting the Coles Foundation, a professor from the University of Rochester came by to discuss the possibility that McKenzie might be interested in a position there to head an economics department with the aim of developing a Ph.D. program. McKenzie later learned that this job of chairmanship had been recommended by P. A. Samuelson at MIT. This was the reason why McKenzie spent his first year at Rochester in 1957 and later devoted his full energy to gradually make Rochester a world-famous institution of mathematical economics. For a detailed story on this point, see McKenzie (1999). My academic relation to McKenzie, a mentor at Rochester, carried over to Pittsburgh; I myself made Sakai (1972) my own lecture note on general equilibrium theory, by occasionally consulting McKenzie (1969) and also introducing some original materials. For the life and work of S. Kakutani who established a famous fixed point theorem in Kakutani (1941), see Hirota (2004).

handwritten manuscripts, which contained a lot of mathematical symbols and complicated equations. As could easily be guessed, the symbols and equations were rather loosely written and sometimes almost incomprehensible. There was something dignified in his teaching; using large blackboards in a classroom, he usually wrote so many definitions and axioms before proceeding to prove a series of mathematical propositions. All the students seemed to be quiet, taking great pains in making their lecture notes faithfully.

Professor McKenzie was very fond of mathematics, thus being a passionate researcher in the application of advanced mathematics to economic science. It is true that he almost always controlled his class authoritatively. No person was perfect, however. There was an occasion when he was a bit stuck in mathematical derivations and pondered for some time while grasping a piece of white chalk in his right hand. Whenever his right hand got up and approached to his face, the color of his lips gradually changed from reddish to whitish: he forgot the inescapable reality that the white chalk happened to touched his lips. Occasionally, he spoke the names of some Japanese economists in heavy (or rather correct) English accents, "Morry-she-ma" (meaning Michio Morishima), "Woo-zawer" (Hirofumi Uzawa), "Inner-da" (Ken-Ichi Inada), "Knee-kwaido" (Hukukane Nikaido), and "Nay-gee-she" (Takashi Negishi). Yes, they should be Japanese names, but sounded to me like American names.

I still remember the occasion when McKenzie did not feel well and unfortunately got struck in a mathematical jungle. This incident happened exactly when he was about to finish the proof of general market equilibrium solution. He knows that the mathematical tool needed was no less than the effective use of the fixed point theorem. Then he stopped walking and began to fold his arms, holding a piece of white chalk with his right hand. After 5 min or so, his cheek suddenly got more brighter than before and nodded his head to himself, "I've got it!". And after completing the existence proof successfully, he convincingly yet rather quietly muttered with sigh, "Oh, it's so beautiful!". This was only faintly heard to me: I was lucky enough to sit on the front row.

It was no doubt that McKenzie's lecture on general equilibrium theory was mathematically so beautiful that it greatly impressed all the students in his class. His inclination toward mathematical beauty seemed too much to us, however. In academic activities, if we seek "beauty" in addition to "logic" and "ethics," we should be demanding too much. Then we could possibly be caught in escapable pitfalls in the sense that we vainly searched for a sort of "utopian capitalism" or rather "elegant nihilism." A will-o'-the-wisp would be burning and sneer at us forever![3]

---

[3]McKenzie (1969) was the handwritten lecture note he used in a graduate seminar in general equilibrium theory at Rochester. It was a loosely written manuscript full of corrections and imperfections. All the students had a very hard time to fully understand his unique writing style, mysterious notations, and complicated equations. Fortunately, it was later typewritten by his efficient secretaries and eventually became a hard-covered book, namely, McKenzie (2002). The time span between the lecture note and the complete book is amazingly 33 years. We strongly feel that his esprit, wit, and human touch have been gone in those long years. As the saying goes, time and tide wait for no man!

7.2.2 The Brouwer Fixed Point Theorem

L.E.J. Brouwer (1881–1966) was a famous Dutch mathematician, who worked in topology, measure theory, and complex analysis. He proved a number of mathematical theorems including what mathematicians later called the Brouwer fixed point theorem. Probably to his surprise, the powerful theorem failed to be fixed at the field of pure mathematics, influencing beyond the mathematical border to a variety of applied areas such as general equilibrium analysis in economic science.

In what follows, let us briefly explain the Brouwer fixed point theorem. Let us consider a set X and a function f from X to X, namely, a transformation of X into itself. We find it very interesting to find the existence of an element x^* such that $x^* = f(x^*)$, namely, an element which does not move in the transformation. Such an element is particularly named a fixed point of the function f.[4]

Let us assume that X is a non-empty, compact, convex set of R^n and then n-th-dimensional real space. It is well known that in the real space, a compact set is equivalent to a bounded and closed set. If we consider a unit closed interval [0, 1], it is indeed non-empty, compact, and convex. For an illustrative purpose, let us consider the following continuous function from [0, 1] into itself.

$$f(x) = x^2 - x + 3/4 \tag{7.1}$$

Then as is seen in Fig. 7.1, the curve f must cross the 45-degree line at least once. Such a crossing point Q constitutes a fixed point, namely, $f(x^*) = x^*$ (= 1/2).

More formally speaking, we can establish the following simple yet powerful theorem which was first proved by Brouwer (1910) more than 100 years ago:

Theorem 1 (The Brouwer Fixed Point Theorem) Let X be a non-empty, compact, convex set of $R^{n.}$ and f be a continuous function from X to itself. Then f has a fixed point: namely, there is an element x^* of X such that $x^* = f(x^*)$.

Although the Brouwer fixed point theorem seems very powerful, it should never be almighty: namely, it does not hold unconditionally. A clear yet rigorous proof is provided by Nikaido (1970). We are only content here to confirm that the following four conditions must be satisfied for applicability of the theorem.

(1) The function f must be continuous on the set X.
(2) X must be a closed set.
(3) X must be a bounded set; namely, X must have upper and lower bounds.
(4) X must be a convex set.

Figure 7.2 shows that if one of those four conditions is not met, the fixed point theorem is no longer applicable. In Panel (A), the curve f is not continuous at $x = 1/2$, whence f does not cross the 45-degree line. Panel (B) stands for the case in which the

[4]Debreu (1959) and Takayama (1974) are very useful in understanding the Brouwer fixed point theorem and its related topics.

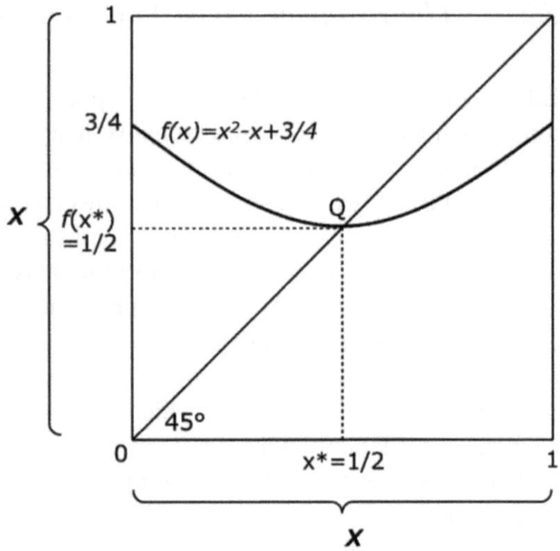

Fig. 7.1 The Brouwer fixed point theorem

set X is an open unit interval (0,1), which demonstrates non-intersection of f and the 45-degree line. In Panel (C), since X is an infinite interval $[0,\infty]$, it is no longer bounded above. If the curve f under question is always increasing above the 45-degree line, then there should be no crossing point between these the curve and the line. Finally, Panel (D) indicates the situation under which X is not a convex case. Suppose that X is the union of the two closed subintervals such that $X = [0,1/3] \cup [2/3,1]$. Then if the curve f jumps at $x = 1/3$ and $x = 2/3$ as is seen the panel, there should be no crossing point.

To sum up, we should be very careful of the effectiveness and limitations of the Brouwer fixed point theorem.

7.2.3 The Equivalence Between the Walras Existence Theorem and the Brouwer Fixed Point Theorem

Mathematics is often called "the queen of sciences"; it has produced so many beautiful theorems since Archimedes (287?–212B.C.), an ancient Greek mathematician. It seems that the Brouwer fixed theorem is one of the most beautiful theorems in modern times. Although the theorem per se is a pure brain product, it has many applications to other fields such as economics and game theory.[5]

In the 1950s and the 1960s, there reemerged a bulk of mathematical economists who found much interest in giving a rigorous proof for the existence of multi-market equilibrium a la Leon Walras (1874), a lonely French pioneer. Among those economists were Arrow (1951), Arrow and Debreu (1954), Debreu (1959),

[5]See Wald (1936) and Von Neumann and Morgenstern (1944), for instance.

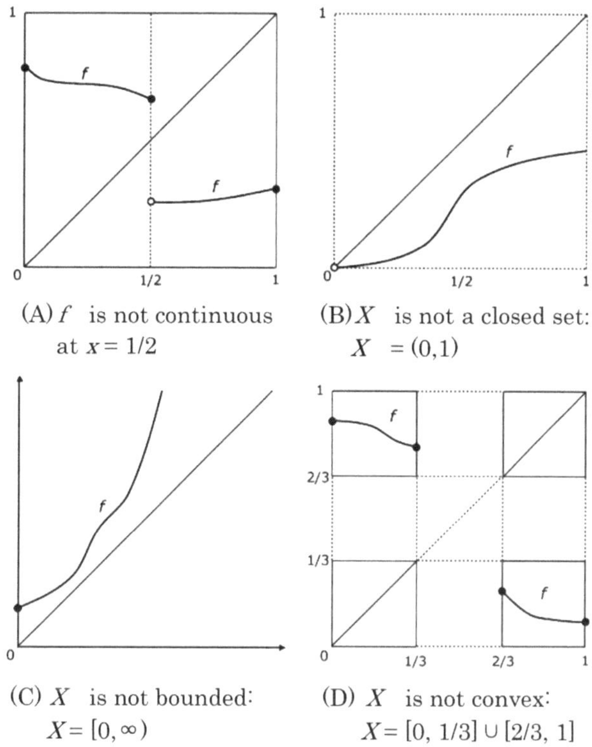

Fig. 7.2 The four cases where the fixed point theorem is not applicable

McKenzie (1954, 1955, 1959), Gale (1955), and Nikaido (1956). Unquestionably, the Brouwer fixed point theorem and its generalizations such as the Kakutani fixed point theorem have been the most powerful mathematical tools employed by those economists.[6]

The purpose of this subsection is to show the equivalence between the Walras existence theorem and the Brouwer fixed point theorem. Uzawa (1962) was the first person to point out such equivalence in a very exact form. In what follows, let us attempt to give an elementary proof by help of simple figures.

[6]From the 1970s onward, very useful advanced textbooks in general equilibrium theory have been appeared. So systematic presentations of the fixed point theorems and their economic applications are now available to any eager graduate student. For instance, see Nikaido (1970), Arrow and Hahn (1971), and Takayama (1974). Also see Lancaster (1968). Compared with those works, McKenzie (2002) was a belated product, yet presumably showed the culmination in thus field.

In what follows, we would like to pick up a very simple, one-good market equilibrium model a la Walras (1874) in order to establish following theorem:

Theorem 2 (Equivalence Between the Fixed Point and the Market Equilibrium) The fixed point implies the market equilibrium and vice versa.

Let the demand function and the supply functions of good x, respectively, be denoted by $x = d\ (p)$ and $x = s\ (p)$, where p stands for the unit price of x. For simplicity, assume that the functions d and s are both continuous and smooth. Then we can write down the excess demand function e of good x as follows:

$$e(p) = d(p) - s(p). \tag{7.2}$$

Common sense tell us that when the price of a good x rises, the demand for the good decreases and the supply increases. Consequently, on the one hand, if the price p is low enough (namely, $p = p^L$), the excess demand for x occurs, so that $e^L = d^L - s^L > 0$. On the other, in case the price p is high enough (i.e., $p = p^H$), minus the excess demand (namely, the excess supply) for x takes place, whence $e^L = d^L - s^L < 0$. Let put $P = [p^L, p^H\ ]$. Then evidently, P is a closed interval; whence it is a non-empty, compact, closed set.

Now, let us consider the following mapping from P into itself:

$$\Phi(p) = p + \alpha \cdot\ e(p) \tag{7.3}$$

It is noted here that α stands for a fraction, namely, a constant between 0 and 1. The mapping $\Phi(p)$ indicates a sort of Walrasian price adjustment process. For example, let us put $\alpha = 1/2$. Then if the excess demand for x occurs (i.e., $\alpha > 0$), we find $\Phi(p) = p + (1/2)\ e\ (p)$, meaning that the price p must go up by 50%. By the same token, if the excess supply takes place, then p must go down by 50%.

Clearly, the mapping Φ: $P \rightarrow P$ is continuous. So if we apply the Brower fixed point theorem here, we may find the fixed point, namely, p^* such that $\Phi(p^*) = p^*$

In the light of Eq. (6.3), we can immediately obtain the following equivalent relation:

$$\Phi(p^*) = p^* \Leftrightarrow e(p^*) = 0. \tag{7.4}$$

Needless to say, Eq. (7.4) above is a mathematical restatement of Theorem 2. Therefore, the Brouwer fixed point theorem implies the Walras market equilibrium and vice versa. Take a look at Fig. 7.3. The point Q^* and the point R^*, respectively, indicate the fixed point and the market equilibrium. It is very obvious from this figure that the existence of Q^* in the upper figure implies the existence of R^* in the lower figure and vice versa. The proposition "the fixed point equals the market equilibrium" constitutes one of the very fundamental ideas underlining the core of general equilibrium theory.

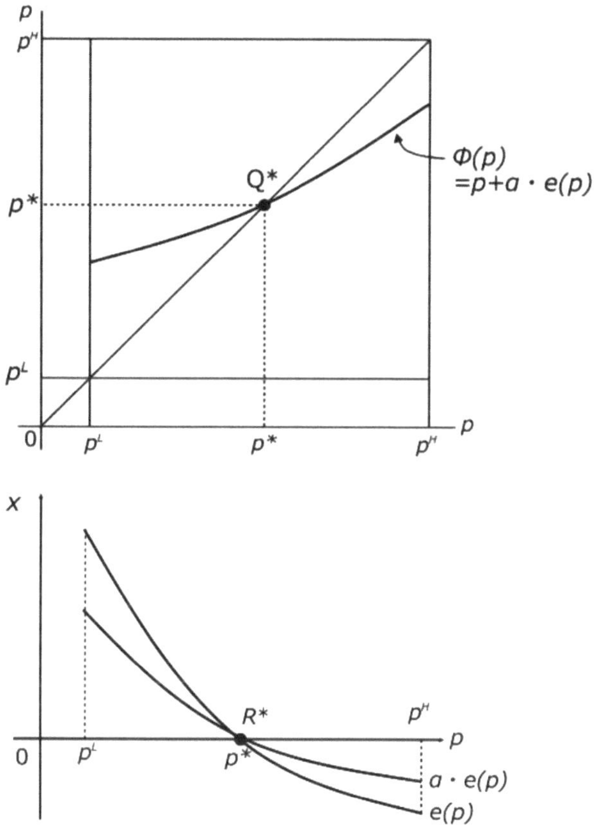

Fig. 7.3 Equivalence of the fixed point Q^* and the market equilibrium point R^*: $\Phi(p^*) = p^* \Leftrightarrow e(p^*) = 0$

7.3 Welfare Implications of General Equilibrium

7.3.1 The Impact of the Cold War on the Economics Profession

Just after the Second World War, we were engaged in another world war named the Cold War. There emerged many political, military, and ideological tensions between the Western Capitalist Bloc (the USA, its NATO allies, Japan, and others) and the Eastern Socialist Bloc (the Soviet Union, its Warsaw Treaty allies, China, and others). The term "Cold War" was intentionally employed since there was no longer large-scale "hot fighting" directly between those two blocs. The importance of the "ideological struggles," however, should not be underestimated.

In the field of economics profession, a sort of "Economics Cold War" took place between what we called modern economics and what we named Marxian economics. It should be recalled that Marxian economics was not only the official economics taught in the Eastern Bloc but also a more or less popular subject in the Western Bloc except the USA. In Japan, most of the major universities were then dominated by Marxian socialists, with modern economists taking a back seat.

Under the circumstances mentioned above, especially in the USA, general equilibrium theory has played a very special role in establishing the proposition that the capitalist economy really works at least as efficiently as its rival, socialist economy. A great number of research projects on mathematical economics were very generously supported by the National Science Foundation, Naval Research Logistics Project, and the like.[7]

The thinking of Immanuel Kant (1785), a famous German philosopher, has influenced moral philosophy a great deal. According to his philosophy, there are three important value judgments in human behavior. They are truth, good, and beauty. General equilibrium theory has taught us that the market economy works and indeed works very beautifully. Contemporary mathematically trained economists have succeeded in truly and beautifully providing the existence proof of a multi-market, competitive equilibrium on the basis of the powerful fixed point theorem. There is something missing in general equilibrium theory, however. In order to make our value judgment a la Kant more complete, we have to demonstrate that the market economy is a very good system, or an even optimal system, from a moral point of view.

It is really remarkable to see the following important theorem has been established by Arrow (1951), Hurwicz (1960), and others.

Theorem 3 (The Fundamental Theorem of Welfare Economics) Let us suppose that an exchange economy be "normal." Then it possesses the following properties:

(1) Every market equilibrium achieves Pareto optimality.
(2) Every Pareto optimal state can be achieved as a market equilibrium position.

The rigorous proof of this theorem is omitted here. We note that in a "normal economy," an increase in the quantity of any good increases the total utility of every person but decreases his/her marginal utility. Besides, in a Pareto optimal economy, it is not possible to make any one person better off without making the other worse off. Whether and to what extent Pareto optimality really represents the "ideal state" of the economy remains to be debatable.[8]

---

[7]Newman (1968) was a nice collection of outstanding papers on mathematical economics. The reader could easily understand how effectively many scientific research funds were used in the 1950s and the 1960s.

[8]The concept of Pareto optimality was first introduced by Pareto(1906). For a nice discussion for the relation between the market equilibrium and Pareto optimality, see Negishi (1960) and Quirk and Saposnik (1968).

7.3.2 Market Equilibrium and Pareto Optimality

The relation between the market equilibrium and Pareto optimality may be easily understood by the box diagram a la Edgeworth (1881). Let us take a close look at two panels in Fig. 7.4. Panel (A) shows Property (1) of Theorem 3 aforementioned: every market equilibrium achieves Pareto optimality. In order to understand this, let us arbitrarily pick up the initial endowment point W and the budget set $B\ (p)$ passing through W. Then the point Q lying on $B\ (p)$ achieves the equality of demand and supply for the two goods, good 1 and good 2, since it is really a point in the box diagram. Moreover, it is apparently a point at which the two persons, Ms. A and Ms. B, can achieve her utility maximization subject to the budget constraint since at the point Q.

Now let us simply look at such a situation and forget the presence of the budget set for a while. Then we immediately see that the two indifference curves I^A and I^B just touch at Q. This shows that Pareto optimality is now achieved at Q.

Fig. 7.4 The market equilibrium and Pareto optimality

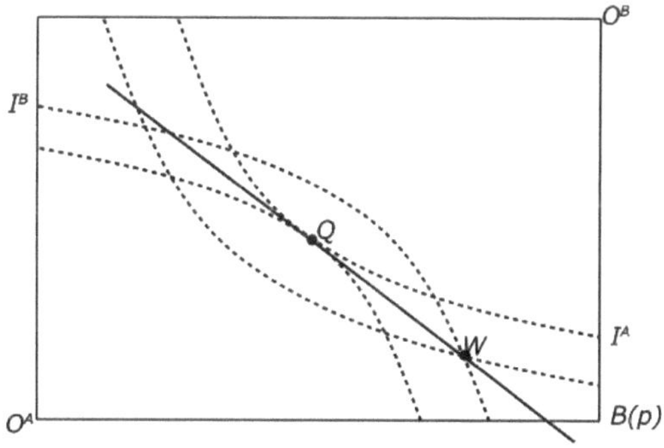

(A) The equilibrium point Q achieves Pareto optimality

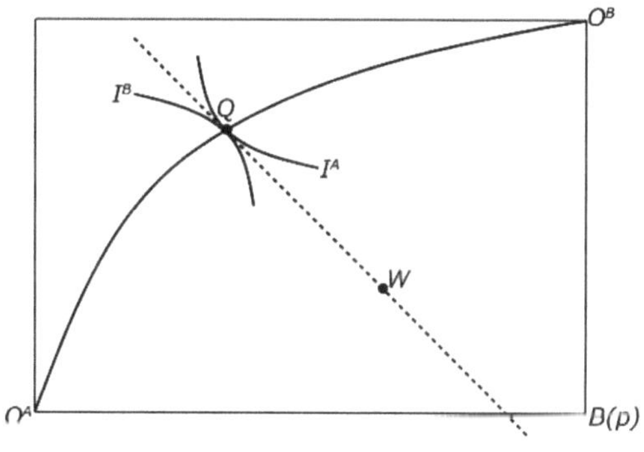

(B) The optimal point Q achieves a market equilibrium

In contrast, Panel B indicates Property 2 of Theorem 3; every Pareto optimal state can be achieved by a market mechanism. Let us pick up a point Q on the contract curve O^AO^B. Since point Q is a Pareto optimal point, it must be the point in which the two convex indifference curves I^A and I^B just touch each other. We can then find a separating line $B(p)$ and an initial endowment W. It is now clear that the Pareto optimal point P becomes a market equilibrium point with the initial endowment W and the common budget line $B(p)$.

I still remember how some graduate students instantaneously reacted when I energetically taught the nice relation between the market equilibrium and Pareto optimality at the University of Pittsburgh in the early 1970s. A clever female student from Turkey had the courage to ask a question to me: "Dr. Sakai, I was really impressed by your lecture to inform me that the market Economy is a sort of the Earthy Paradise. The three virtues of true, good and beauty seem to be perfectly achieved there. I would like to tell you, however, that I am from a less developed country located between Asia and Europe. I wonder whether and to what extent your today's talk is relevant to the present state of my country."

I was then really shocked by this question: it seemed to be a bolt out of the blue. I took a short pose and eventually managed to answer it. "This is really a very good question. As you know, I am also from the country of tradition and culture like you. Although Japan now might be a bit more advanced than your country, I am sure that it is not, and will never be, the Earthy Paradise. Now, all my fellow students, let us together think of the validity and limitations of general equilibrium theory. Man is a thinking reeds!"

This was part, though by no means the whole, of the reason for the change in my research area from general equilibrium to risk and uncertainty.

7.4 F. H. Knight's Strong Objections Against the Capitalist Economy

7.4.1 Knight's Unique Position: A Pluralist Insight

Frank H. Knight was perhaps one of the deepest thinkers and the most critical economists in the twentieth century. When I joined the economics faculty at Pittsburgh in the 1970s, I was surrounded by many people who had mixed feelings for general equilibrium theory and fondly talked about Frank Knight's philosophical pluralism.[9]

[9]The philosophical and economic thought of Knight was intensively discussed in Sakai (2010, 2015).

Knight was often called the "Grand Old Man" of Chicago, playing a central role in setting the character of "the early Chicago School." Interestingly enough, Patinkin (1973) vividly recalled the days when Knight was a teacher at the University of Chicago (1941–1947):

> A the Chicago of my student days it was, ironically enough, the socialist Oskar Lange who extolled the beauties of the Paretian optimum achieved by a perfectly competitive market—and Frank Knight who in effect taught us that the deeper welfare implications of this optimum were indeed quite limited. (Patinkin 1973, p. 801)

At Chicago in the 1940s, there were the two economics giants: Oskar Lange and Frank Knight. While the market socialist Lange extolled the beautiful equivalence of a competitive equilibrium and Pareto optimality, the reluctant capitalist Knight raised serious objections against it. Lange simply believed that human behavior was rational in the sense that a consumer maximizes his/her utility subject to the budget constraint, while a producer maximizes his/her profit subject to the technological constraint. In contrast, Knight's view of human nature was more complicated and more realistic than such a simple-minded view. As Boyd (1997) noted, the intellectual legacy of Frank Knight was a study in paradox. Although he could be regarded as an outstanding scholar in neoclassical economics, he nevertheless stood high as it harsh critic as well.

Knight (1925) once remarked:

> It is time to admit that while the craving for a monistic view of the world is real, the project of resolving either minds or objects into the other type of existence is futile. ...... Both realism and idealism are, in the vernacular, "the bunk"; monism is moonshine! In the human and social sciences, most clearly, the only possible point of view is pluralistic. (Knight 1925, p. 255; 1999, p. 121)

Generally speaking, there are two views of the worlds, a monistic view and a pluralistic view. According to Knight, monism is too simplistic and tends to view the world either white or black. The situation, however, is not a matter of black and white. Between black and white, there should be many complicated colors. If monism is regarded as weak moonshine, pluralism is sunshine and sheds a stronger and more colorful light into the world.

It is in such a pluralistic view that Knight very critically discussed the ethical foundations of the market economy.

7.4.2 *Knight's Strong Objections Against the Market Economy*

Throughout his career, Knight never regarded the capitalist system as ethically defensible. In fact, he fondly adopted his pluralistic view in order to critically investigate the ethical foundations of the market economy. According to Knight (1935), we can enumerate the following 12 reasons why the market economy cannot be defended from a moral point of view:

(1) The assumption that the economy is made up of freely contracting individuals is quite questionable. All minors, the aged, and some others must be taken care of by adult persons. The family, but not an individual, is still the unit in consumption and production.
(2) An individual is in large measure a product of the cultural environment. Human beings are not accurate mechanisms of desire satisfaction: human activity is largely impulsive, a relatively unthinking and undetermined response to external stimulus and rumors. When the family is the social unit, the inheritance of wealth and educational advantages tend toward the progressive increase of inequality. Therefore, the results which a competitive economy brings about are often far from being ethically ideal.
(3) The traditional assumption that all goods and services are perfectly divisible and freely mobile is based on mere supposition, thus being far from the actual economy.
(4) One of the most important prerequisites to perfect competition is complete knowledge on the part of every individual. A perfect market would involve perfect, instantaneous, and costless intercommunication among all the traders. This would be existent only in a fictitious world.
(5) Competition further assumes that every buyer of every good knows very accurately its properties to satisfy his/her want. The competitor must perfectly foresee things as they will be, a too unrealistic assumption.
(6) We have to find the proper relation between efficiency and equity. The social order must be judged ethically rather by the wants which it generates than by its efficiency in satisfying wants.
(7) The workings of competition educate men progressively for monopoly. This is being achieved not merely by producers but by labor and in many branches of agriculture. In short, free competition will destroy itself!
(8) In reality, what is desired is more largely a matter of human relations than goods as such; we want things because other people have them or cannot have them. A typical illustration is the improvement or use of property in ways which may add or subtract value from neighboring property.
(9) An exchange system cannot work at all according to theory without a control unit. With the use of credit highly developed, the control of banking and currency involves a large measure of control over all business, but really free banking would soon reduce all exchange relations to chaos.
(10) An economic organization must employ its available productive power in part to provide for present needs of society and in part to provide for future growth. In an individualistic system, provision for progress depends on the interest of present individuals in future individuals, which is being engendered to uncertain extent and with uncertain consequences by a change of the social and historical condition.

(11) All human planning and execution involve uncertainty, and a rational social order can be realized through individual action only if all persons have rational attitude toward risk and uncertainty. As can be seen in gambling and speculative behavior, however, the general human attitude tends to be nonrational, and much social limitation is required.
(12) We have to closely examine the ethical foundations and consequences of unbounded individualism and competition. In the capitalist economy, productive contribution can have little or no ethical significance from the standpoint of absolute ethics. For instance, no one contends that a bottle of old wine is ethically worth as much as a barrel of flour or a fantastic evening wrap for a powerful person's mistress as much as a substantial dwelling house. Besides, Knight has noticed that the ownership of personal or material capacity is based on a complex mixture of inheritance, luck, and effort, probably in that order of relative importance.

Because of those reasons aforementioned, the competitive system, viewed simply as a want-satisfying mechanism, falls short of our highest ideals. Knight thereby concludes that unlimited individualism and free competition cannot bring about the ideal utilization of social resources. We have to find the right proportion between individualism and socialism and consider their various varieties.

7.4.3 Inheritance, Luck, and Effort: A Graphical Interpretation

Knight does not believe that individualism can automatically bring about an ideal utilization of economic resources. He contends that the welfare results of trading are based rather on initial endowment and chance than on hard work.

In what follows, let us attempt to graphically interpret some of his objections against the market economy. Let us compare the two boxes in Fig. 7.5. The upper Panel (A) represents the trade of the two goods, good 1 (rice) and good 2 (fish), between Mr. Land and Mr. Sea. The initial endowment W is represented by point W, which is located in the south-east of the center Z. Mr. Land is a farmer who possesses a large amount of rice yet a small amount of fish, whereas Mr. Sea is a fisherman who has a large quantity of fish yet a small quantity of rice.

It would be nonsense to say that one of the two persons is absolutely richer or poorer than the other: in fact, each person is relatively rich in one good, but relatively poor in the other good. The trade between Mr. Land and Mr. Sea makes both much better off; the point Q, a Pareto optimal point, indicates the position after the trade. To sum up, gains in the exchange of rice and fish between a farmer and a fisherman are very large for the two persons. So far so good!

Such a sort of win-win situation would vanish if the initial endowment position is in the north-east position as is seen in the lower Channel (B). This is the trade between Ms. Rich and Ms. Poor. Ms. Rich is absolutely more affluent than

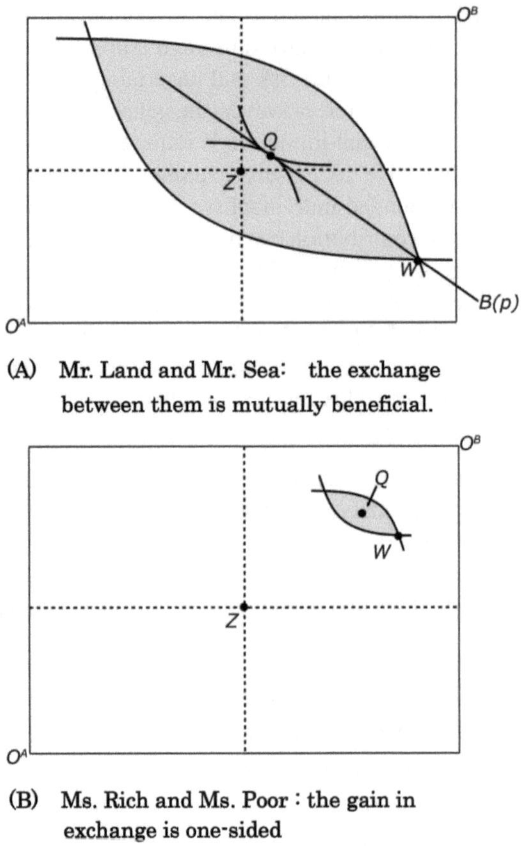

Fig. 7.5 Is a starting point before the exchange fair enough?

Ms. Poor: the former possesses more rice and more fish than the latter. Under such a lopsided situation, a gain in trade, if it exist, would be minimal for both parties. In fact, the movement of position from point *W* to point *Q* in Panel (B) would be too small to be identified. Our natural guessing is that after the trade with Ms. Rich, Ms. Poor would reconfirm her miserable position, thus psychologically more unhappy than ever. The have-not would go unrewarded. Certainly, this should not be a win-win situation. Our natural guessing is that after the trade with Ms. Rich, Ms. Poor would reconfirm her miserable position, thus psychologically more unhappy than ever. The have-not would go unrewarded. Certainly, this should not be a win-win situation.

7.4.4 *Risk, Uncertainty, and Moral Hazard: A Graphical Analysis*

According to Knight, all human planning and execution can be realized through individual action only if all persons have a rational attitude toward risk and chance. The general human attitude, however, is not necessarily very rational, and individual knowledge is more or less limited. The traditional assumption that every buyer of any good perfectly knows its properties to meet his/her want would not be satisfied in reality.

One of many interesting problems is how we relate quality uncertainty to the market mechanism. As Akerlof (1970) noted, the existence of a single good with several grades may pose a very serious problem for the working of a market. In this case, there emerges the possibility that a seller has an incentive to tell a lie to a buyer: he/she may supply a poor-quality good rather than a good-quality good. As a result, dishonest dealings may tend to drive honest dealings out; indeed, the market per se may shrink and will eventually vanish. This is what Akerlof has wisely called the lemons principle.

Figure 7.6 enables us to understand how the market for travel accident insurance works. There are two persons in the market: Mr. Fair as an insurance provider and Mr. Foul as an insurance purchaser. There are two contingent goods: X_1 as the amount of money when no accidents occur and X_2 as the one contingent on a travel accident. With accidents or without them, Mr. Fair receives a certain amount of insurance fee from Mr. Foul. If and only if an accident such as theft or loss occurs, Mr. Fair must pay a promised amount of insurance money to Mr. Foul. Let point W be the initial endowment point. Then point Q is the market equilibrium point, with the exchange price ratio being associated with the budget set $B(p)$. The honest dealing between the two persons can be characterized by the bold arrow "W ➡ Q";

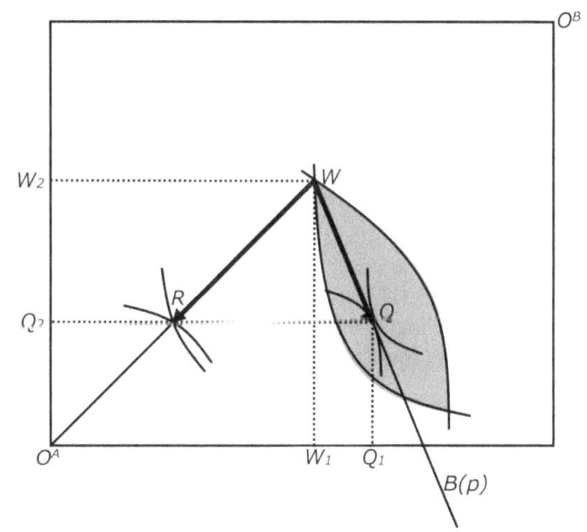

Fig. 7.6 The exchange of contingent goods between Mr. Fair and Mr. Foul: the bold arrow "W➡R" represents a dishonest dealing and the market may break down

Mr. Fair is entitled to receive from Mr. Foul the insurance fee W_1Q_1 in exchange for the payment of the net insurance money W_2Q_2 that equals the gross insurance money minus the insurance fee.

Let us first consider the ideal situation under which both the insurer and the insured are fully informed of any travel accident. If the two contingent goods X_1 and X_2 are exchanged between the two persons, the market equilibrium is achieved at point Q that is also Pareto optimal. So far so good!

Unfortunately, the world where we live is not so idealistic; in fact, we are rather involved in the situation where nonsymmetric information prevails. Mr. Fair as an insurance agent is not in a position to know whether and to what extent Mr. Foul, a customer, is really engaged in a travel accident. The reliable tie between the two parties might be honesty. The reality may be severe, and human trust may be rather weak, so that the insured is likely to have an incentive to tell a lie, taking advantage of the insurer's ignorance. Let us suppose that such betrayal really happens: Mr. Foul would claim that he has been involved in theft although the truth is not so. If Mr. Fair is a man of good character and accepts Mr. Foul's claim, the *actual* trade between the two persons would be indicated by the bold arrow "$W \Rightarrow R$" rather than the bold arrow "$W \Rightarrow Q$." Apparently, R is the point in which Mr. Fair becomes worse off. Consequently, the market is doomed to shrink and possibly vanish.

In the light of the history of economic thought, the economics of imperfect information has been greatly developed since the 1970s. Akerlof (1970) was generally regarded as one of those outstanding promoters. We must bear in mind, however, that far back in the 1930s, Knight already did a significant contribution to this field, so that he could also be thought of as one of important founders.

7.5 The Disappointing Performance of the Economics Profession:

Final Remarks

Shigeto Tsuru, the late Japanese economist, once attended with Paul A. Samuelson the graduate seminar conducted by Joseph Schumpeter at Harvard University. In the first page of a challenging book, Tsuru (1961) cited the following remark made by Dr. Seishi Kaya, chairman of the Japan Science Council:

> On reflection it is really ridiculous that mankind cannot live on thus globe peacefully with each other when they possesses the knowledge and know-how even of making a round trip to the moon. The most important thing from now on seems to be to join our efforts in making the time nearer when we can all visit the moon as friendly tourists, instead of being involved in the clash between communism and capitalism. (Tsuru 1961, p. 1)

In the 1960s and the 1970s when I myself stayed first as a graduate student and later as an assistant professor at American universities, the clash between communism and capitalism was very severe in every aspect of human life; indeed, the Soviet Union and the USA competed neck and neck for the first landing on the moon. When the Berlin Wall collapsed in 1990 and the Soviet Union disintegrated into Russia and many other smaller countries in the following year, it appeared to many people that the Cold War was clearly over.

Later in 2008, however, the world banking system collapsed, and we found ourselves involved in the biggest economic crisis after the Great Depression of the 1930s. The failure of socialism was never equivalent to the success of capitalism. A failure, if not the failure, of capitalism became a fashionable topic again. In a popular book, Richard A. Posner (2009) has recently remarked:

> My focus is on the course, causes, and offered cures of the depression. But I also emphasize some points that have received relatively little coverage in other accounts: the depression's political dimensions, the disappointing performance of the economics profession in regard to anticipating and providing guidance to responding to the depression, how ideology can distort economic policy, the inherent limitations of depression economics, how the self-interested decisions of rational businessmen and consumers can give rise to a depression.... (Posner 2009, Preface, p. xiv)

Posner's remark aforementioned is both very serious and greatly challenging. We all have seen the disappointing performance of the economic profession in regard to the breakdown of the market economy. It is recalled here that Keynes (1936), a noted contemporary of Knight, once lamented the disappointing performance of the economics profession and devoted his full energy to establish a new way of thinking.

In historical perspective, the two great economists, Knight (1921, p. 35, 99) and Keynes (1936), did outstanding contributions on the ethical foundations and consequences of a competitive economy. We believe that it is now high time to have serious reconsiderations of the logic and ethics of the capitalist economy. We need a Knight and/or a Keynes. Regrettably, neither a second Knight nor a second Keynes appears to be in sight yet. A completely new approach to the logic and ethics of the market economy would urgently be needed.

References

Akerlof GA (1970) The market for 'lemons': quality uncertainty and the market mechanism. Q J Econ 84:488–500

Arrow KJ (1951) An extension of the basic theorems of classical welfare economics. Contained in Neyman J (ed) Proceedings of the second Berkeley symposiums on mathematical statistics and probability, 507–532. University of California Press, Berkeley

Arrow KJ, Debreu G (1954) Existence of equilibrium for a competitive economy. Econometrica 22:265–290

Arrow KJ, Hahn FH (1971) General competitive analysis. Holden Day, New York

Becker G (1976) The economic approach to human behavior. University of Chicago Press, Chicago

Boyd R (1997) Frank Knight, ethics and competition: introduction to the transaction edition. Transaction Publishers, New York

Brouwer LEJ (1910) Über Abbildungen von Manningfaltigkeiten (in German). Written at the University of Amsterdam. Published in Mathematische Annalen, 71, 1911

Debreu G (1959) Theory of value: an axiomatic analysis of economic equilibrium. Wiley, New York

Edgeworth Y (1881) Mathematical psychics. Kegan Paul, London

Gale D (1955) The law of supply and demand. Mathematica Scandinavica 3:155–169

Hicks JR (1939) Value and capital. Oxford University Press, Oxford

Hirota M (2004) In memory of Professor Shizuo Kakutani: his work on pure mathematics and mathematical economics (in Japanese). Econ Semin J 597:10–11, Nihon Hyoronsha Publishing Company

Hurwicz L (1960) Optimality and informational efficiency in resource allocation processes. Contained in mathematical methods in the social sciences. Stanford University Press, Stanford

Kakutani S (1941) A generalization of Brouwer's fixed point theorem. Duke Math J 8:457–459

Kant I (1785) Grundlegung zur Metaphysik der Sitten (in German). English translation: groundwork of the metaphysics of morals

Keynes JM (1936) The general theory of employment, interest and money. Macmillan, London

Knight FH (1921) Risk, uncertainty and profit. Houghton Mifflin Company, Boston/New York

Knight FH (1925) Fact and metaphysics in economic psychology. Am Econ Rev 15:247–266

Knight FH (1935) The ethics of competition. Harper and Brothers, Boston/New York

Knight FH (1999) In: Emmett RB (ed) Selected essays by Frank H. Knight, volume 1: what is truth in economics? The University of Chicago Press, Chicago

Lancaster K (1968) Mathematical economics. Macmillan, London

McKenzie LM (1954) On equilibrium in graham's model of world trade and other competitive systems. Econometrica 22:147–161

McKenzie LM (1955) Competitive equilibrium with dependent consumer preferences. Contained in the second symposium on linear programming, Berkeley

McKenzie LM (1959) On the existence of general equilibrium for a competitive economy. Econometrica:27, 54–71

McKenzie LM (1969) Lecture notes on general equilibrium theory. Unpublished manuscript, University of Rochester

McKenzie LM (1999) A scholar's progress. Keio Econ Stud 36(1):1–12

McKenzie LM (2002) Classical general equilibrium theory. MIT Press, Boston

Negishi T (1960) Welfare economics and existence of an equilibrium for a competitive economy. Metroeconomica 12:92–97

Newman P (1968) Readings in mathematical economics, volume 1: value theory. Johns Hopkins Press

Nikaido H (1956) On the classical multilateral exchange problem. Metroeconomica 8:135–145

Nikaido H (1970) Convex structures and economic theory. Academic Publishers, New York

Pareto V (1906) Manuale di economia politica (in Italian). Società Editrice Libraria. French Translation (1909): manuel d'économie politique. Paris, Giard, 1909

Patinkin D (1973) Frank Knight as teacher. Am Econ Rev 63(5):787–810

Posner RA (2009) A failure of capitalism: the crisis of 2008 and the descent into depression. Harvard University Press, Boston

Quirk J, Saposnik R (1968) Introduction to general equilibrium and welfare economics. McGraw-Hill, New York

Sakai Y (1972) Lecture notes on mathematical economics I : general equilibrium theory. Unpublished manuscript, University of Pittsburgh

Sakai Y (2010) The economic thought of risk and uncertainty (in Japanese). Minerva Publishing Company, Kyoto

Sakai Y (2015) Keynes versus Frank Knight: how the two economic giants dealt with 'the age of uncertainty' (in Japanese). Minerva Publishing Company, Kyoto

Sandel M (2012) What money can't buy: the moral limits of markets. Allen Lane, New York

Takayama A (1974) Mathematical economics. Cambridge University Press. Second edition (1985)

Tsuru S (ed) (1961) Has capitalism changed? an international symposium on the nature of contemporary capitalism. Iwanami Publishing Company, Tokyo

Uzawa H (1962) Walras's existence theorem and Brower's fixed point theorem. Econ Stud Q:8, 59–62

Uzawa H (2013) Can economics make people happy ? (in Japanese). Toyo Keizai Publishers, Tokyo

Von Neumann J, Morgenstern O (1944) Theory of games and economic behavior. Princeton University Press, Princeton

Wald A (1936) Über einige Gleichungssysteme der mathematischen Ökonomie (in German). Zeitschrift für Nationalökonomie 7:637–670. English translation: Wald (1951) on some systems of equations of mathematical economies. Econometrica 19:368–403

Walras L (1874) Eléments d'économie politique pure (in French). Corbaz, Lausamme. English Translation (1954) Elements of pure economics. Irwin Publishing Company, Illinois

Chapter 8
An Application to Nuclear Power Generation: From Daniel Bernoulli to J.M. Keynes and F.H. Knight

Abstract This paper aims to discuss the problem of nuclear power generation from the viewpoint of the economics of risk and uncertainty. Although we have experienced the two major nuclear disasters, Chernobyl and Fukushima, in recent times, it is quite unfortunate that risk-economic studies in nuclear power generation have been extremely rare so far. This may show intentional neglect in the academic circle.

The purpose of this paper is to duly mend such a regrettable tendency. Before 11 March 2011, there were many people who more or less believed in the myth of absolute safety. The Great East Japan Earthquake, however, has completely changed their concept of risk for nuclear power generation, thus requiring the need to take a new risk-economic approach to nuclear energy. As the saying goes, we can learn new lessons from old teachings: we have to reexamine the economics of J.M. Keynes and F. H. Knight. There are surely new possibilities for future research.

Keywords Nuclear power generation · Risk-economic approach · Psychological factors · J.M. Keynes · F.H. Knight

8.1 "Strong in the Rain": Fukushima and Chernobyl

The purpose of this paper is to carefully discuss the problem of nuclear power generation from the viewpoint of the economics of risk and uncertainty. In recent times, we have experienced the two major nuclear plant crises—Chernobyl in 1986 and Fukushima in 2011. Those crises have repeatedly reminded us of the dangers of reactor explosions and their consequences such as radioactive soil, polluted areas, and abandoned towns. It is quite unfortunate, however, that risk-economic studies in nuclear power generation have been amazingly rare although the economic theory of risk and uncertainty has been developed well since Daniel Bernoulli, J.M. Keynes, and Frank H. Knight. Presumably, this paper is a bit ambitious attempt to fill in such a regrettable gap.

This paper is a revised version of Sakai (2017).

Y. Sakai, *J.M. Keynes Versus F.H. Knight*, Evolutionary Economics and Social Complexity Science 18, https://doi.org/10.1007/978-981-13-8000-6_8

Miyazawa Kenji (1896–1933) is a very popular Japanese writer who spent his whole life in Iwate Prefecture, one of the stricken areas of the 2011 Great East Japan Disaster. Out of his famous poem "Strong in the Rain," let us write down some leading sentences:

> Strong in the rain.
> Strong in the wind.
> Strong against the summer heat and winter snow.
> He is healthy and robust.
> Unselfish.
> He never loses his temper.
> Nor the quite smile on his lips. (Miyazawa 1931)

In 11 March 2011, Japan experienced a tremendous trauma: a massive earthquake, followed by a big tsunami and a tragic nuclear disaster. As is seen in Miyazawa's poet, some of the Japanese people might be strong in the rain and the wind and also strong against the summer heat and winter snow. They might never lose their tempers and the quiet smiles on their lips. Understandably, the rain, the wind, the summer heat, and the winter snow are those natural risks that can easily be expected and endured by the local people. We must point out, however, that the 2011 East Japan Earthquake demonstrated the scale of the disaster which was perhaps beyond the bounds of Miyamoto's imagination. What was once regarded as unthinkable is now a thinkable reality.[1]

George A. Bonanno (2011), a noted journalist, wondered how much trauma Japan could take in the Fukushima nuclear disaster and wrote the following impressive report in the *Newsweek*, a world-famous journal:

> First Japan was hit by a triple whammy. The country of 127 million has just endured one of the largest earthquakes in recorded history, followed by a shockingly voracious tsunami. Together, these two brutes of nature wreaked havoc on the towns and villages of the northern Japanese coastline. If only the damage had stopped there. When the deadly combo of earthquake and tsunami breached the protective barriers and engulfed one of Japan's oldest nuclear power plants, a nuclear nightmare began, one that at this point has shown no clear signs of ending. (Bonanno 2011, p. 8)

Five years have passed since the Fukushima nuclear accident. As McCurry (2016) has noted, in those 5 years, cleanup of Fukushima's reactor remains a far distant goal. Interestingly enough, perhaps to the ears of non-Japanese people, Fukushima might sound like Hiroshima, the place in which the first atomic bomb was dropped over a great number of innocent residents. Those two similar names, Hiroshima and Fukushima, will eternally be recorded as devastating nuclear tragedies in human history.

It is recalled that another nuclear accident, even worse than the Fukushima disaster, took place in Chernobyl, the Ukrainian Soviet Republic, on 26 April

[1]Birmingham and McNeill (2012), well-known reportage writers, have offered the reader many interesting stories concerning the relation between Kenji Miyamoto and the Fukushima disaster.

1986. When Japan still struggled with its nuclear disaster, Robin McKie (2011), a noted British reporter, returned to the scene of the 1986 reactor explosion and found many evils such as radioactive soil, abandoned towns, and polluted lakes. Another 5 years have passed. On the 30th anniversary of the nuclear accident, we can still eyewitness many traces of the Chernobyl disaster. Surrounded by barbed wire, completely abandoned by men, the Chernobyl exclusion zone may be regarded as a sort of hell. Authorities are said to make reconstruction plans beyond the twenty-first century.[2]

As the saying goes, history repeats itself. A disaster may conveniently be forgotten, but is likely to repeat itself. Both the 1986 Chernobyl and the 2011 Fukushima nuclear plant accidents share the infamous distinction of recording the Level 7, the highest scale of nuclear accident. A second Chernobyl or a second Fukushima might occur in the not too distant future.

The contents of this paper are as follows: Section 8.2 will discuss the role of risk and/or uncertainty in economics. The quality of risk distinct from the quantity of risk and the interaction between psychology and economics will be on the agenda of our discussions. Section 8.3 will deal with the traditional expected utility theory under risk and its economic applications. In Sect. 8.4, we will attempt to adopt a risk-economic approach to nuclear power generation, with a comparison of the two opposing views, the pros and cons of "the peaceful use of nuclear energy." Section 8.5 will turn to the world on true uncertainty, with a discussion of the selection problem of appropriate projects. Final remarks will be made in Sect. 8.6.

8.2 The Place of Risk and Uncertainty in Economics

8.2.1 People's Concept of Risk in Daily Life

Let us begin our discussion with people's concept of risk in daily life. In historical perspective, there exist two different concepts of risk—old and new. In old times, Japanese people used to regard the following four items as very risky and fearful:[3]

Earthquakes, thunders, fires, and arrogant fathers.

Geographically speaking, Japan is a long archipelago spreading from the northern a subarctic zone to the southern subtropical one, being surrounded by so many seas and having so many volcanoes. Earthquakes may be felt by the local resident almost every month. Most people live at wooden houses, thus always being afraid of thunders and fires in the neighborhood. Although arrogant fathers are now almost nonexistent, there remain some governmental officials who behave in high-handed fashions.

---

[2]See Oliphant (2016).

[3]For a detailed discussion on the relation between risks and daily lives, see Sakai (1991, 2006). Also see Beck (1986), Taleb (2007), and Birmingham and McNeill (2012).

Time has changed so drastically since then. In modern times, the following four items can be regarded as a new set of risk factors:

Radioactivity, global warming, garbage, and AIDS.

Before the 2011 Great East Japan Earthquake happened, most people attached the myth of absolutely safety to a nuclear power plant. They are told that the nuclear power generation could guarantee them an ideal set of cheap cost, stable power supply, secure jobs, and above all absolute safety. The reality, however, is sometimes more cruel than the fiction: the tragic nuclear disaster which happened 6 years ago completely changed people's concept of nuclear power risk. What they once thought of as unthinkable evens are no longer beyond imagination: there should be no "black swans" in scientific minds. Radioactivity is now the most fearful item in the minds of the Japanese people.

In ordinary people's minds, the old set and the new set of risk factors exist together. The question of much interest is weather and to what extent those factors are numerically measurable or comparable with each other. Although some factors may be relatively measurable, others are almost non-measurable. Non-measurable risks are sometimes referred to uncertainty. When a risk-economic approach to nuclear power generation is adopted, all the risks including natural and human risks must be considered.

8.2.2 *Individual Decision-Making Under Risk: The General Framework*

Let us consider the problem of individual decision-making in the presence of risk. Its general framework may be depicted in Table 8.1. The set of possible choices is denoted by the row $(a_1, \ldots, a_i, \ldots, a_m)$ and the set of possible states of the world by the column $(s_1, \ldots, s_j, \ldots, s_n)$.[4]

Table 8.1 The individual decision-making under risk: the general framework

	States of the world				
Alternative choice	s_1		s_j		s_n
a_1	y_{11}	...	y_{1j}	...	y_{1n}
...	...		...		...
a_i	y_{i1}	...	y_{ij}	...	y_{in}
...	...		...		...
a_m	y_{m1}	...	y_{mj}	...	y_{mn}
Probability	p_1		p_j		p_n

[4]For the economic thought of risk and uncertainty with a focus on the expected utility theory, see Sakai (1982, 1991, 2010).

Let us take a look at Table 8.1. When the individual has chosen a specific choice a_i, and when the nature reveals a specific state s_j, we will have the specific outcome that is represented by the element y_{ij} ($i = 1,.., m; j = 1,..., n$). All the combinations of those elements form the outcome matrix (y_{ij}). The probability that any particular state s_j actually occurs is denoted by p_j. Note that $p_j \geqq 1$ for each j and $\Sigma_j p_j = 1$.

We live in the world of risk and uncertainty. The knowledge of natural and human risks is imperfect and limited. When we face the payoff matrix as shown in Table 8.1, we have to do the best possible judgment subject to the technological and informational constraints. Which is a better allocation for the thermal power plant, in the city or in the country? This is certainty a very important question we face in the modern world.

We are in a position to introduce a particular form of judging criterion. In the field of the modern economics of risk and uncertainty, presumably the most popular criterion is provided by the *expected utility rule*, which was first introduced into human science very long time ago by Daniel Bernoulli (1738), a very famous Swiss mathematician.[5]

For any $i = 1,..., m$, we define the expected utility level of a choice a_i as follows:

$$\begin{aligned} EU_i &= \sum\nolimits_j p_j\, U(y_{ij}) \\ &= p_1 U(y_{i1}) + \ldots + p_j U(y_{ij}) + \ldots + p_n U(y_{in}) \end{aligned} \tag{8.1}$$

We can state the expected utility rule as a lucid rule by which we make the best possible choice in the sense that we select the act yielding the maximum value among those expected utilities $EU_1,..., EU_i,..., EUm$. In other words, we are engaged in doing the following maximizing operation:

$$\mathrm{Max}_i\, EU_i = \mathrm{Max}_i \left\{ \sum\nolimits_j p_j U(y_{ij}) \right\}. \tag{8.2}$$

As will be shown, the expected utility theory a la Bernoulli constitutes the standard framework for the economics of risk and uncertainty.

8.2.3 *The Allocation Problem of a Power Plant*

As an interesting application of the general framework of individual decision-making, let us consider the allocation problem of a thermal power plant. In order to meet additional electricity demand, suppose that we are going to construct a new thermal power plant. As is seen in Table 8.2, assume that there are two allocation choices available: the densely populated city or the depopulated country. The thermal power plant is not an absolutely safe facility and may break down because

[5]The general framework of individual decision-making under risk and uncertainty was systematically discussed by Sakai (1982).

Table 8.2 The allocation problem of a thermal power plant: the city or the country?

Alternative choice	States of the world	
	Non-accident	Accident
The city	2	−2
The country	1	−1
Probability	$1-p$	p

of an accident. There are two states of the worlds: The state of non-accident and the one of accident, with the rate of accident being p.

The construction of a thermal power plant in the city instead of the country represents the case of "high return and high cost." On the one hand, if no accidents occur at all, residents can enjoy the benefit of a shorter distance from the power supply site to the power demand place: the transportation cost would be less. We assume that the payoff of the pair (the city, non-accident) is as great as 2 (see Table 8.2). On the other hand, the thermal power plant may produce air pollution and noise in the neighborhood. Moreover, if an accident occurs in the crowded city, the resulting damage would be very serious. Hence the payoff of the pair (the city, accident) must be a negative value, say (−2).

The construction of a thermal power plant in the sparsely populated countryside will give us a different story: in fact, we will enter the world of "low return and low cost." In the case of non-accident, the net benefit will surely be positive yet small because the power transmission to the consumption area will not be so expensive: the payoff is assumed to be 1. In the case of accident, the resulting damage would be relatively small: the payoff is (−1).

We are ready to apply the expected utility rule to the allocation problem of a power plant. The levels of expected utility attainable from the power plant in the city and in the country are, respectively, given as follows:

$$EU(\text{city}) = (1-p)U(2) + pU(-2), \tag{8.3}$$

$$EU(\text{country}) = (1-p)U(1) + pU(-1). \tag{8.4}$$

Which one gives us a greater value, *EU* (city) or *EU* (country)? The answer to this question should be like this: it depends! Indeed, it depends upon the shape of the utility function U, the accident rate p, and several other factors. As is naturally expected, the greater the degree of risk aversion or the value of the accident rate, the more likely do the people select the country as a cite for the thermal power plant.

The allocation problem of a thermal power plant is depicted in Fig. 8.1. For the sake of presentation, let us intentionally put $p = 1/5$, which is a larger value than usual. Then the point J on the line segment BC and the point K on the line segment DE, respectively, indicate the value of *EU* (city) and *EU* (country). Note that $BJ : JC = DK : KE = 1/4$. Since J is located higher than K, we can conclude that the city

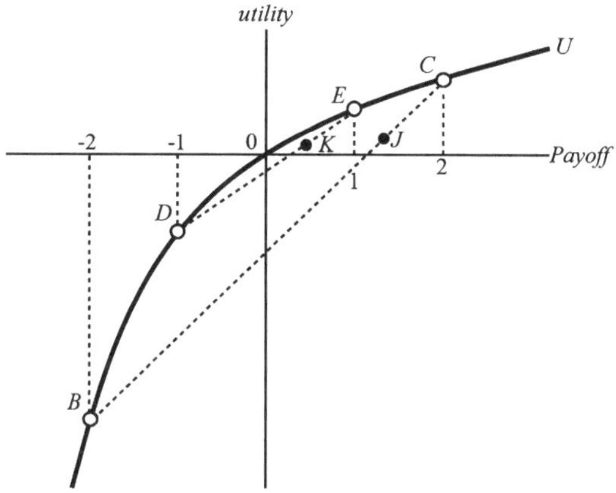

Fig. 8.1 A graphical interpretation of the allocation choice of a thermal power plant

is a better plant cite than the city. Needless to say, the opposite conclusion would come if *K* is located higher than *J*, which is another possible conclusion under other circumstances.

8.3 Nuclear Power Generation: The Interactions of Economic and Psychological Factors

8.3.1 The Two Opposite Views: Pro and Con

We are now in a position to discuss the problem of nuclear power generation, which is a very sensitive and even political issue and has been more or less neglected in the literature. For instance, around 40 years ago, Kikuo Iwata (1981), then a rising star in Japanese economics profession, frankly remarked with embarrassment:[6]

> I have so often been asked: 'What do modern economists think of nuclear power generation? What on earth are they doing right now?'... Alas, modern economists gave up the idea of raising such an question per se. At present, there are very few economists who do research in the problem of nuclear power generation. This tells us that the Japanese academics has a fragile philosophical base, thus deliberately keeping from such an important issue. Honestly speaking, this might represent a sort of academic sabotage by irresponsible persons. (Iwata 1981, p. 81)

To be fair, Iwata was not the only person to be blamed for keeping us from the problem of nuclear power generation. While Diamond and Rothschild's (1978) paper was an excellent collection of influential papers in the field of risk and uncertainty, none of the selected papers did not seriously discuss the possibility of nuclear power accidents. I myself was also to be blamed in my earlier papers (see

[6]As of 2017, Kikuo Iwata serves as one of the vice presidents in the Bank of Japan. Time flies like an arrow!

Table 8.3 The technical cost of power generation (officially announced): the positive view by the METI (2010)

Type of power generation	Power generation cost (¥/kWh)
Nuclear	5~6
Thermal	7~8
Hydro	8~13

Sakai (1982)), but later could successfully deal with the issue of nuclear power generation from the viewpoint of risk and uncertainty.[7]

There are two opposing views on the efficiency and safety of nuclear power generation: the positive view and the negative view. Before the Great East Japan Earthquake took place in 2011, the majority of the Japanese took the positive view. In fact, many people believed in the "myth of absolute efficiency and absolute safety": nuclear power is presumably cheaper and safer than any other means of power generation. Although the influence of such an optimistic view has considerably declined in recent times, it is nevertheless officially supported by the Japanese government and thus cannot easily be ignored.

The second negative view was initially taken by a limited number of scientists including Takagi (1986) and Koide (2011). It has become more popular since the 2011 Fukushima disaster. It would be fair to say that the myth of absolute safety is now almost gone. The question whether and to what extent a nuclear power plant is economical, however, remains a very controversial one and requires the collection of more reliable data as well as more interdisciplinary analyses. Not only economic factors but also psychological and cultural factors must be taken into consideration.

Let us suppose that there are three types of power generation; nuclear, thermal, or hydro. Presumably, the key questions to ask are simple and straightforward. How much does each type cost in economic terms? How reliable is it in psychological terms? As mentioned above, there are two opposing views, optimistic and pessimistic ones, on those issues. What makes our analysis really complicated is that each view offers a different answer to each of those questions.

Let us start our inquiry with the positive view. Table 8.3 indicates the list of the technical cost of power generation, which was officially announced by the Japanese Ministry of Economy, Trade and Industry in 2010, just 1 year before the Fukushima disaster. According to this METI data, nuclear power is the most economical among the three (exactly, 5–6 yen for kilowatt hour), followed by thermal, and hydro the most expensive. Since METI has been strong and influential in the Japanese society, the conclusion that nuclear is the best type of power generation has been more or less trusted by the majority of people for a long time.

Let us turn to the negative view. Professor Kenichi Ohshima (2011), an independent and energetic researcher, has conducted a more comprehensive inquiry than METI, having come to an entirely opposite conclusion. His method of analysis and acquired data can clearly be seen in Table 8.4. According to his opinion, the real cost of nuclear power generation should be the sum of the direct technical cost a la METI,

[7]See Sakai (2004, 2006). While Arrow (1970) was a monumental work in the economics of risk and uncertainty, he did not discuss the economics of nuclear energy.

Table 8.4 The comprehensive cost of power generation (independently reevaluated): the negative view by K. Ohshima (2011)

Type of power generation	Direct cost	Policy cost		Total cost
		R & D cost	Site subsidy	
Nuclear	8.53	1.46	0.26	10.25
Thermal	9.87	0.01	0.03	9.91
Hydro	7.09	0.08	0.02	7.19

the policy cost, and possibly the environmental cost. The policy cost is calculated as the sum total of all R & D expenditures and the site location expenditures including all subsidies necessary for the site promotion to the local residents. The environmental cost includes all expenditures associated with environmental damage caused by the construction of power generation facilities. Among those costs, Ohshima characteristically emphasized the importance of the policy cost, which was quite outside what the METI people had calculated, and succeeded in making Table 8.4 to show his own list of the comprehensive cost for each type of power generation.

As can immediately be seen in Table 8.4, the introduction of the new policy cost was quite effective in the calculation of the comprehensive cost of power generation. In fact, the total cost of nuclear power generation was calculated as 10.25 yen for kWh, which clearly exceeded the thermal power (9.91 \/kWh) and the hydropower (7.19 \/kWh).

As Ohshima himself has noticed, the list of direct and policy costs enumerated in Table 8.4 is certainly less than perfect. Indeed, there remain still missing items that must be taken into account for the sustainable operation after the construction of power plants. One of those missing items is what we may call the backend cost, which mainly consists of the expenditure necessary for reprocessing and safekeeping radioactive wastes. And still another item to be mentioned is the expenditure needed to carefully handle the phase-out process of nuclear power. Remarkably, such a phase-out process may be involved in a series of many difficult and long processes that no one may exactly foresee. Besides, if any radioactive leakage occurs, then many residents will have to be evacuated from the local area; the resulting expenditures for economical and mental compensations, hospitals, and possibly civil trials would be incalculably huge.

8.3.2 *Psychological Factors: Their Effects on Payoff Matrices and Probabilities*

Let us now introduce several noneconomic and psychological factors into our model analysis of power generation. For simplicity, there are only two choices of the type of power plants: namely, thermal and nuclear. Besides, as was mentioned above, there are two opposite views on the analysis—the positive view and the negative

Table 8.5 The two opposite views of nuclear power generation: how to deal with psychological factors

Type of power generation	Payoff (probability) Non-accident	Accident	Psychological factors
(A) The positive view			
Thermal	2	−1	None
	(1−*p*)	(*p*)	
Nuclear	4	−2	Myth of absolute safety (q is zero)
	(1−*q*)	(*q*)	
(B) The negative view			
Thermal	2	−1	None
	(1−*p*)	(*p*)	
Nuclear	2	−(4+α)	Unknown and dreadful risks
	(1−*q*)	(*q*)	

view. Those views can easily be modeled in Table 8.5: the positive view in the upper Panel (A) and the negative view in the lower Panel (B).

Let us begin to take a look at Panel (A). We would naturally expect that the rate of accident differs between the two types of power plants. Let us, respectively, denote the accident rate of a thermal power plant and the one of a nuclear power plant by p and q. According to the official view of the government authority, "going nuclear" is much safer than "going thermal," so that q is considerably lower than p. We suppose that $p = 1/5$ and $q = 1/10$. It is needless to say that local residents and liberal scientists may have serious objections against such an optimistic view.

We assume that the thermal power plant gives all the persons concerned (both the optimists and the pessimists) the solid payoff 2 if no accidents occur and the small loss (−1) if an accident occurs. Besides, we also assume that the reliability of the thermal power plant, the rate of accident p, is largely objective and commonly shared by all the persons; therefore, there are no special psychological factors working behind.

The difference of positions between the optimists and the pessimists appears when the reliability question of nuclear energy is on the agenda. According to the optimists or the people having the positive view, "going nuclear" is much more efficient than "going thermal." After all, they are all strong believers of the "myth of nuclear energy"; the rate of nuclear accident may be regarded as substantially zero. It is assumed here that the nuclear power guarantees four units of money, a handsome amount of gain, in the case of non-accident, whereas it may yield (−2), a manageable amount of loss, in the case of accident.

The whole situations would be drastically change if the local people decide to take the negative or critical view. In a sense, "the wind against nuclear" will blow strongly. The people are no longer believers in the nuclear myth, but are really concerned with the "nuclear enigma" which can be neither measurable nor predictable. As is seen in Panel (B), there are strong psychological and cultural factors working behind. Although a nuclear power plant can yield two units of money when no accidents take place, it will cause a huge and perhaps non-measurable amount of loss shown by minus (4+α) unit when an accident occurs. Presumably, the "α factor" represents the non-measurable dimensions of unknown and dreadful damages.

8.4 A Generalization of the Expected Utility Theory: J.M. Keynes and F.H. Knight

In the above, we have intensively discussed the effects of psychological factors on decision-making under risk. How to deal with those factors is really a controversial question. Since there are the two opposing views of nuclear power generation, it seems clear that a mere application of the traditional expected utility theory a la Daniel Bernoulli does not work at all. In the history of economic thought, there are several economists who had serious doubts about the applicability of the traditional Bernoulli principle. Among those economists are J. M. Keynes and Frank Knight. Keynes (1936) once remarked:

> Human decisions affecting the future, whether personal or political or economic, cannot depend on strict mathematical expectation, since such calculation does not exist. (Keynes 1936, pp. 162–163)

The traditional expected utility theory may be a good example of "strict mathematical expectation." We have to go beyond such a narrow framework. It would be high time for us to establish a more ambitious theory—a sort of generalized expected utility theory a la Keynes and Knight—by appropriately incorporating psychological and cultural factors into our theoretical framework.

In what follows, let us adopt a generalized expected theory. Within such an expanded framework, the utility function U is no longer a function of one variable x such that $U = U(x)$ but a more complicated function of a variable x and a parameter β so that $U = U(x; \beta)$. The new parameter β measures the degree of human sentiments, which may go in both ways—negative or positive. Presumably, the presence of fear or unknown risk would shift a person's utility curve downward, whereas the optimistic sentiments such as animal spirits would shift the curve upward. When we evaluate the frequency of risky events, what matters is not the objective probability p per se but rather the subjectively weighted value $\omega(p)$ filtered through a certain subjective filter ω. On the one hand, when the local residents feel uneasy about unknown and dreadful risks associated with nuclear generation, they may not totally trust the officially announced accident rate, so that the weighted value $\omega(p)$ tends to be higher than p per se. On the other hand, as far as they believe in the myth of absolute safety, they tend to regard the accident rate p as near zero.

It should be noted that our generalized expected utility theory is even more general than the prospect theory of Kahneman and Tversky (1979). While they have newly introduced "the weighted filter of probabilities" into the traditional

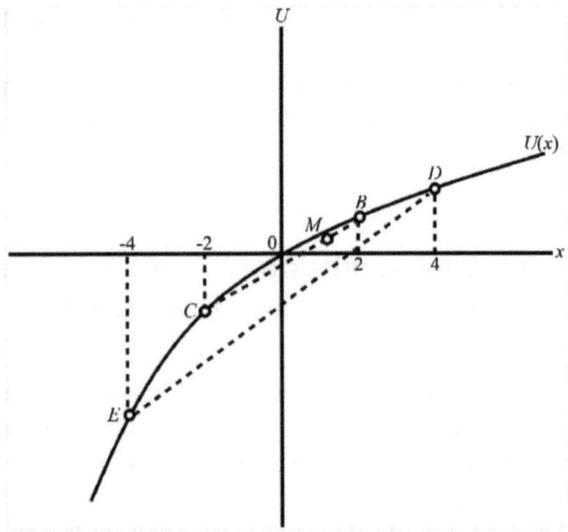

Fig. 8.2 The positive view: a graphical presentation

expected theory, we go even beyond their approach in that we take account of "the possibility of lower or upper shifts in the utility function." After all, there should be many possibilities to expand any existing approach.

We are now in a position to get back to Table 8.2 in which the two opposite views of nuclear generation are presented in the form of tables. First of all, according to the positive view, the weighted values *WV* of the two power plants—thermal and nuclear—are provided in the following manner:

$$WV(\text{thermal}) = \omega(1-p)U(2;\beta) + \omega(p)U(-1;\beta), \tag{8.5}$$

$$WV(\text{nuclear}) = \omega^*(1-q)U(4;\beta^*) + \omega^*(q)U(-2;\beta^*). \tag{8.6}$$

Figure 8.2 evidently demonstrates the positive view indicated by Panel (A). For the sake of graphical convenience, we put $p = 1/5$, which is definitely larger than the real value. Since no special psychological factors are considered for the thermal power generation, no special attentions of the weighted filter of probabilities are necessary, so that we should have $\omega(p) = p$ for any p. Therefore, for the case of the thermal power generation, Eq. (8.5) may be simplified as follows:

$$WV(\text{thermal}) = (4/5)U(2;\beta) + (1/5)U(-1;\beta), \tag{8.5*}$$

The case of nuclear power generation requires a different treatment from the one of thermal power generation. While the weighted probability filters should be considered here, the myth of absolute safety leads to the simplification of $q = 0$. Hence for the case of nuclear generation, if we note that $\omega*(1) = 1$ and $\omega*(0) = 0$, Eq. (8.6) may be overly simplified as follows:

$$WV(\text{nuclear}) = \omega^*(1)U(4;\beta^*) + \omega^*(0)U(-2;\beta^*) = U(4;\beta^*). \tag{8.6*}$$

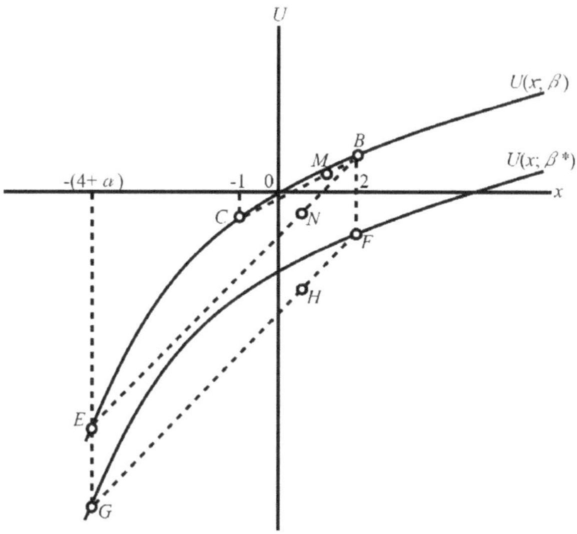

Fig. 8.3 The negative view: a graphical presentation

As is clear in Fig. 8.2, according to the positive view, the midpoint *M* lying on the line segment *BC* stands for the value of *WV* (thermal), whereas the end point *D* on the line segment *DE* indicates the value of *WV* (nuclear). Because the point *D* is located higher than the point *M*, the value of *WV* (nuclear) is greater than the one of *WV* (thermal). Therefore, the optimists are encouraged to tell us that "going nuclear" is the best policy conceivable.

Now let us turn to the negative view, which is graphically presented in Fig. 8.3. This figure is apparently more complicated than Fig. 8.2 and thus requires a more careful analysis than before. As far as the thermal power generation, there should be no fundamental difference between the negative and positive views. Hence as before, the midpoint *M* on the line segment *BC* indicates the value of *WV* (thermal). When we are dealing with the nuclear power generation, however, the negative view is definitely at variance with the positive view. The critical people do not believe in the myth of nuclear energy. Even if no nuclear accidents occur, the payoff we can obtain is no longer four units but merely two units, which is the same amount of money we can get from the thermal power generation. Besides, the nuclear accident ratio q is no longer near zero but rather may be substantially larger than p, the thermal accidental ratio.

At this stage, we must not forget the fact that the pessimists have extraordinary fears against nuclear energy such that their utility curves are no longer stable but may shift downward. If the utility curve shifts downward from $U(x, \beta)$to $U(x, \beta*)$ under the heavy stress, then the value of *WV* (nuclear) is no longer indicated by the midpoint *N* but rather the midpoint *H* on the shifted curve. It is noted that as the point *H* lies in the fourth quadrant, *WV* (nuclear) is forced to take on a negative value. In short, we may enter into the world where nuclear generation per se is a negative asset.

To sum up, a risk-economic approach involves a fundamentally difficult problem. First, human attitude toward nuclear generation differs from person to person: there exist a variety of optimists and pessimists. Second, the utility curve per se may not be stable but possibly shift downward. Third, the official opinion for the reliability of nuclear generation may not necessarily supported by the local people. To be fair, there remains still a long way to go in this field.

8.5 Selection of Appropriate Projects in the World of True Uncertainty

8.5.1 Paul Slovic and F.H. Knight: Beyond Measurable Risks

When we are dealing with the problem of nuclear energy, we sometimes wonder if the risks under consideration are really numerically measurable. It is necessary but not sufficient to consider the "quantity of risk" only. We have to take account of the "quality of risk" as well.

Paul Slovic (1987), a famous psychologist, once reported the results of his empirical research on many risk perceptions of the American people. The list of 17 items adopted by him is as follows:

> Nuclear power plant, radioactive fallout, nuclear waist, DNA engineering, supersonic transport, man-made satellite accident, nuclear war, natural gas explosion, mine accident, air plane accident, pistol, dynamite, microwave, oven, caffeine, aspirin, smoking, bicycle.

Interestingly enough, Slovic classified those 17 items into just 2 items, unknown risk and dreadful risk. His research results were edited and summarized in Fig. 8.4. Nuclear power plant is located in the first quadrant, meaning that it is both highly unknown and highly dreadful risks. Psychologically speaking, it is the most dangerous thing the people want to avoid. Although mine accident represents highly dreadful risk, its danger is rather known to all the people. In contrast, the risk of microwave is highly unknown but not so dreadful. Finally, bicycle is the most familiar and the most risk-free good.[8]

In his well-known book (1921), Frank Knight (1921) emphasized the role of uncertainty in the working of the market economy. For instance, he once remarked:

> Uncertainty must be taken in a sense radically distinct from the familiar notion of risk, from which it has never been properly separated. ... A measurable uncertainty ... is so far different from an un-measurable one that it is not in effect an uncertainty at all. We shall accordingly restrict the term 'uncertainty' to cases of the non-quantitative type. It is this 'true' uncertainty, and not risk, which forms the basis of a valid theory of profit and accounts for the divergence between actual and theoretical competition. (Knight 1921, pp. 19–20)

[8]Also see Kahneman, Slovic, and Tversky (1982) and Michel-Kerjan and Slovic (2010). Akerlof and Shiller (2009) is an interesting book which deals with the question how human psychology drives the economy and why it matters for the market economy.

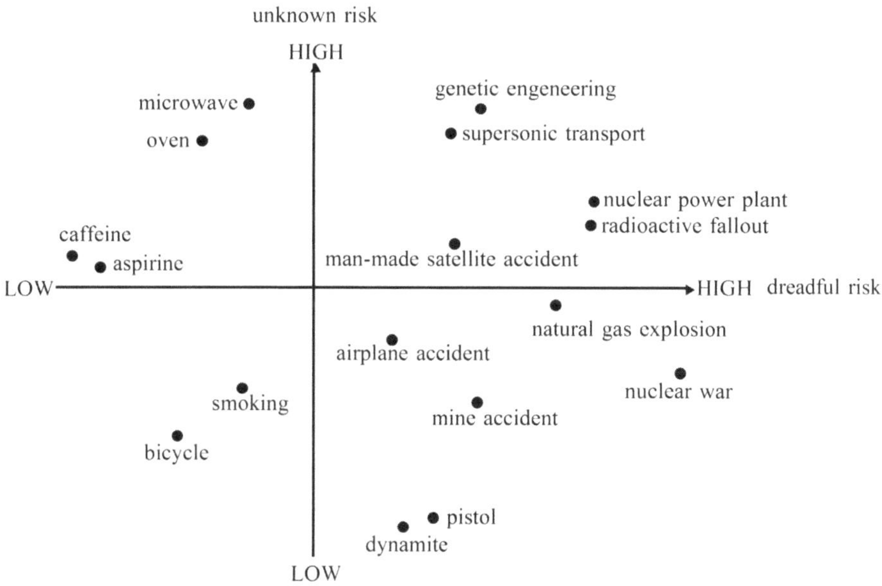

Fig. 8.4 Slovic (1987) on the quality of risks: unknown and dreadful risks

According to Knight, risk is a measurable concept in the sense that it can be represented by the normal or other specific distribution functions. Uncertainty, however, is radically different from risk since the former is no longer measurable at all. The notions of psychological risks including unknown and dreadful risks are very closely related to the one of non-measurable uncertainty. We might to add that it is this true uncertainty, but not risk, which may form the basis of a valid theory of nuclear generation from the economic-psychological viewpoint.[9]

8.5.2 Application of the Maximin Rule to the Selection of Power Plants

As we have noticed before, the myth of nuclear energy is now vanished among the people. Let us go with Knight's argument. Then we are ready to investigate the selection problem of power generation with special reference to with non-measurable uncertainty.

One thing is certain. The direct application of the traditional expected utility theory is not appropriate. In the world of true uncertainty, risks may not be

[9]For Knight on true uncertainty, see Sakai (2015, 2016).

measurable, so that many formulas of mathematical probabilities are now worthless. In order to conduct our analysis further, it is necessary to introduce some forms of selection rules. There might be the plain average rule or the very aggressive maximax rule. We do think, however, that the more prudent maximin rule is the best selection rule when the people face unknown and dreadful risks.

Let us discuss the maximin rule in greater detail. In plain English, it requires the people for playing safe in uncertain situations. We must first think of the worst possible scenario for every project and proceed next to find the best one out of those worst scenarios. Suppose that there are m projects, $a_1,\ldots, a_m$, and n states of the world, $s_1,\ldots, s_n$. Note that no probabilities p_j are associated with the state s_j. Further let y_{ij} be the payoff we can get when the project i is taken and the state j is realized. More mathematically, let us define the worst scenario N_i for the project i in the following way:[10]

$$N_i = \mathrm{Min}_j \quad \{y_{i1}, \ldots, y_{ij}, \ldots, y_{in}\}. \tag{8.7}$$

Then the maximin rule requires that the project yielding the maximum value of N_i must be chosen:

$$\mathrm{Max}_i\, N_i = \mathrm{Max}_i\, \mathrm{Min}_j\{y_{ij}\}. \tag{8.8}$$

Now, let us get back to Table 8.2. We are dealing with the selection problem of power generation types, thermal or nuclear. In the world of true uncertainty, numerical probabilities become meaningless, so that the accident rates such as p, $1-p$, q, and $1-q$ should not be referred at all. If we side with the positive view, as is seen in Panel (A), the payoff of the thermal power takes on the minimum value (-1) when an accident occurs, whereas the one of the nuclear power is the minimum (-2) also in the case of accident. While those two values are both negative, (-1) is larger than (-2). Therefore, according to the minmax rule of decision-making, the thermal power generation is better than the nuclear. Presumably, a stronger argument would be applied to the negative view. As in Panel (B), while the payoff of the thermal power takes on the minimum value (-1) when an accident occurs, the one of the nuclear power is the minimum $(-(4+\alpha))$ also in the case of accident. Between those two values, (-1) is clearly a much better value. This shows the superiority of the thermal power over the nuclear.

It is noted that the above argument is totally dependent on the reliability of the minmax rule of decision-making. In the world of non-measurable uncertainty, the people are involved in many risks of unknown and/or dreadful types. As common sense tells us, the principle of "safety first" constitutes one of the golden rules in human life.

[10]For the maximin rule, see Sakai (2004).

8.6 Louis Pasteur Versus Torahiko Terada: Concluding Remarks

Louis Pasteur (1822–1895), a renowned French chemist and microbiologist, once remarked:

Chance favors the prepared mind.

This maxim is important and persuasive when we are eager to discover hidden laws in the field of natural science. Its applicability may be somehow limited, however, if we take a look at the history of natural and human disasters. Even if we focus on nuclear disasters in modern times, there are too numerous to list. Among them are the Three Mile nuclear accident (1979), the Chernobyl nuclear accident (1986), the Great Hanshin-Awaji earthquake (1995), and the Great East Japan disaster. It is fair to say that when those disasters stroke the local people, they were not prepared at all.

Torahiko Terada (1934), a legendary Japanese scientist and essayist, noted that a natural disaster unexpectedly struck the people who were so busy in their daily lives and conveniently forgot the past experience of disasters. Therefore, in line with Pasteur's famous sentence aforementioned, we might say the following:

Disaster strikes the forgetful mind.

As we repeatedly noticed, it is quite unfortunate that risk-economic studies in nuclear power generation have been extremely rare so far. In closing this paper, we would like to point out one important exception. In his outstanding book, E.F. Schumacher (1973) was brave enough to regard the problem of nuclear energy as the one to choose the way to salvation or damnation. In fact, he once remarked:

> No degree of prosperity could justify the accumulation of large accounts of highly toxic substances which nobody knows how to make 'safe' which remain an in calculable danger to the whole of creation for historical or even geological ages. To do such a thing is a transgression against life itself.... It means conducting the economic affairs of man as if people really did not matter at all. (Schumacher 1973, p. 154)

In spite of Schumacher's warning, the main stream economics has consistently ignored the important problem of nuclear energy under uncertainty. It is recalled that Schumacher was once a research associate under J.M. Keynes. Moreover, we would like to point out that Schumacher's view of nuclear energy as incalculable danger is in line with Knight's notion on non-measurable uncertainty.

This paper may be just one step forward toward a more systematic approach to nuclear power generation. No doubt, so many unsolved problems remain. They will be left for future research.

References

Akerlof GA, Shiller RJ (2009) Animal spirits: how human psychology drives the economy, and why it matters for global capitalism. Princeton University Press, Princeton

Arrow KJ (1970) Essays in the theory of risk-bearing. North-Holland, Amsterdam

Beck U (1986) Risikogesellschaft: Auf dem Weg in eine andere Moderne (in German). Suhrkamp Verlag, Frankfurt am Main. English translation by Ritter M (1992) Risk society: towards a new modernity. Sage Publications, London

Bernoulli D (1738) Specimen theoriae novae de mensura sortes. Commentarii Academiae Scientiarum Imprials Petropolitanae (in Latin), vol 5, pp 175–192. English translation by Sommer L (1954) Exposition of a new theory on the measurement of risk. Econometrica 22:23–36

Birmingham L, McNeill D (2012) Strong in the rain: surviving Japan's earthquake, tsunami, and Fukushima disaster. Palgrave Macmillan

Bonanno GA (2011) Japan: too much trauma? Newsweek:8–9

Diamond P, Rothschild M (eds) (1978) Uncertainty in economics: readings and exercises. Academic, New York

Iwata K (1981) What are modern economists doing now? (in Japanese). Sci Thought 10:18–31

Kahneman D, Tversky A (1979) Prospect theory: an analysis of decision under risk. Econometrica 47:1–21

Kahneman D, Slovic P, Tversky A (eds) (1982) Judgment under uncertainty: heuristics and biases. Cambridge University Press, Cambridge

Keynes JM (1936) The general theory of employment, interest and money. Macmillan, London

Knight FH (1921) Risk, uncertainty and profit. Houghton Mifflin Company, Boston/New York

Koide H (2011) The lie and enigma of nuclear power generation (in Japanese). Huso Publishing Company, Tokyo

McCurry J (2016) Five years on: cleanup of Fukushima's reactor remains a distant goal. The Guardian. March 2016

McKie R (2011) Chernobyl 25 years on: a poisoned landscape. The Japan Times, April 2, 2011. Adapted from The Observer, April 2011

Michel-Kerjan E, Slovic P (eds) (2010) The irrational economist: making decisions in a dangerous world. Public Affairs, New York

Miyazawa K (1931) Ame nimo makezu (in Japanese). Private Notebook of Kenji Miyazawa. English Translation by Japan Medical Association (2011) Strong in the rain. Contained in Nabeshima N (ed) (2011) The galactic realm of Kenji Miyazawa. Ryukoku University Press, Kyoto

Ohshima K (2011) Cost of nuclear power generation (in Japanese). Iwanami Publishing Company, Tokyo

Oliphant R (2016) Chernobyl disaster: on the 30th anniversary of the nuclear accident: authorities plan for the next century. The Telegraph, April 2016

Sakai Y (1982) The economics of uncertainty (in Japanese). Yuhikaku Publishing Conpany, Tokyo

Sakai Y (1991) Risk and information: towards a new economics (in Japanese). Keiso Publishing Company, Tokyo

Sakai Y (2004) Risk, environment, and economy (in Japanese). Keiso Publishing Company, Tokyo

Sakai Y (2006) Risk society: a pluralistic view (in Japanese). Iwanami Publishing Company, Tokyo

Sakai Y (2010) Economic thought of risk and uncertainty (in Japanese). Minerva Publishing Company, Kyoto

Sakai Y (2015) J.M. Keynes versus Frank Knight: comparing the two economic giants in the age of uncertainty (in Japanese). Minerva Publishing Company, Kyoto

Sakai Y (2016) J.M. Keynes versus F.H. Knight on uncertainty: reflections on the miracle year of 1921. Evol Inst Econ Rev 13(1):1–21

Sakai Y (2017) A risk economic approach to nuclear power generation: from Daniel Bernoulli to Keynes and Knight. CRR Discussion Paper A-23. Shiga University, Japan, pp 1–22

Schumacher EF (1973) Small is Beautiful: economics as if people mattered. Blond & Briggs, London
Slovic P (1987) Perception of risk. Science 236:36–51
Takagi J (1986) Nuclear power accident: will it take place in Japan? (in Japanese) Iwanami Publishing Company. Tokyo.
Taleb NN (2007) The black swan: the impact of the highly improbable. Random House, New York
Terada T (1934) Natural disaster and national defense (in Japanese). Keizai-Ohrai Journal, Tokyo

MIX
Papier aus verantwortungsvollen Quellen
Paper from responsible sources
FSC® C105338

If you have any concerns about our products,
you can contact us on
ProductSafety@springernature.com

In case Publisher is established outside the EU,
the EU authorized representative is:
Springer Nature Customer Service Center GmbH
Europaplatz 3, 69115 Heidelberg, Germany

Printed by Libri Plureos GmbH
in Hamburg, Germany